The Policy State

The Policy State

An American Predicament

Karen Orren

Stephen Skowronek

Harvard University Press

CAMBRIDGE, MASSACHUSETTS • LONDON, ENGLAND

First Harvard University Press paperback edition, 2019
First printing

Library of Congress Cataloging-in-Publication Data
Names: Orren, Karen, author. | Skowronek, Stephen, author.
Title: The policy state : an American predicament / Karen Orren,
Stephen Skowronek.
Description: Cambridge, Massachusetts : Harvard University Press, 2017. |
Includes bibliographical references and index.
Identifiers: LCCN 2017014601 | ISBN 9780674728745 (cloth : alk. paper) |
ISBN 9780674237872 (pbk.)
Subjects: LCSH: Policy sciences—United States. | Political culture—
United States. | United States—Politics and government.
Classification: LCC H97 .O77 2017 | DDC 320.60973—dc23
LC record available at https://lccn.loc.gov/2017014601

To our brothers,
Lowell Orren and David Skowronek

Contents

The Policy State

Part I

Introduction

Public Policy and State Formation

PUBLIC policy keeps government current with changing times. It is the state's reflexive instrument for dealing with issues and problems as they arise. Policy is also a spur to changes within government, as new applications will, by degrees, affect received relations of power and authority. Since the turn of the twentieth century, novel demands for policy have multiplied exponentially, and the accompanying changes in American government have reached transformative proportions. The modern American state is the historical expression of those adaptations. Its organization and operation reflect the vast expansion of policy's domain.

Government's accommodation of a larger role for policy is apparent today in every particular. The fallout from these changes preoccupies contemporary discussions of law, rights, relations among the branches, and American politics at large. But general assessments are rare.[1] Perhaps because individual policies are so diverse, generalization seems forbidding, or maybe impacts so widely dispersed appear to resist clear characterization overall. Perhaps a measure of unity is taken for granted, assumed to follow from the continuity of the Constitution and principles of policy making that have been there all along. Or perhaps attention is drawn more readily to the "veto points" that complicate policy making and impede doing more. Whatever the reason, policy has become an enigmatic omnipresence, the always implicit but seldom addressed mainspring of this state's reformation.

Our objective in this book is to open this reformation to more direct interrogation. As a first step, we have given the emergent state its proper name. *The Policy State* considers the cumulative consequences of our long history of collective problem solving. It examines the systemic impact on law and politics of repeatedly taking the policy cure. In these pages we pull together concerns usually addressed in discrete sectors of contemporary American government. We apply analytic tools of our own to subject them to a fresh assessment, and we elaborate a view of the whole. Looking at the expansion of policy's domain, we take the measure of American government as we find it now.[2]

An American Predicament

Inquiry along these lines will entail a bit of conceptual spadework. That said, the analytic concerns we bring to *The Policy State* are in no sense removed from the political fray. We write at a time of widespread distrust of the institutions of American government. Political disagreements have deepened and aligned nationally on policies across the board. The problem-solving ethos has itself become a bone of contention. Political debates routinely move beyond the discussion of policy alternatives and escalate to bare-knuckled contests over the government's working assumptions. Pundits write of the raw, emotive character of the national mood, of a public frustrated by what it sees as the cynical gamesmanship and empty promises of officeholders. There is widespread speculation about the dawn of a new era, of a "post-policy politics."[3]

For those who would press ahead on the received path of development, all this turmoil is a dangerous distraction. The priority of policy is, for them, just common sense: the nation faces serious problems on every front; it is the responsibility of government to respond and where necessary to adapt; refusing to engage in the constructive search for solutions is not a legitimate option. President Barack Obama pegged his leadership to the broad, intuitive appeal of this outlook. His frequently stated purpose was to find ways to "get stuff done,"[4] or at least to "move the ball forward."[5] When political and institutional obstacles blocked his way, he used the policy imperative to justify unilateral action: "We can't wait for Congress to do its job; so where they won't act, I will."[6] For Obama, as for progressives generally, policy "is not a matter of if, it is a matter of when." The only real question is "do we do it in a smart, rational, sensible way?"[7]

Those who would abandon this path and set a different course invoke first principles. They reject the primacy of policy, with its insatiable plea to "do something," and propose instead to restore "limited government."[8] Justice Scalia's dissent in the Supreme Court's 2012 decision upholding the Affordable Care Act put it this way: "Article I [of the Constitution] contains no whatever-it-takes-to-solve-a-national-problem power."[9] John Boehner, the former Republican Speaker of the House, was equally direct: "Congress should not be judged by how many new laws we create. We ought to be judged on how many laws we repeal."[10] For conservatives mobilized against the prevailing regime, the fix-it impulse has spun out of control; the expanding scope of policy has compromised constitutional foundations and jeopardized the nation's future. This competing diagnosis has figured in a series of operational crises—debt-ceiling face-offs, government shutdowns, appointment blockages, siege-like investigations—each engineered to arrest this state's compulsive, allegedly self-destructive meddling.

The predicament expressed in this standoff appears to us more profound than either side admits. It has been nearly forty years since Ronald Reagan declared government problem solving itself to be the problem; still, an alternative remains elusive.[11] Tactical assaults on the policy state's operations have repeatedly threatened their instigators with political marginalization; by the same token, the commitment to limits has been compromised by repeated accommodations that defer to norms of governmental engagement. George W. Bush, scion of the Reagan Revolution, spearheaded major extensions of policy-making authority. At times, he was moved by the sheer force of events—a terrorist attack, an imminent financial collapse. "If we're really looking at another Great Depression," he said of the economic crisis of 2008, "you can be damn sure I'm going to be Roosevelt, not Hoover."[12] Other initiatives showed the political attractions of policy in more mundane ways: a bid to redress the sorry state of the nation's schools; a plan to augment Medicare with prescription drug coverage. Confusion approached a new high point in 2016 when the party of Reagan was taken over by an outsider with a penchant for populism and when the rhetoric of limits morphed into "repeal and replace."

Prospects are hardly less daunting for progressives. Though generally forward moving, policy is also known for turning back and biting its most ardent advocates. In recent decades, progressives have been playing defense, fighting on all fronts to repel policy encroachments on victories seemingly won—labor's right to bargain collectively, African Americans' right to vote, women's "right to choose," everyone's right to health care and security in old age. Options abound in a policy state, and that makes achievements provisional, protections unreliable, and commitments dependent on who is next in charge. Compounding these anxieties are doubts about how the business of this state gets done: presidential "aggrandizement," judicial "activism," administrative "overreach," congressional "dysfunction." Policy is the bait in this trap, and solutions peddled by experts look suspiciously like the lure. Now that policy has infiltrated every aspect of American life, now that it spews out of every corner of the state apparatus, now that there is little agreement about how pressing problems should be addressed, or in what order and at what expense, the promises of progressivism are wearing thin.

American government has always made policy. Our intent in calling the current system a "policy state" is to focus on the implications of doing more over a broader range of affairs. To that end, we offer a descriptive theory, one that identifies developmental dynamics inherent in this buildup and brings them to bear on the current political scene. Put simply, we argue that policy has expanded its role in American government and society by eroding the boundaries and dissolving the distinctions that once constrained policy's reach. As we show, greater reliance on policy has the consequence of rendering all aspects of state authority more homogeneous and making each more difficult to pin down. A protracted history of collective problem solving has in this way created a set of problems for American government that more policy is unlikely to remedy.

Our proposition is that policy has not filled a void in governance; rather, it has dislodged governance previously in place. Examining the matter that way points to the impact of policy's expansion on the fundament of rights and on formal structures of decision making. Rights and structure, we contend, grow more attenuated and uncertain as policy proliferates and assumes dominance. When we call this troubled accretion a "policy state," we are referring to the effects on elements and modes of government that in earlier times bore little resemblance to policy, indeed represented an opposite set of governing principles. In accommodating more and more policy making, those elements have shed their historic purposes and attributes to take on policy's own distinctive earmarks.

One advantage of thinking about American state formation in this way is that it pulls us deeper into some of the issues that currently pit the political Right against the political Left. Another is that it avoids political caricatures. America's policy state is not, as some conservatives would have it, an evil empire out to quash the republic bequeathed to us by the founders. Assessing its actual development dispels the illusion of halcyon days. Early American government was less fully occupied with policy, but it was also no state of grace. Policy's domain expanded at the same time—and often because—older hierarchical forms of governance became inoperative and unacceptable. Their abandonment was not a mistake. Policy innovations reestablished authority that was more inclusive and popularly responsive. The call to restore constitutional limits might support a more devastating critique of the policy state if it did not elide democracy's greatest achievements. On that score, there is no question of going back.

It should be equally plain, however, that the progressives' no-regrets reliance on policy solutions has not been as benign as they would have us believe. Programmatic government expands uneasily within a Constitution originally framed with limited policy objectives and extensive provision for keeping them that way. When purposes change and authority is redeployed, underlying principles of organization come under pressure. Adverse consequences, many of them unintended, are compounded over successive policy-making episodes. The same solutions that have proven this government's adaptability and underwritten its great success have also set it at cross-purposes, mangled its forms, helped polarize its politics, and eroded confidence in its basic operations.

The founding of the American republic is as much a benchmark of these dynamics as it is the beginning. Caught up in the late-eighteenth-century British Empire's unprecedented expansion of policy making over commercial and military affairs, the American Constitution sought to provide national initiative and control over those same areas. By the same token, the framers at Philadelphia were careful to leave the rest of American society governed as it was, as undisturbed as possible by creative actions from the center. The balance they struck between authorizing policy making and checking its spread, between empowering problem solvers and reining them in, turned out to be an intervention midstream. Forward from that point, timely extensions of policy's domain have grappled with time-bound provisions hammered out for its containment. America's policy state is a product of the succession of adjustments and the muddle of compromises that ensued.

Much as this government has had good reasons along the way for expanding policy's domain, so too have governments around the world. Policy states are now common. We suspect, however, that each bears the marks of its particular path of development. In that regard, the United States is not an exceptional case but, like others, one that wrestles with less programmatic values according to its own history. Issues of structure in a policy state present themselves differently in Britain, where constitutional provisions were less firmly set; the problem of rights plays out differently in Germany, scarred in living memory by totalitarianism. The case of the United States is framed by a written text, seldom changed over two centuries. The nation is culturally identified with that document, making it the premier symbol of unity for a diverse and contentious people.[13] When, through the actual operations of American government, it becomes more difficult to assert and defend common understandings—when persistent negotiations over practical solutions to national problems destabilize those rights and hollow out that structure—this state finds itself, and the polity it governs, unhinged, unmoored, adrift.

Blind Spots

A veritable industry devotes itself to policy research, tracking and modeling public programs to understand varieties of the instrument and the factors that determine their effectiveness. That enterprise speaks for itself. Foreign policy, defense policy, monetary policy, trade policy, tax policy, immigration policy, family policy, environmental policy, health-care policy, labor policy, energy policy, science policy, education policy, information policy—this is the urgent business of the day. Policies command our attention because so much depends on keeping them "smart" and up to date.

Our interest in this book is not the analysis of these "policies," singly or sequentially. We aim, rather, to describe the regime that supports this seemingly consuming interest. Submerged in the reign of the adjectives is the rule of the noun. Our definition of policy, further elaborated in Chapter 2, is this: policy is a commitment to a designated goal or course of action, made authoritatively on behalf of a given entity, and accompanied by guidelines for its accomplishment. "Policy analysis" developed precisely when policy in our meaning became the government's dominant, driving motive, the raison d'être of its entire operation. We will have more to say about "motives" later. Suffice it here to point out that policy research has been an integral part of the sea change we are examining, and that as such, it does not offer a clear or secure vantage point for our analysis. Because it regards the new state that has emerged matter-of-factly, moving directly to its exemplars, it offers no alternative point of reference, no opposing governing principle, against which we might follow the transformation or gauge its significance.[14]

A related point concerns the "state" as it is commonly invoked to designate clusters of policy: the welfare "state," the national security "state," the regulatory "state," the fiscal "state," the carceral "state," the litigation "state," the privatized "state." Aggregating policies, along with their institutional supports, modes of operation, and interest group clienteles, is a fruitful way of illuminating important sectors of activity in modern American government. But the very multiplicity of labels suggests their limitations. Syntheses achieved by way of categorization are, by design, partial, each grouping bound by its affinities. The "state" appears in these usages to be little more than a tag attaching special significance to the policies included. There is value in identifying clusters that amount to more than the sum of their parts, but these scattered subsystems can only gesture at the background system that comprises governance in its entirety.

In our usage, the "state" refers to authority relations that embrace the entire population, including all of the many forms found among government officers and citizens. Our interest lies in changes in those relations that have affected government operations as a whole. The "policy state" is not an amalgam of other, more common usages; it is a specific proposition about the thrust and consequences of these developments. We delve into particulars to uncover changes submerged in more familiar formulations, changes that have prioritized policy over other motives that, historically, constrained its reach.

As usual, when looking for system-level changes, it is advisable to widen the time frame. In fact, standard accounts in history textbooks move us closer in on the political development we seek to address. As these indicate, American government over time becomes more national, more democratic, more bureaucratic, more hegemonic. Working through any one of these patterns will highlight changing political aspirations and corresponding institutional reforms. Yet again the feature they share—policy's own expanding terrain—goes largely unnoticed, the consequences of its rise to prominence never productively registered. Here, too, until we figure out a way to focus on policy as a distinct instrument of rule, policy's significance in state formation will be glimpsed only in passing.

Part of the problem lies in policy's own nature. We seek to understand a multifaceted change reaching across the institutional landscape and eventually permeating the field, but evidence of policy's impact is everywhere and is far easier to accumulate than to assess. A simple inventory of its incidence and scope will not be sufficient. If the state that policy built is authentically new, if it has reconfigured a prior state of affairs, then it can best be observed from the vantage point of its historical predecessors. Policy, we will show, is one way of governing among others, and not the principal way in which America was governed originally.

Past and Present

Heightened political concern over the assumptions and travails of modern American government has led scholars from a number of fields—constitutional theory, political science, history—to scrutinize the connections between past and present more intensely. Some of the projects underway afford a fuller view of the impact of public policy on state formation. The approaches of special interest to us, though very different from one another, look, as we do, to the significance of policy overall, not just the impact of this policy or that. By pulling their insights together, we can capitalize on common concerns; by pointing to loose ends, we can clarify our own line of advance.

No academic endeavor has been more fully attuned to the foundational issues that surround the coming of the policy state than constitutional theory. Questions about the relationship between past and present lie at the heart of this work, and a burgeoning band of scholars has produced a widening variety of responses. We share with them a focus on the two most important dimensions of American government on which policy impinges, namely, rights and structure. These two dimensions not only contain the basic elements of constitutional law; they also comprise the loci through which policy is regulated. As an initial matter, we will add that they are also conceptually distinct, with characteristics that are in many respects opposed to those of policy. The question we ask, then, is how constitutional rights and structure themselves have changed as policy's domain has expanded.

A good indicator of this expansion is the recent proliferation of constitutional theories. Quite apart from any consideration of their individual merits is the significance of their unprecedented number, the quickening pace of their appearance, and the sobering recognition of just how thin the intellectual consensus on foundations has become. The current literature on the Constitution is replete with new angles of approach, with new methods of sorting through provisions and precepts at a time when these are increasingly less self-evident as written or formally understood. By the same token, any guidance for current practice turns directly on the specific perspective adopted. "Originalism," "realism," "dualism," "legal process," "popular constitutionalism," "the living Constitution"—each presents the relationship between past and present differently. More to our point, these theories, different as they are, are all focused on the question of how much of constitutionalism remains *besides* policy.

For the most part, when constitutional theorists approach this question they are looking to discover, or to reestablish, a coherent account of government authority in operation. Their enterprise is largely dedicated to making the Constitution work better, either by formulating new standards of performance or by reinvigorating old ones. History is used to determine baselines for the fidelity of current constitutional events and practices, which means their description of the past is riddled with prescriptions concerning how, by what logic, the changes they discern can be regarded as lawful.[15] Thus, when William Eskridge and John Ferejohn describe the United States as a "republic of statutes," they are not simply characterizing "the new American Constitution";

they are setting a historical standard of "deliberation" that can elevate certain "super-statutes" to constitutional status.[16] When Bruce Ackerman declares the sweeping innovations of the New Deal to be a "constitutional moment," he aligns them in a historical pattern that justifies their avoidance of Article V's amendment procedures and, at the same time, forecloses the idea of their easy reversal.[17] In their history of the "unitary executive," Steven Calabresi and Christopher Yoo are not just documenting the bipartisan consistency with which presidents have resisted encroachments on their office by the other branches; they are interpreting the constitutional design to justify greater presidential control over policy making in the executive branch.[18]

Constitutional theory combines elements that we intentionally keep separate. Bracketing the question of what is to be done allows us to distinguish description more clearly from prescription and to gain a firmer hold on why that question has become so urgent and seemingly intractable.[19] In their bid to resolve issues that arise in the policy state, constitutional theorists offer fixes and cures touching all aspects of political life. At the same time, their divergent approaches to upholding constitutional principles and standards reflect the difficulties of reaching any decisive resolution. A descriptive theory of America's policy state should, as a matter of course, include the push and pull of alternative theoretical responses to the constitutional problems that have emerged. It should also stand outside the elastic bubble within which options accumulate and contend, first and foremost, on the value of constitutionalism itself.

Within the discipline of political science, the subfield of public policy approaches the relationship between past and present very differently. At least until recently, it has shown more consensus than has constitutional theory. Interested most of all in the systemic effects of economic and political changes in the twentieth century, this work describes a state that is politically restricted over time by its prior choices. From the classic writings of E. E. Schattschneider and Theodore Lowi comes the reigning theoretical insight of this literature: policies create their own politics.[20] Later elaborations by scholars like Paul Pierson and Suzanne Mettler have drawn out the effect on state formation. Once implemented, policies are "locked in" by the arrangements and interests that support them.[21] Policy's entrenchment renders political development "path dependent," narrowing the range of responses to the new problems that inevitably arise.[22]

Path dependence shows, for instance, in the complexities of the American health-care system. New health-care arrangements have not replaced the old; they have, rather, been successively "layered" on, multiplying the different systems in operation.[23] Path dependence also highlights conditions at large: a sprawling array of subgovernments, resistance to change by incorporated interests, the mounting frustrations of centralized management. The concerns captured by these dynamics are serious and endemic. To borrow a phrase, path dependence creates "an unwieldy state," strewn with encumbrances of its own making and often working at odds with policy's problem-solving rationale.[24]

That said, the historical perspective provided is strikingly one-sided. The focus on self-generated obstacles to more effective policy making obscures the historical transformation that has occurred in standards of responsiveness. Consider a prior state of affairs: in the nineteenth century the most significant constraints on policy were not imposed by political interest groups; they were legal, based on common law rules internalized by legislators and enforced by judges who, by turns, foreclosed the occasional bid for change. "Domestic"—family and labor—relations, well understood to be at the heart of what John Dewey called "the public and its problems," were effectively "locked out" of policy consideration.[25] These relations were in their own way "path dependent," but they had nothing meaningful to do with prior "choices."

A more circumspect history tracks a course of American state development that we find more trenchant than path dependence: path clearance. In a pattern centuries old, pivotal events toppled fixed relations of authority and pried the door open to programmatic solutions.[26] The subgovernments that arose in the twentieth century reflect the collapse of these ancient enclaves and the extension of public policy. Some policies did "lock in"—an "iron triangle" here,[27] a "third rail" there[28]—but the surer basis for relating public policy to state formation prioritizes the expanding scope of government's intervention, its historical opening to choice. This analysis better matches what are widely seen as policy's own energetic attributes. In place of sclerotic images of path dependence are "shifts" in policy, tides of opinion, and jostling for "attention."[29] Policy alternatives "stream" through "networks" of issue activists who exploit "windows" of opportunity.[30] Fitting here, too, are the "conversions" of policy missions by ambitious elites,[31] and "drifts" when lawmakers with other priorities neglect necessary updates.[32] Implicit throughout is the recognition of proliferating routes to innovation.

Another group of scholars who have been busy reassessing the importance of policy in state formation are political historians. Their interest in nineteenth-century developments serves to sharpen our own. Ironically, while political scientists have been pondering path dependence and the weight of the past, political historians have underscored the futuristic, creative character of policy making, and for them, policy's forward-leaning, problem-solving disposition has narrowed the differences between past and present. In a summary assessment, William Novak uses evidence from new histories of nineteenth-century government to debunk, once and for all, "the myth of the weak state" in early America.[33] He attributes this misguided characterization to comparisons with the apparatus of developing states in continental Europe, against which early American government appears undernourished, detached, attenuated, and ineffective. The new histories, Novak observes, shift the focus from apparatus to activity. They light on the spirit of instrumentalism that runs throughout American state formation, documenting the government's persistent, extensive, and indispensable engagement.

This new work refutes the notion that the strong activist government of today is a cultural aberration, a foreign import, a betrayal of principles, a break in pattern, or anything other than the tried-and-true American way. In so doing, it also raises doubts about the "big-bang" transformational moments of Progressivism and the New Deal. The takeaway after all is that little about modern American government is fundamentally new, that in one way or another, this state has always been a robust promoter of great national projects,[34] that it has always regulated the economy and supported national administrative discretion,[35] that it was always in the business of providing welfare,[36] that since the advent of the Constitution itself, the aim was to support and expand a great commercial empire.[37] At the very least, differences between government then and now need to be drawn with greater precision.

The new histories employ an authentically American method, one that can be traced back to the early champions of pragmatism.[38] It was John Dewey who elevated action over form, John R. Commons who defined the state as "officials-in-action," James Willard Hurst who confessed, "I do not find it profitable to distinguish 'law' from 'government' or from 'policy.'"[39] For us, the question raised by that lineage is whether a single-minded focus on creative activities will discount well-insulated, resistant pockets of authority, relegating their overthrow to little more than changing "technologies of practice."[40] Our answer is "yes." The character of the early American state is revealed more fully by paying closer attention to the obstacles the early pragmatists sought to remove: custom, tradition, legalism. That angle does not discount evidence of extensive policy making in early America, but it does better clarify and delimit its range. Our descriptive theory of American state formation will indicate that government in the nineteenth century was not all one thing, that the development of a policy state was not seamless, and that more policy is not just more policy.

The pragmatists of the early twentieth century were dedicated to breaking down distinctions. As we show, "law" and "government" have indeed shed many of the characteristics that once set them apart from each other and from "policy." But fierce contests were waged over how far policy might extend its reach, and that historical resistance attests to critical differences. Coterminous with the expansion of policy's domain, legal relations in society experienced massive shifts. To a large extent, negotiating these constituted politically the well-rehearsed historic breakpoints in American state development. To observe these displacements, we need a method attuned to aspects of early American government that were *not* policy and that specifically protected *against* policy. In other words, if we are interested in what sets modern American government apart, we will need to revisit the distinctions that pragmatism collapsed, for they lie at the heart of the prior arrangement.

No Bigger Than a Man's Hand

The Constitution of 1789 acknowledged the rising importance of policy making in statecraft and provided for its operation within defined limits. Equally emphatic was its endorsement of approaches to government other than policy. The first move is seen in the Constitution's detailed provisions for Congress, expected to be the creative body, the source of new law; the second is found in provisions for the judiciary, the guardian of existing rights. The president, as "chief magistrate," was made responsible for enforcing the decisions of both. Policy's allotment was set in designated authorizations and prohibitions— commerce, the military, the slave trade, religion.[41] Against the vast expanse of American governance outside the nation's capital and indeed outside the legislatures of the states, policy's domain was the proverbial man's hand held up to the sky. The subsequent enlargement of this sphere is the growth of the policy state.

In Chapter 2, "The Policy Motive," we provide the analytic tools needed to track and evaluate this process. When we speak of government in early America that was mostly "not policy," we mean something more than that policy was not enacted in a given area. We refer instead to the operation of institutions and rules that governed differently from, and substituted for, policy as we define it. We distinguish the programmatic, intentional character of "the policy motive" from governance more broadly, exercised by private as well as public authority. Although private authority in early America operated within legal limits and yielded predictable outcomes and effects, it was unlike policy in that it did not interrupt business as usual. On the contrary, it was itself business as usual, the foundation for much else that happened in government, including policy. This system proceeded for many centuries on the principle of rights, which we identify as the most encompassing countermotive to policy. We juxtapose these two systems—policy, limited but bent on expansion, and rights, socially entrenched but increasingly challenged. These initial arrangements did not make the early American state in any sense a simpler state, much less a weaker one, but they made it a very different state from the one we know today.

In Chapter 3, "Rights in the Policy State," we consider the impact of the expansion of government by policy on government by rights. This relationship sits at the heart of our developmental story, and assessing it will necessitate a fairly fine-grained treatment. With the "rights revolution" still ongoing in the United States, it is evident that government by policy has by no means extinguished its ancient counterpart. On the contrary, the United States recognizes more rights today than it did previously. The goal of this chapter is to demonstrate that the nature of rights has changed, that they have shed much of their historically distinct character as social and political demarcations. They now bestow authority on individuals—both citizens and government officers—less predictably and independently of policy considerations. In their practical operations, rights have become integrated into the scheme of programmatic government.

In Chapter 4, "Structure in the Policy State," we examine constraints on policy lodged in the formal arrangement of the institutions of American government. While the erosion of the division of labor set by the structure of the three constitutional branches has been well documented, surprisingly little attention has been paid to the pattern of change overall, or to the identification of common drivers, or to drawing general lessons from specific episodes. Our survey shows that the Constitution has come to operate over time less as a containment structure for policy than as an opportunity structure, that incumbents in every office have become policy entrepreneurs, advancing programs to secure their positions and enhance their power. This shift from containment structure to opportunity structure has itself opened new pathways to policy, creating outlets for results-oriented actions that work around the Constitution's divisions and weaken the rules of institutional behavior. Today's policy entrepreneurs treat rules as extensions of their programmatic ambitions, as resources to exploit and obstacles to overcome.

Chapter 5, "Politics in the Policy State," widens the perspective further still. Here we identify some additional components of a policy state in action and reflect on what the effective operation of such a state might require. That takes our analysis to the authority of science and expertise and to the responsibilities of citizenship. We consider the importance of information sharing, civic-mindedness, and consensus in the operation of representative bodies and in the political community at large. We point out how America's policy state has by its own development undermined these preconditions for its success. Looking at the prescriptions of scholars who have been privy to the inner workings of modern American government, we consider various arguments for sticking with the current course, and we ask how effective they are against the strains mounting on governmental authority. We conclude with some thoughts about the systemic problems that now loom large, the ones that more policy is unlikely to resolve.

CHAPTER TWO

The Policy Motive

STATES vary in their approach to policy. Emperors of the Han dynasty in third-century China were schooled in the virtues of "nonaction." They idealized a center of calm, an ascetic sovereign, a state that could function without the intrusion of new directives. Modern states are less abstemious. The United States boasts "popular sovereignty," a principle that, however reticent its beginning, promotes agency, choice, and intervention. Citizens participate actively in determining the course of affairs, and politicians compete for their favor. The center of government is raucous, alive with initiative; the policy motive courses through the polity, strong and aggressive.

That said, scholars still distinguish modern states by the extent of their restraint. Although the ancient Han might find American government's approach to policy reckless, contemporary observers count it one of the more circumspect. Judged strictly "on paper," it is easy to see why. Rights and liberties, divided powers, local control, staggered elections, multiple modes of representation, procedural safeguards— these emblems of reserve have been integral features from the original design. The American idea has always been to mobilize other motives to slow the conversion of initiatives into programs, or block them altogether, setting the policy motive in a perpetual bid for priority.

By "motive" we have in mind more than its colloquial use as a personal reason for acting. We use the term to mean an animating premise or theme, a "motif," drawn from the political culture and supported by the state. A "policy motive" is embedded in the apparatus of a government just as a "profit motive" is embedded in the organization of an industry. Policy is one of many lines of action available to office-holders and citizens, lines they are encouraged by various means to pursue. Some motives are shared by all states: law and order, for instance, and national security. Others, like democracy or civil liberties or power checking, may be in play strongly or weakly or not at all.

Motives can connect to one another differently: rights, for instance, may be connected to the preservation of hierarchy or to its elimination; representation may work to bolster or loosen local control; the motive of policy may cut for or against democracy. Motives find expression in innumerable particulars, and in every instance, they call on, underscore, and channel authority. Motives convey values, activate commitments, and interrogate political practices.

Working together, motives articulate the polity at large, joining the formal arrangements of government to politics and society outside. Attending to motives in this way opens analysis to the full range of political activity without dissolving the state into an undifferentiated realm of "action" that obscures its distinctive and contradictory features. By the same token, an approach through motives is well adapted to the study of change. Motives that are supported, not to say enshrined, within a given constitution will be difficult to dislodge, but mere persistence does not imply a fixed model. As they are enacted, downplayed, revived, and redeployed, they shape and reshape the state. The simultaneity and mutual impingement of different motives suggest the perpetual contention and uncertain resolution characteristic of politics.

The potential for change inherent in these interactions alerts us to the parameters of development. By examining motives as they clash over time we can identify systemic shifts of great practical significance, even in a state like the United States, otherwise characterized by extraordinary historical continuity. Were all government's motives in perfect equipoise, then actions and principles, operations and rules, outcomes and norms would also stay in rough alignment, each motive holding the others in place. The American Constitution was specifically designed to tap these mutually reinforcing effects, empowering policy while simultaneously engaging other motives to discipline and contain it. Exactly how public resources—intellectual, material, institutional—accumulate around different motives over time and redistribute themselves throughout the state is an empirical question. Each adjustment tests the correspondence of principles with actions, rules with operations, norms with outcomes. While a state's motives may remain nominally the same, accommodations among them may be uneven. As their relative positions change, so, too, their practical effects.

On inspection, we find that the policy motive has far outstripped its place in the original design. This development is testament to policy's unique affinity to problem solving in a world of rapid economic and demographic changes. Of particular interest to us is the systemic political impact of policy's historically attained dominance, a de facto priority foisted uneasily on arrangements of governance principally associated with other values and legitimating norms. The results that ensued were not all—or even mostly—planned or calculated; the policy space has been constructed pragmatically, to a large extent experimentally. Nor were the trade-offs entailed locked in some imaginary zero-sum "game." Rather than close off avenues for other motives like representation, say, or democracy or citizens' rights, proponents of the policy motive have characteristically promised to enlarge the expression of these others and spread their benefits more widely.

The historical shift to policy affects not only the relative strength and position of other motives but also the character of those other motives. The aggrandizement of policy causes these others to become both more policy-like and increasingly dependent on government policy for their own vitality. Insofar as these effects are unsettling, it must in part be attributed to a widening disparity between how these other motives are experienced and how we continue to talk about them, to a disparity between the discourse of "rights," "checks," "representation," and so on, and their implementation in practice.

Everything in Its Place

Debates about "more" or "less" government turn out, on closer look, to be disputes about the kind and location of public authority. As a general proposition the authority of government in a nation state may be described as plenary.[1] The shorthand contrast drawn between an early era of "limited" government and a modern era of "big" government refers more meaningfully to the government's authority to make policy, to purposely and programmatically intervene in society's ongoing operations, than to the range of enforceable rules. The same goes for the notion that the United States began as a "weak" state and became a "strong" one. In some respects and for many people, government in

America was more imposing at the time the Constitution was written than it is today.

The framers of the Constitution did not change every aspect of American government as they found it but dealt with the parts of most immediate concern. They also did not contemplate a partial system of laws or a less obtrusive government than what they already had. They were interested above all in widening the scope of authority to make national policy, as it was then envisioned, more effective, and they prudently shifted around bits of authority within the larger governing scheme to achieve that objective. Their debates focused on these shifts, what they proposed to relocate, what would remain where it was, and how to keep things in their place in the future. Many of the prior arrangements came through the commotion largely unaffected.

The failings of the Articles of Confederation had been clear for all to see. Having resolved to correct them, the framers were not modest in their ambitions. Taking their cue from the great commercial nations of the day, they fortified the government of the United States with military command and control, a reliable revenue stream, and the final say over currency, foreign trade, and interstate commerce.[2] This they joined to the cause of a nation capable of acting on behalf of its people and, ultimately at least, responsible to their will. Their defeat of a proposal to give the national government a veto over state-level legislation brought the construction project into sharper relief. Providing shelter to local authority was as important to the majority at the Constitutional Convention as creating a national government that could act without state permission. In that sense, the Constitution was above all an allocation mechanism, its authority superior to the others to the extent that it divided operations among the parts and promised due support for each. The distinction between government and policy rested in significant measure on the degree of independence preserved for different systems of rule.

The major elements of the constitutional design—federalism, bicameralism, the enumerated powers, the different forms of representation, the separation of powers, checks and balances—as well as the negotiations that surrounded their adoption, ratification, and amendment all worked to the same ends. The higher purpose was to restrain tyranny; an immediate objective, to reassure all involved that policy would be contained. Consider Congress, policy-wise the most dangerous branch. The single unamendable guarantee in the Constitution is the equal representation of each state in the Senate. In the House of Representatives, with incumbents elected from smaller districts, protection was sought in the difficulty of forming majorities on a continental scale and augmented by a three-fifth's supplement in representation for localities with slaves. The framers allowed for some degree of elasticity. The purpose was, after all, to substitute the hamstrung Confederation with a national government having the leeway to perform its newly assigned roles. Elasticity, however, was meant to be a hedge against unexpected events, not a plan for future development.[3] The balance struck among institutions assumed their permanent operation, a message reinforced by the framers' new science of statecraft. The built-in capacity to stretch and rebound promised long-term responsiveness without fundamental change. Once set in motion, the republic was to sail forward with only minor listing.

To further assuage doubters, it was agreed to buttress this vessel with a second set of provisions in the form of ten amendments, known from then on as the Bill of Rights. Likewise understood as checks on tyrannical ambitions and protections for hard-won liberties, they present, from our perspective, the same combination of policy enactment and policy prevention as the constitutional text itself. The Fifth Amendment's provision of just compensation for "takings," modeled on the English law of eminent domain, was a policy choice over "allodial"—absolute—property rights preferred by settler interests. The Sixth Amendment guarantee of assistance of defense counsel was a departure from English practice. The Seventh Amendment endorsed civil jury trial for suits "at common law" over access in some states to jury trials for all disputes. The Ninth and Tenth Amendments in particular bore on policy at the level of declared principle: liberty will not be shut down by actions of the center. All posited attributes of a free state. Many would not be legally clarified—even authoritatively addressed—for more than a century.

Once locked into the Constitution, these limits established a formidable barrier to the advance of policy beyond where it stood at the time of ratification. In particular, the jurisdictions of common law authority that William Blackstone labeled "the private relations" became in America "vested rights," unreachable by legislation—master and servant, husband and wife, parent and child, guardian and ward (James Kent, Blackstone's American equivalent, would add domestic slavery[4]). Unlike the Bill of Rights, which increased the number of constitutional provisions, the authority lodged in these constrained policy at the government's core social foundations. Virtually all were located in the states,[5] governed on-site by the superior party in each pair, according to rules often centuries old, internalized by those involved, and, in the occasional case of resistance, enforced by courts of law. Authority at this level operated, both in letter and in spirit, at the furthest remove from programmatic intrusion; the rules, as inherited, were thought to be, for all practical purposes, timeless. As events would show, resistance to the encroachments of policy would prove stiffest when it threatened authority so deeply entrenched.

"Conjuring Tricks"

Immediately upon ratification, fierce contests broke out over the precise scope of the government's authority to meet new demands. Where the Constitution's provision for policy was uncertain, national leaders sometimes enlisted "implied" powers, as with the Neutrality Proclamation; sometimes "the general welfare" clause, as with the Sedition Act; sometimes the "necessary and proper" clause, as in the case of the national bank; and they "combined" powers for public works. Although none of these early initiatives moved beyond the areas of national security and commerce already carved out for policy making by the framers, they were resisted by many as perilous intrusions on protected areas. The countermove was to amplify existing methods of "we the people" by organizing political parties dedicated to states' rights and strict constitutional construction. In the near term, these parties would clamp down on national policy ambitions.

Political parties developed so quickly in the new republic that they now appear integral to its operation. Nonetheless, they were a portentous development. Perhaps elites were bound to collide over principles still arguable. But once their disputes were taken to the public at large, their alternative interpretations of free government magnified the insecurities of all concerned. If states' rights and national power were to be contested electorally, it followed that either cause might be defeated. For those defending strict construction, the act of organizing nationally carried additional risks. Although Jeffersonians and Jacksonians tended to out-organize their opponents and beat back the most aggressive nationalist advances, they did so by connecting separated institutions and facilitating collective action. Parties by their nature aggregate interests across localities, coordinate actions across branches, and thus empower national majorities. Whatever their ideological impetus, the natural tendency of parties is not to defend boundaries but to transgress them and push limits outward. Put within our larger perspective, parties had a born affinity with policy making.

Tying the cause of strict construction to national party calculations caused special apprehension in the slaveholding South. As national demographics tilted against the region, Southern elites found themselves precariously dependent on cross-sectional alliances and the balance of party power to protect their region's uniquely vulnerable institutions. Long before the turmoil of the 1850s, the pull of coalition, spoils, and majority rule led them to worry about prospects for keeping their most basic interests aloof from the struggle over national initiatives. They gradually lost confidence in the Constitution's promise of consensus, the idea that what common interest might be had for action at the center would be found by independent representatives deliberating in separate institutions.

The coming of the policy state was foretold by Southerners expressing buyer's remorse. John Randolph of Virginia, for example, was a prominent victim of misplaced faith in a party preaching limited government. His bruising collaboration with the Jeffersonians convinced him that no party could be trusted to respect the Constitution's enumerated powers, that the temptation of organized majorities to stretch their warrants and trample rights was irresistible. In his increasingly strident assaults on the policy motive, he renounced "the lust of innovation"[6] and issued militant calls for nonaction: "For my part, I wish we could have done nothing but talk . . . give me fifty speeches, I care not how dull or stupid, rather than see one new law on the statute books."[7] After the Missouri crisis, his fury reached the very foundation of the regime. The 1824 tariff on plantation staples was well within Congress's powers in Article I, yet Randolph assailed it as proof of the

Constitution's uselessness: "I have no faith in the abracadabra of the constitution. . . . If, under a power to regulate trade, you draw the last drop of blood from our veins; if *secundum artem,* you draw the last shilling from our pockets; what are the checks of the constitution to us? A fig for the constitution!"[8]

The enlistment of tariffs in a program for national economic development—raising revenue beyond that needed to run the national government and advancing a coalition to build the home market—brought on the most serious constitutional crisis prior to the Civil War.[9] But this time the Southerner behind the confrontation did not, like Randolph, renounce the Constitution outright.[10] After a failed collaboration with the party of Jackson, John C. Calhoun set out to show how the constitutional project might be saved from the threat of nationally organized electoral machines. Calhoun met the rising strength of the policy motive with a proposal to erect more imposing impediments—concurrent majorities, minority vetoes, plural executives, and state nullification. All this he regarded as fully in step with the founders' intentions for representation, local control, and national consensus, but strengthened for the fast-changing field of play. The added provisions he advocated would shore up all authorities, preserve rights, and restore constitutional faith.[11]

The fear of policy expressed by Randolph and Calhoun heavily weighed the loss of political and legal privileges enjoyed by slave masters. But their grievances and formulations reached beyond slavery to other governance left untouched by the settlement of 1789. Essentially the same point was made in the wake of the New Deal by the French theorist Bertrand de Jouvenel as he observed the movement of America's industrial workers out from under the governance of their employers. As if channeling Randolph, de Jouvenel argued that the protections offered by intricate constitutional contrivances were liberal illusions, "conjuring tricks," and that the only real force behind so-called limited government was the isolation of large segments of the citizenry beyond the control of lawmakers ready to make policy on their behalf. If legal protections for these, what de Jouvenel called social "make weights," were no longer able to block policy solutions, then the supposed hold of constitutions would be lost, left to the con-

tingencies of political power.[12] This was the South's analysis brought
up to date.

What Is Policy and What Is It Not?

Randolph, Calhoun, and de Jouvenel each appealed to forms of governance that have passed into history. The Constitution, on the other
hand, endures. The design for inhibiting would-be policy makers did
not evaporate; American government continues to be characterized by
"veto points," not to mention "gridlock." Still, there is reason to think
these cranky prognosticators were onto something.[13] Up until the
1970s, divided authority inside government—in federalism and in the
separation of branches—continued to derive staying power from traditional authority relations outside. Episodic elimination of those arrangements and the expansion of the field for government's programmatic
intervention has affected both, including the "veto players" who vie to
impede this policy or that. That these changes fundamentally altered
the American state cannot be dismissed on evidence that policy initiatives regularly run a difficult obstacle course. Rather, the question to be
answered is whether the Constitution today protects anything substantial *besides* policy. For that inquiry, we need to sharpen definitions
grown fuzzy with usage.

We turn first to the centerpiece, "policy" itself. What exactly is
"policy"? What are its distinguishing attributes? What are we thinking
when we call policy a "motive" of government? In our understanding,
*policy is a commitment to a designated goal or course of action,
made authoritatively on behalf of a given entity or collectivity, and
accompanied by guidelines for its accomplishment.*

"Commitment" suggests that policy is supported and endorsed—
actively—by its makers. This does not mean policy might not be inherited in the sense that it was devised and passed on by others, or that
a policy might not be accidentally stumbled on through trial and error.
But policy is not compulsory; it entails discretion and assumes options,
if only to do nothing. Officers of government may choose to pursue
policy in a particular area or not, or this policy over that; circumstances—
resources or public support—may make one policy possible and rule

out another. "Commitment" also speaks to duration. Policy is fixed for some period of time, though the span will vary; implied here too is the idea that policy will have a beginning, a period of continuance, and, at least in principle, an end. "Designated goal or course of action" refers to projected and not unintended consequences. A goal may be sparsely or fully articulated, more or less immediate, and it may encompass an array of outcomes, but policy is characteristically an intervention seeking to change an existing state of affairs. Policy will be monitored, adjusted, and evaluated accordingly, with reference to its performance.

"Made authoritatively on behalf of a given entity or collectivity" highlights the element of representation always present in policy decisions. Policy makers do not act, at least not openly, on their own behalf; they are anchored in institutional settings that lend legitimacy to their actions. This aspect also presumes that policy will command some measure of social resources, including the cooperative actions of others. This brings our definition of policy close to "legislation," whether this be done by legislators proper or by judges, administrative agencies, and executives at various levels of government. "Guidelines for its accomplishment" means that policy anticipates a road map, from here to there, with an idea of steps in between. Though policies are generally associated with instructions and rules, "guidelines" better conveys policy's flexibility, its openness to maneuver and adjustment around the edges. When greater discipline is imposed on policy operatives, it is more often to achieve greater efficiency of performance or a rebalancing of goals than to enforce obedience to rules for its own sake. Guidelines also establish limits beyond which a policy may be said to have shifted its goals or gone off track.

All these attributes—goals, discretion, representation, intervention, performance, flexibility—suggest policy's orientation to the future. Policy is animated by discontent with the status quo, by circumstances as they unfold, by problems as they arise. The policy motive is open-ended, instrumental, calculating, and creative; it seeks efficiency and anticipates more policy to come. This brings us to an another attribute: each policy moves on its own tangent. Although a policy may build on or coordinate with another, the impetus, goals, and guidelines tend to be discrete, particularized, and, to a meaningful degree, indepen-

dent. This fact complicates the extent to which the future is susceptible to control. A policy state will strive to achieve central direction,
to impose some overhead management of its many commitments and
goals, but this capacity is not easily cultivated. In the United States
the effort confronts an underlying structure of authority that is fragmented, conflict ridden, and battered regularly by elections.

Policy as we define it, then, is not meant to appear as anything different from what it is commonly thought to be. By our definition, a
single statute may contain many policies, and that is often in fact the
case. To pick one out of the hat, the Violent Crime Control and Law
Enforcement Act of 1994 dealt with prisons, police, judges, city youth,
gun owners, and abortion providers. Our definition of policy excludes
"rogue" projects, outside the guidelines altogether, but this boundary
is not always clear-cut. President Reagan, for instance, expressed support for rebels in Nicaragua, but he disavowed the "policy" pursued
independently by his staff to provide assistance from arms sales to
Iran. In general, policy purports to be, at least in some respects, new;
however, here, too, boundaries cannot be sharply drawn. Actions routinely seen as "housekeeping" may, under unforeseen conditions,
explode into a pressing policy choice. In 1861 provisioning a fort in
Charleston Harbor raised the monumental decision of Civil War; recent
resistance to raising the national debt ceiling has one party accusing
the other of "holding policy hostage" by refusing to countenance business as usual. The policy motive may be mixed with others; we saw
that earlier in the Bill of Rights. Policies enhance as well as encroach
on authority. In a history of American policy spread over more than two
centuries of social change, mixes like these are commonplace.

The opposing term to policy in our analysis, the counterpoint
motive—what policy is not—is rights. This does not mean that policy
and rights are the only motives active in American politics. We have
already mentioned democracy, representation, checks, and others, and
we return to them again shortly. But the interplay of policy and rights
brings into focus the policy state's development. In our definition,
*rights are claims that one person, in or outside government, may make
on the person or actions of another, enforceable in a court of law.*

"Rights are claims": this signals that rights are decidedly unlike
policy in several ways. Whereas policy looks ahead to the future, the

orientation of rights is backward, affirming or reclaiming something already due. A right may be variously acquired—through a constitution, common law, a statute, a contract. A right might be inherited at birth or legislated or agreed on last week. But once in existence, there is no expectation that it will be reevaluated or modified. The expectation, rather, is that the right will be found, acknowledged, proven, upheld, or enforced. Policies, too, may be upheld and enforced, of course, but only contingently, according to future objectives. "That one person, in or outside government" distinguishes rights from policy by their being attached to or possessed by individuals. This personal attachment, no deputies or substitutes permitted, exists even when the right arises through group membership or a class action in court.

Our inclusion of government officers among persons who enjoy rights might seem odd until one remembers that under the Constitution judges hold their offices for life, that presidents have a right to appoint them, and that U.S. senators have a right to confirm them. Rights claimed by officers are routinely opposed to rights claimed by citizens; the procedures by which citizens assert their constitutional and statutory rights in court, for instance, through writs of habeas corpus, presume this juxtaposition.[14] In this respect, as always, rights exist in relation to "the person or actions of another," with the claimant demanding that someone do something, or stop doing something, or turn something over. Such interdependency is missing from policy, where initiatives operate, as it were, automatically, on their own track and impersonally on those affected.

If the legislature is the natural locale of policy, the judiciary is the natural locale of rights. "Enforceable in a court of law" indicates that rights are affirmed or denied, post hoc, by judges or in judgelike proceedings. The phrase also speaks to the fact that these agencies are anticipated, provided for in advance, available to perform their function. New agencies or officers are not required. New courts might be created, but rights presume their availability in advance. "Enforceable in a court" also reflects the fact that claiming rights today is always entwined with the actions as well as the rights of government officers, whether as the instrument of trial or as party to a suit. The idea of enforcement implies the all-important aspect of rights that they are prescribed in fixed rules to which obedience is anticipated. The degree to which such rules are "absolute" will, as we show, vary according to their context, but rights are never admitted to be mere guidelines. Rights may involve balancing among one another and be subjected to different levels of enforcement, but no particular right is understood as flexible or accommodating in itself.

Like the motive of policy, the motive of rights is comprehensive, capable of coordinating the operations of government in its entirety. Feudalism, for example, was an all-encompassing system of rights. Readers will recognize a family resemblance between the motive of rights and the concept of a *Rechtsstaat*, the nineteenth-century European idea of a morally sanctioned government organized under the rule of law. Our construct, unlike that one, does not give pride of place to the protection of property, nor do we conflate the motive of rights with the achievement of justice. We place the dominance of the rights motive earlier in history than the nineteenth or even the seventeenth century, and see it significantly eroded by the nineteenth, indeed, by policy affecting property in particular.

As we emphasized in the case of policy, our definition of rights does not exclude hybrids, crossovers, and overlaps. King Henry II, the great organizer of the common law in the twelfth century, was nothing if not a policy maker. The idea that common law judges in England were arbiters of rights without regard for policy was derided by Bentham as "nonsense on stilts."[15] Legislation today that is unquestionably policy will frequently create rights going forward; sometimes policy will bestow rights on persons authorized to defend the just-created rights in court. Within government, authority within jurisdictions is regularly divided, for instance, as it has been for centuries, between ministerial rights exercised by mandates and rules, and judicial rights exercised purely by discretion, on the pattern of policy. Even in settings where, on the record, rights were rigidly enforced—say, in nineteenth-century family relations—there was not the total absence of legislation or of policy, but this was mainly found at intersections of categories (wives and property ownership, for example) or limited to details. The Missouri controversy of 1820, nothing if not a dispute over rights, began with a legislative policy of depriving slaveholders of the right to automatically own their slaves' offspring.

As all of this should indicate, rights by no means disappear in the policy state. However, we shall argue that rights demonstrate progressively less "rightness" as they take on attributes associated with policy. We will call attention to the "endowment" of rights in different social settings over time. By endowment we mean the contents of a given right that may be successfully asserted at law. We will also be interested in "valence," how much a given right is weighed against another given right in different disputes or sets of circumstances. Through these two qualities we will be able to follow the changing character of rights as well as their place in the developing policy state. At issue always is the extent to which rights constrain official discretion, foreclosing programmatic goals.

Structure and Opportunity

The predominance of the policy motive, increasingly marked over time, implicates all aspects of modern American government, including its constitutional structure. For every conservative who laments "parchment barriers," there is a frustrated progressive who perceives this structure as a lamentable obstacle to accomplishing the public's business. What, then, is structure?

The term is harder to define than either "rights" or "policy." Arguably, the Constitution was a "policy," a future-looking product of collective deliberation and political compromise, a programmatic intervention meant to alter course and attain stated purposes. This alone suggests a closer affinity between structure and policy than between policy and rights. That said, structure is not policy. Although structure can enable action, it is not itself a "goal," or even a motive of government in our meaning. If the structure of American government is broken up and examined in its separate elements, it will appear to have less in common with policy than with rights. As we indicated in the previous section, the Constitution is, among other things, so-many-rights, each part answerable to claims that officers in a given branch or agency can make on and against the actions of other persons, in and outside of government. Under a rule of law, structure-as-rights keeps policy and its advocates contained.

To the extent that structure is more than the sum of such parts, it refers to an entire ensemble, a comprehensive scheme of interrelated pieces with its own discernable "principles" of organization. For instance, incumbents in one branch of American government may, in the course of their transactions with those in another, assert "the symmetry of privileges," or "coordinate power," or "concurrent exercise," or "separate obligations."[16] None of this is spelled out in the Constitution's words, but each principle may be inferred from the manner in which the institutions are arranged. Each is a proposition about how they are intended to work together.

In this respect, structure is a set of conjectures or extrapolations derived from an arrangement of parts. It is more abstract and theoretical than both rights and policy, but exerts influence over both. The structure of the U.S. Constitution, perhaps all constitutions, has a twofold rationale. First, it promotes a range of motives: policy, rights, representation, democracy, decentralization, separation, efficiency, stability, law and order. Second, it distributes the work of government and sets the relations—the rights—among officers accordingly. Contention and ongoing "construction" stem from the conjectural aspect, the inherent possibility of different inferences about practical operations.[17] In this way, structure provides a framework for strategic action—a set of opportunities, incentives, resources, and risks—supporting whatever motive of government, legitimate or otherwise, incumbents pursue. Actions less directly tied to the written text, more speculative in their interpretation of it, will render the framework more flexible, which is to say that greater uncertainty will be introduced over permissible outcomes.

At the time of the Constitution's framing this was well understood. *The Federalist Papers* countered the risks of disembodied reasoning with reference back to rights. By tying the "interests" of the institutional actors to "the constitutional rights of the place," Publius argued that "ambitions" would be, as if mechanically, held in check.[18] The Anti-Federalists were quick to point out that the same logic could be inverted to predict a different future: the less strictly jurisdictional lines were enforced, or the less tightly the constitutional structure of officers' rights defined the interests of incumbents, the less confidence one could place in its assurances about restraint. On both sides, there was basic agreement that rules governing institutional interactions were only as dependable as the rights behind them.

The greatest ambiguity surrounding the alleged correspondence of officers' interests with officers' rights arose from the placement of all institutional 'assignments on the same popular foundation. Each of the Constitution's several parts was regarded as the common possession of "the people," on a new idea of popular sovereignty. This was perhaps the ultimate abstraction. Popular sovereignty all but invited officeholders to leverage their own powers against rights held by their counterparts. Charged to serve the will of the citizenry outside of institutions, they might discount norms of comity, deference, and mutual restraint on the inside. Action on behalf of the people at large virtually committed the structure to permanent negotiation.

The expansion of policy's domain has drawn heavily on projections like this. Exploiting the conjectural qualities of structure lends the legitimacy of constitutional principles to new arrangements. Motives present in the original document can be relocated, moved from one place to another, creating novel configurations. The expansion of presidential policy making has been accommodated structurally by recasting the presidency as the nation's most "representative" institution; the enlargement of administrative policy making has been accommodated structurally by "separating" agency rule making from agency adjudication. When lines of action supported by the Constitution are transposed onto new forms, structure operates less as a hedge against change than as a goad to further development.[19] By the same token, authority becomes harder to pin down.

Tracking Development

The dilution of rights and the erosion of structure are twin features of state formation in modern America. As we argue, both entail a relaxation of constraints on the policy motive. The pertinent events begin in the second half of the nineteenth century and accelerate through the twentieth. Energetic as it was, antebellum government deployed policy within expected lines, for reasons of national security and to promote commercial expansion. Intimations of wide-ranging policy to come shaped the political discourse of the period until the nation literally burst its bounds.

In retrospect, the path of subsequent development may look like simply more policy. What distinguishes the "policy state," however, is that its central motive has weakened others, not only rights and structure but with them representation, accountability, public deliberation, and the like. These alterations have greatly complicated the prospect that a different state of affairs might be achieved by further rearranging the furniture. The complication is this: although the policy state opens government to a wider range of options, it also makes it less likely that government can be tied down to any one of them. Rearrangement is policy's beat, promoting an inveterate hostility to fixed relationships of any kind. The dilution of rights and the erosion of structure are in this regard only symptomatic. The perpetual churning saps the personal and material resources that make the system secure. Attaching the "interests of actors" to "the rights of place" can be effective only if rights and place are stable.

The chapters that follow concentrate on what we consider prototypical advances along this path and what they reveal about the thrust and direction of change. We are not attempting a history. If we were, we might dwell on the events of the Civil War and Reconstruction, where we find the nineteenth century's most conspicuous departure from previously constrained policies. The Civil War amendments to the Constitution proclaimed a categorical shift in authority over race relations, a violent and sweeping opening to new programmatic initiatives: "Congress shall have power . . ." But in the face of this opportunity, the Supreme Court narrowed Congress's authority, the radical wing of the Republican Party melted away, and reaction in the shape of Jim Crow stymied social reforms that at least some Northerners anticipated.[20] For decades afterward, policy worked to keep race relations as close as possible to their prior condition. The breakthrough moments for the policy state are in the middle of the twentieth century. For the most part, those are the developments that command our attention.

A second point concerning selection follows on the above. In Chapters 3 and 4, on "rights" and "structure," we focus on the historic incorporation into the policy state of personal relations. Matters of commerce and security, already firmly established there in 1789, were, by definition, the vibrant core from which the new policy state would spring, but we follow them only secondarily. Our discussion of policy "auras" in Chapter 3 shows that programmatic action in policy matters already "inside" are never far removed from the fierce contests in "outlying" regions. Change often stems from these points of contact. The decades-long resistance encountered in extending policy-making authority over commerce could not exempt itself from the turmoil of labor relations; the civil rights movement was inevitably affected by the national security concerns of the Cold War; the current war on terror puts new strain on free speech and the writ of habeas corpus.[21] We touch on these interchanges but do not explore them in any depth.

Finally, the policy state is plainly visible in the sprawl of agencies and commissions at all levels of government. It is evident in the provision and continuous proposal of new goods and services and in the dense networks of organized interests that depend on them and nourish them. It appears in the proliferation of offices charged with directing operations overall—with agenda setting, priority budgeting, expert forecasting, performance monitoring, and institutional coordination. It is implicated in the emergence of an elaborate "parastate"[22]—the complex of think tanks, graduate schools, private foundations, professional societies, watchdog groups, and rating services, all dedicated to monitoring performance, updating old prescriptions, developing new applications, and setting standards of best practice.

Our intent is not to exclude these or other aspects of policy-state development. We deal with them, however, only as they arise in a dogged pursuit of our basic proposition. *The Policy State* is not meant to summarize all the pertinent things the state is doing and their effects. What it intends to document is a historical reconfiguration of—in our usage—the government's driving motives, or for a more familiar word, government's meaning.

Part II

The Policy State

CHAPTER THREE

Rights in the Policy State

STUDENTS of the Han Empire aside, the contemporary reader may well find it hard to imagine a government without policy. It is likely easier to imagine a government without rights. Yet historically, the political background of the United States presents a picture exactly contrary to these intuitions. England from medieval times was a place where the intellectual and political energies devoted to rights—the rights of monarchs, officers, freeholders, towns, guilds, churches—dwarfed the very small allocation devoted to policy, at least in the definition of the forward-looking, problem-solving expenditure of mental and material resources we provided in Chapter 2. Rights, on the other hand, comprised the touchstone, the method, the rules by which the entirety of English society and government was constituted, organized, made to obey.

During the Middle Ages, and until the great social upheavals of the sixteenth and seventeenth centuries, the world was presumed to be in most ways an unchanging place, preordained and inviolate. The natural calamities and the ebbs and flows of trade that are today commonplace occasions for policy making were regarded then as temporary interruptions of the settled order. The very premise of English common law was that judges decreed nothing new but instead affirmed rights according to existing rules and customs. The system of common law anticipated all predictable, which is to say most, human situations that arose, regulating the activities of every person under its sway, from the monarch and his officers to the lowly villein; foreigners when they were in the country; aboriginal inhabitants of colonies; even Jews, who since the fourteenth century had been officially banished.[1] Parliament for its part was understood to smooth out uncertainties left in what the law courts had already decided.[2]

An arguable exception to this pattern was foreign affairs. We say arguable because the idea that even here monarchs prior to the Glorious

Revolution of 1688 were committed to some sustained project or
instrumental strategy to which they adhered more than sporadically—
beyond religious quarrels, dynastic exigencies, and the blandish-
ments of this or that group of merchants—would be an exaggeration.[3]
England's benign neglect where foreign affairs were concerned was experienced by the North American colonies firsthand, much as they
also knew a rude awakening when royal attentions spiked upward in
the eighteenth century. Moving ahead from that point, foreign policy
making was emphatically "on," full-bore, in the so-called age of mer-
cantilism. For the first time, national economic advantage became the
preoccupying purpose in relations among nations. Foreign and domestic affairs joined forces to promote manufacturing and trade, to
control money and wages, to expand foreign colonies, the entire effort
propelled by new political theories infused with the scientifically
driven idea of "progress."[4] Of a piece with this broad mobilization, the
national legislature achieved the status of principal policy maker.
Flying the banner of parliamentary sovereignty, it openly defied the
commercial rigidities imposed by the monarchy and the courts of
common law and assumed authority over commerce as its own favored
area of operations.

As distant as it may seem, this chronology is critical for understanding the discussions that follow here and in the next chapters.
Commerce among nations was at the center of policy making in the
new United States—first among reasons for independence and then for
the abandonment of the Confederation, in pursuit of becoming a continental power. Commercial affairs constituted the principal content
of domestic policy as well, from the era of the framing straight through
the first half of the nineteenth century. National debt, banking, tariffs, land sales, canals and toll roads, pensions, immigration, railways,
antitrust, the interstate movement of slaves: all were pressing business
of the federal government prior to the Civil War. Afterward, as we have
said, the policy space can be seen to widen, in stages, to take in relations of society formerly configured by rules—rights—of inherited English law, that is to say, the workplace, the family, and, to an extent
not always appreciated, among the white and black races.[5]

These stages, punctuated by successive social upheavals, were not
mutually airtight. Each development represented a loosening of di-

rectly applicable rules, of closely associated rules, of rules governing the making of rules, and, at every point, a loosening of rules against loosening rules. In that sense, each stage led to the one that followed and each along the way gave clear signals of additional loosening to come. We will not recount this larger history even in abbreviated form, for although it proceeds in tandem with the growth of the policy state, it entails causes and actors far beyond our focus. Our interest in this chapter, rather, will be with what we have called the *valence* of rights, the effectiveness of a given right to determine—in practice—the legal outcome when asserted or contested in court. Examining valences allows the assessment of how rights as such have changed their character, and, further, how this change bears on our larger argument that the dominant *motive*—the energizing and organizing theme—of American politics has shifted from rights to policy.

To this end, let us begin with the most influential contemporary definition of rights, the definition offered by the late political philosopher Ronald Dworkin: rights are "trumps."[6] Trumps, according to Dworkin, are preferences that legitimately override preferences or goals that other persons, whether the same in number or even the polity as a whole, might embrace or pursue. Realistically speaking, and even setting aside the obstacles involved in defining the preferences of the polity as a whole, does this chime with lived experience? Our answer is, in a word, "no." To continue the gambling metaphor, we propose that rights in the policy state are not trumps but "chips." By chips we mean tokens or vouchers, in this case of legal and moral value, which are regularly countered by other chips of parallel or correlative standing, leaving the outcome in any particular legal conflict undetermined. In Dworkin's defense, it can be said he intended his analysis normatively, not empirically. But that merely muddles things more, for it obstructs our view of the historical progression from an earlier time when some rights were—as demonstrable fact—trumps, whereas today they are almost never so.[7]

Our reliance on two categories, trumps and chips, in no way implies the absence of gradations, or the fact that some rights-as-trumps may not be more embedded, harder to dislodge, than others, or that some particular rights-as-chips may not be routinely balanced against other rights-as-chips in patterns that take on a semblance of permanence.

Also, the source of any given right—in common law, in legislation, in constitutional provision—can affect its efficacy relative to others. Some rights are expressly fortified at their origins, even as rights-as-chips have become the norm. For example, the modern Supreme Court has afforded certain rights-as-chips protections under the rubric of "substantive due process," allowing them to be abridged by legislation for only the most exigent of reasons. By the same token, the presence of legislation concerning a right does not in itself signal change in this regard. The fact that certain subjects were, in our understanding, outside the policy space in early America did not preclude statutes intended to enhance the enforcement of common law rules, for instance, and to bolster certain moral teachings, providing only that existing trumps remained intact. Our purpose is not to put rights into boxes but to understand their permutation as a category over time.

As society becomes more contentious, rights change their character as well as their putative source. In Blackstone's era, the mid-eighteenth century, understood widely to be the "classical" or high point in the history of rights, many, perhaps most, rights were, in Dworkin's meaning, trumps. That is, they were rights denoting stable arrangements, regularly contested but still well defined, expected by society to decide disputes and, more generally, to rule social relations on an everyday basis. Rights-as-chips, prevalent later on, will, by degrees, cut against their predecessors. In America, this will be on the whole to the benefit of citizens as opposed to government officers, to slaves as opposed to their owners, to laborers as opposed to their employers, to women and children as opposed to men. Each of these changes entailed major social dislocation, driven by dedicated popular movements, with rights—new rights—the objective in view. At the same time, rights—existing rights—were the chief roadblock to their success. In every instance the vehicle of change was policy. In the policy state emerging, rights-as-chips were—are—still assigned by law through the same institutions as before, but now they are loosely defined, contingent, "balanced," "proportioned," ensuring no single principled outcome.[8]

This does not mean arguments that one or another chip should be treated as a trump have been eliminated; they are, in fact, commonplace. Whether a right is a chip or a trump is also a different question from what we have called the endowment of a given right, for content can vary within both forms. For instance, First Amendment freedom of speech is far more generously endowed today than when it was written. In the framers' time, it meant mainly "prior restraint" or censorship; today it protects speech before and after, spoken or written, excluding only child pornography, "fighting words," some defamation and commercial speech, little else. The endowment of a right, on the other hand, does not determine its valence, that is, whether a given right will be affirmed when certain other rights are claimed by opposing parties under particular circumstances; think, for instance, of rights asserted in the setting of national security. We are alert to both in our analysis. The most important question for us, however, is not the endowment of a given right or the changing priority afforded one right over another over time, but the strength of rights as a category within the polity overall. In the policy state, the motive of rights is subordinated to the motive of policy. This goes hand-in-hand with the prevalence of rights-as-chips, which is the entryway through which our demonstration proceeds.[9]

Dependence on Policy

In keeping with our intention to examine the contemporary effects of political development rather than offer a full history of the policy state, we begin the discussion of rights with the present-day American family, an institution that in recent decades has experienced rapid and profound rearrangement. A family-law decision issued by the U.S. Supreme Court in 2006, *Town of Castle Rock v. Gonzales*, shows the policy state at full mast. Still valid, the decision is reckoned a significant setback to persons, especially women, fearful of violence by former spouses or partners. In the majority opinion, Justice Scalia's summary of events opens with the words "the horrible facts of this case"—an almost certain signal that the party most fully in agreement with this sentiment is about to experience severe disappointment.[10] *Town of Castle Rock* rewards analysis in some detail, for it offers a fitting introduction to rights in the policy state. American courts by their nature adjudicate rights; in the policy state, they continue to do so, but less by the motive of rights than by the motive of policy.

The "horrible facts" Justice Scalia recites occurred some six years earlier. Over a period of several hours, the plaintiff, Jessica Gonzales, telephoned the police station in Castle Rock, Colorado, and begged officers to arrest her estranged husband, who, she informed them, had taken their three daughters away from home contrary to a restraining order issued by a state trial court in connection with ongoing divorce proceedings. At one point she provided a location, an amusement park in nearby Denver, where, based on a phone call from her husband, she believed the group might be found. The officers declined to take any action, instead advising Gonzales to wait for the children to be returned home. In the early morning, her husband arrived at the police station and began firing a semiautomatic handgun, whereupon officers shot back, killing him. Checking his truck, they found the three daughters in the cab, murdered. Gonzales sued the town of Castle Rock and several individual officers for damages under U.S. Code Title 42, Chapter 21, Section 1983. She claimed injuries to both her "substantive" and her "procedural" constitutional rights of due process.

Section 1983 provides an action in federal court for damages and injunctions against any officer of a state, territory, or the District of Columbia who violates a right that is guaranteed by the Constitution or laws of the United States.[11] The basis for Gonzales's claim that she was denied her rights of due process under the Fourteenth Amendment was a statute passed in 1994 by the Colorado legislature.[12] A goal of a national campaign under way since the 1970s to reform and redress women's legal subordination within the family, the statute was lobbied for by the Battered Women's Movement and their allies in "the second wave of feminism." By the time *Town of Castle Rock* was decided, thirty-five states and territories had enacted similar laws. The statute's stated purpose was to overcome the slowness and reluctance of police to intervene in cases of domestic violence, and the means to achieve this end was spelled out in detail. For restraining orders, the statute called for the following instruction to police to be printed on the back: "You shall use every reasonable means to enforce the restraining order. You shall arrest, or, if an arrest would be impractical under the circumstances, seek a warrant for the arrest of the restrained person."[13]

Gonzales claimed that by ignoring this instruction the police injured her constitutional rights. Section 1983 reiterates legislation first passed by Congress in 1871, origins that throw considerable light on rights-as-chips and on the structure of modern rights litigation generally. Before Reconstruction, slave masters and other whites normally exercised their rights with respect to African Americans directly, acting in a long legal tradition known to the common law as "self-help."[14] When slave masters sought to punish or recapture a slave, they were free to do so on their own, without resort to further legal assistance. To the extent that law played a part in the actual transaction, it conformed to the pattern of subordination by withholding normal remedial actions like habeas corpus and assault charges. When slavery ended, however, and African Americans sought to exercise their new rights in the face of whites who violated their free status in various ways, self-help was no longer an option. As legal "equals," they were forced to depend on policemen, prosecutors, and judges, who often were not inclined to oblige them. It was this situation that Congress sought to ameliorate.

For the first century of its life, courts interpreted Section 1983 as covering mainly race-related constitutional injuries. Until the 1960s its protection extended only to a small segment of officers' adverse acts, and even afterward it continued to be hampered by jurisdictional and procedural roadblocks. In short, rights under Section 1983, while valuable, were nonetheless "chips," far less potent that the "trumps" previously bestowed on masters by "self-help." When, during the 1970s, the benefits of Section 1983 spread beyond race relations to other persons formerly subordinated in law, they too inherited, through the force of precedent, the same rights-as-chips, dependent on what various officers—legislators, judges, police officers, and others—within their own spheres of legal authority were prepared to provide. This included wives. It was Gonzales's situation when her children were taken from their home, and when she stood before the Court seeking damages.

In *Town of Castle Rock*, the justices held, 7–2, that Gonzales lacked legal standing, that is, she failed to demonstrate the threshold elements necessary for the case to be heard on the merits. The Court found she had not suffered the requisite injury to a property right under the due process clause of the Fourteenth Amendment, neither a "substantive" right—she was not entitled, a priori, to her husband's arrest absent a legitimate reason for the police to arrest him—nor a "procedural" right—she had not been deprived of any identifiable legal process due her by either the statute or the Constitution. The Court's opinion has been widely criticized as incoherent, circular, and disrespectful of precedent. Our interest is restricted to the reasoning by which the decision was reached, again because of what it tells us about the policy state and the state of rights therein.

The core holding of *Town of Castle Rock*, that Gonzales's constitutional right was not injured, rested principally on the justices' parsing of the words in the Colorado statute, in particular the word *shall*. The majority agrees that *shall* is mandatory in some contexts but not in others, and therefore is insufficiently forceful on its own to overcome the established custom of police discretion in enforcing restraining orders.[15] The opinion goes further, to refute the idea that Gonzales's claim was invalid owing to a deficiency in legislative authority, that is to say, in legislators' rights: legislators are not "powerless to provide victims with enforceable remedies."[16] The opinion provides no specific guidance as to how the statute might be rewritten to afford Gonzales what she seeks: the people of Colorado were "free to craft such a system under state law," but the policy as stated in the 1994 statute did not clear the bar.

Nor does the opinion make any affirmative findings about Gonzales's right vis-à-vis the police. Instead it avers that the authors of the Fourteenth Amendment and of Section 1983 did not impose liability "generally" on police departments for their discretionary actions, leaving matters for the time being with the residual rights of officers, including their rightful discretion when enforcing restraining orders. Notably, however, the majority views the existing discretion of police not as a right of office but in prudential—that is, in policy—terms. The competing duties of police, they opine, "counsel decisively against enforcement in a particular instance . . . particularly when the suspected violator is not actually present or his whereabouts unknown."[17] In short, the legislators were poor craftsmen, the police are very busy, and the judges best not interfere. The Court also turns away the idea, put forward by the court below, that its decision left Gonzales with a restraining order of no value: "The order rendered certain otherwise lawful conduct by her husband both criminal and in contempt of court." Even if those sanctions failed in this instance, this fact does not affect Gonzales's right, since they serve "public rather than private ends."[18]

Altogether, these highly circumstantial, tenuously associated, and largely default explanations contain no clear rules about anybody's rights. Similarly, the capstone reason the majority give for the holding in its summing up engages the same policy logic as the rest, having nothing specific to do with "the horrible facts" or with Gonzales herself, except as she is included within a category of persons, as the phrase has it, "similarly situated." On the theme of why "the benefit a third party may receive from having someone arrested . . . does not trigger protections under the Due Process Clause," the opinion explains: "This result reflects our continuing reluctance to treat the Fourteenth Amendment as 'a font of tort law.'"[19] Justice Scalia means by this that not every ordinary and potentially actionable wrong by a state officer need or should be treated as a constitutional injury, thus reflecting the persistent worry among many federal judges that Section 1983, which by the mid-1970s had come to constitute one-tenth of their total caseload, would further inundate their courts.[20] (Federal judges are busy, too.)

It is instructive that Gonzales's claim would not have landed in an entirely different atmosphere had the dissenters' view prevailed. Justice Ginsburg and Justice Stevens agreed with the majority that no substantive injury had occurred; but they thought "at this early stage," in a hearing on legal standing, procedural claims should be construed "liberally."[21] This, note, was a matter of judicial policy and not of right. Moreover, the dissenters devote the major part of their opinion to why the Court should have deferred to the other tribunals involved: "The majority's decision to plunge ahead . . . departs from this Court's long-standing policy of paying 'deference [to] the views of a federal court as to the law of a State within its jurisdiction.' This policy is not only efficient, but it reflects 'our belief that district courts and courts of appeals are better schooled in and more able to interpret the laws of their respective States.'"[22] Alternatively, they argue, the case might have been certified to the Colorado Supreme Court: "The considerations that weigh in favor of certification—federal-state comity, constitutional avoidance, judicial efficiency, the desire to settle . . . an issue of state law—transcend the interests of individual litigants, rendering it imprudent to cast them as gatekeepers to the procedure."[23]

Finally, had *Town of Castle Rock* been decided on a close vote, we might be tempted to ascribe its rationale to ideology—to a conservative distaste for the mushrooming of Fourteenth Amendment rights and for the new rights holders, including women. But the *Castle Rock* majority included Justice Souter and Justice Breyer, not easily associated with such an outlook. In their concurrence, these two justices were, if anything, the more emphatic that judicial policy, and not Gonzales's rights, must shape their decision. The facts of *Town of Castle Rock*, they write, display no functional separation between the arrest of Gonzales's husband and the "procedure" she argued was constitutionally due; the complaint and the process were one and the same thing.[24] They cite *Board of Regents v. Roth*, a decision about university tenure that broadened the meaning of property in the Fourteenth Amendment to reach state-created entitlements on which persons "rely in their daily lives",[25] and they argue that if the Court held that Gonzales suffered a "procedural" injury, it would go beyond *Roth* to "federalize every mandatory state-law direction to executive officers whose performance on the job can be vitally significant to individuals affected."[26]

It was highly unlikely that Gonzales's claim could have survived this blizzard of nonrights, poorly executed rights, and ill-advised rights in better condition than it did. Still, it did survive, as a "chip." It was not a total loss. Based on its *dicta*, it seems the Court believed that had the legislature spoken more forcefully and the husband's whereabouts that fateful night been known for certain, police might have been required to arrest him. Win some, lose some; this is in the nature of rights-as-chips. Lest it be thought this uncertainty is a function of the many veto points of the American political system, however, it is useful to compare Gonzales's situation with that of her husband a century earlier—indeed, in many American states only a half century ago. Her husband may well not have faced a restraining order, let alone potential arrest for leaving the premises with his children. Although restraining orders to husbands on behalf of wives or children were available during divorce proceedings (and only then), they were sparingly issued.

The theory of the husband's "trump" position changed over the years. By the middle of the nineteenth century, the basis of the judges' grudging rationale shifted from a belief in the husband's authority to an ideology of family privacy.[27] This comported with the broad understanding in the law of a society organized according to jurisdictions, private as well as public, to be protected against intruders, "outsiders" unauthorized by law. In the case of the family, this was reinforced by the English, and later American, doctrine of coverture, as defined here by William Blackstone: "The very being or legal existence of the woman is suspended during the marriage, or at least is incorporated and consolidated with that of the husband: under whose wing, protection, and cover she performs everything."[28] Out of coverture arose the "absurdity" that one might sue oneself. This, too, was on a larger pattern. Workers were likewise seen as fused with their masters for some legal purposes, much as the workplace was protected against its own species of intruder.

Blackstone's depiction survived the passage of statutes known as the Married Women's Property Acts in the 1840s, distinguishing husbands and wives insofar as the matter affected the legal rights of third parties, but still holding husbands immune from suits by their wives. When, after the Civil War, twelve state courts were asked by plaintiffs to abandon the rule against "interspousal torts," that is, injuries husbands and wives might legally cause one another, all rejected the invitation.[29] Nor was the husband's trump here subject to effective interference through legislation. Following reversals in court, women and their allies in several states and the District of Columbia successfully lobbied the legislature for statutes that gave married women the power to sue "for torts committed against them, as fully and freely as if they were unmarried."[30] In every case, the statutes were struck down by their respective judiciaries, each of which, like the U.S. Supreme Court in *Town of Castle Rock,* found legislators' wording insufficient to override husbands' rights at common law.

Judges during the period were not insensitive to the consequences of these rulings. In striking the statute for the District of Columbia, Justice Day, in his majority opinion for the U.S. Supreme Court, writes that ruling to the contrary would bring disharmony and disrepute to the family unit; besides, adequate remedies already existed for the parties in divorce and alimony.[31] Such public-regarding defenses of the status quo, reinforcing the law rather than, in the manner of policy, redirecting it, appear regularly in the history of common law jurisprudence. Judges attributed the same salutary effects to rules of family self-help. For instance, should the wife abscond, with or without the children, to the home of a friend or relative, the husband enjoyed the common law right of "recaption," strictly on his own authority to retake her and the child by force, so long as it did not result in an illegal trespass or a disturbance of the peace. By the same token, friends or relatives attempting to free women or their children held against their will by husbands were legally prohibited from obtaining writs of habeas corpus.[32]

Going further: under the state law of a century earlier, Gonzales would not likely have had legal custody of her daughters to begin with. In the words of a Gilded-age Colorado court: "The father, unless unfit by reason of immorality, is held entitled to the custody and control of his minor children. Nor is the rule departed from except in cases where the court finds it would be greatly to the welfare of the child that it should have some other custodian."[33] Admittedly, were judges gifted with prophecy, the Gonzales family would have qualified for this exception; but routinely, the custody of children was located in "the empire of the father."[34] While this phrasing of the husband's right fairly begs characterization of children concretely, as "property," it is more accurately understood as endorsing just another trump. Neither the husband's immunity to suit nor his paternal rights as custodian were absolute; judges from ancient times were assigned a backstop role in overseeing the welfare of children. But all other things being equal, except where extreme cruelty or immorality was conclusively proven, the husband's right would prevail.

Like the child-custody regime in place at the time of *Castle Rock*, the laws immediately preceding it provide evidence for how rights-as-chips and the subordination of rights to policy go together. During the first half of the twentieth century, virtually every state jurisdiction established, either by statute or at common law, "mother's preference" as the standard legal stance toward custody, especially insofar as younger children were concerned; this last was known as "the tender years doctrine."[35] In practice, "mother's preference" envisioned an equal footing of the two parents in custody disputes, with settlements reached by judges who weighed into the making of each award factors like the child's age, whether some other male relative would be present to perform necessary educational functions, and how well the mother had performed her role as nurturer. "Mother's preference" was full-on policy in our meaning, stimulated at the turn of the twentieth century by the new profession of social work, by the widespread spirit of social engineering, and, where applicable, a suspicion of immigrant fathers. Notably, lawmakers themselves denied that "mother's preference" was a legal right, treating it only as a rebuttable evidentiary presumption; formally, at law, the rights of the two parents remained unchanged.[36]

The instability of this prior situation was brought to a climax in 1973, when the Family Court of New York declared "mother's preference" to be a violation of the father's right to equal protection under the Fourteenth Amendment. Again, the influence of a growing profession, this time psychologists and other mental health experts; greater public attention to the formative influence of childhood; and the movement for sexual equality in family roles all argued for a reformed child custody policy. The response, the principle embraced by both courts and state legislatures, was the "the best interests of the child." How far this approach was from either rights possessed one-sidedly by the father or presumed more recently on behalf of the mother is suggested in a comment by one of the period's most respected legal expositors:

> In the last decade, while some commentators have attacked the breadth of discretion granted judges in resolving custody disputes, the limited role of appellate review, and the inadequate protection of normal procedural safeguards, courts, legislators, and other commentators have shown enormous hostility towards the development of rules that provided tight substantive standards for custody disputes. The differences among families generate great pressure to treat each case on its own facts. Indeed, the old presumptions and rules based on the sex of the parent, the age of the child, or the status of a contestant as a natural parent have all been criticized. Although some commentators have suggested rules are needed, American custody law has come to require a highly individualized determination of

what is in the best interests of (or least detrimental to) a particular
child.[37]

Since this was written in 1975, the custody picture has become im-
mensely more complicated. For instance, the 1980s movement toward
joint parental custody has layered a favored arrangement upon the "best
interests" policy without actually displacing it. Almost every state
has provided statutory guidelines for joint custody, and many list
factors to be taken into account in their devising, but typically factors
are assigned no priority and judges are free to make additions. The
constant flow of legislative suggestions from expert quarters and the
eschewing of all fixed presumptions has eroded even the terminology
involved. "Parenting" replaces "custody" and "parenting plans" replace "visitation"; a 2013 statute in Arizona has defined "legal custody" as "legal decision-making."[38] None of this has reduced rights
claims or their dependence on policy for affirmation or enforcement.
What is different is that policy itself has become increasingly less
dependable.

The Unbearable Lightness of Standards

Legal commentary distinguishes "bright lines"—rules that allow for
no ambiguity, that are subject to up-or-down tests, that are commands
and not propositions—from "standards"—norms, desired conditions,
guidelines for future efforts. In the fluidity of family governance, where
lawmakers have self-consciously avoided setting priorities and establishing metrics, even standards in this wider meaning are an anomaly.
The opposite is true in the case of race. Here, constitutional guarantees
are straightforward, and the question of standards—how to estimate
legal progress or its opposite, how to situate gains against goals, who is
designated to make these calls and by what procedures—has never
been far from the center of controversy. One of the most vivid of
"bright lines" in constitutional history was strung in Section 1 of the
Thirteenth Amendment, between slavery and freedom. No sooner did
this occur, however, than the shadow of "standards" was cast forward.
In Section 2 of the same amendment, we read that the realization of
Section 1 will be accomplished through "appropriate" legislation by

Congress. These two designations correspond to our own division of rights into trumps and chips. The slaves' liberation from personal ownership by their once-masters was assuredly a right-as-trump. However, whatever else might remain "appropriate" with respect to white society, including former slave masters and Congress itself, was, by constitutional design, left undetermined, quintessential rights-as-chips.

This quandary has attached to the rights of free African Americans throughout their history. Witness Justice Bradley in his 1883 opinion for the U.S. Supreme Court, striking down the public accommodations sections of the federal Civil Rights Act of 1875. Justice Bradley writes that a time must arrive in the elevation of the former slave when the latter "ceases to be the special favorite of the laws" and "takes the rank of a mere citizen."[39] Among his brethren, Justice Harlan alone dissented. To the degree that Bradley implied the time in question was now, and that the freed slave for all intents and purposes was ready to be a citizen without additional protections, Harlan disagreed. The Fourteenth Amendment, he insisted, gave Congress the express power to eliminate the "practical subjection" of one class of human beings to another, and it was to the policy (and wisdom) of Congress that "everyone must bow," including members of the Court.[40] Over the period of more than a century following this exchange, and allowing only for episodes when the Court majority and the Congress traded positions, the terms of the argument remained essentially the same. At what point can laws to promote racial equality be deemed to have achieved their end? At what point, indeed, might their continuance counteract mere citizenship, not only of the slaves' descendants but of other persons in American society with rights to equal treatment? How should this all be decided?

The emancipation of some four million black slaves, roughly one-third of the total population, marked the first major expansion of the policy state under the auspices of American nationhood. Little space need be devoted here to documenting the master's rights-as-trumps in the slave states before the Civil War. In this regard, slaves were indeed "favorites of the law," though differently from Justice Bradley's suggestion. As other forms of property, once bestowing rights-as-trumps on their owners, were further liberalized through new rules of alienage and inheritance, slave property lagged behind. Caveat emptor, for instance, did not apply to the sale of slaves; nor did the easing of the fellow-servant doctrine that assigned greater liability to masters for workers' injuries, for that rule did not embrace black labor, free or unfree. Humanitarian pressures on the ante-bellum South typically worked to underscore the slave's continuing subordination. In some states, for instance, slaves were permitted to testify in court but only for the purpose of confessing to a capital crime; elsewhere, they were afforded jury trials, with all the jurors slave masters. Manumission was liberalized, though regularly balanced with heightened barriers in neighboring states to entry by free blacks.[41]

The slave masters' rights over slaves at the time paralleled those of the husband's common law rights over his wife and children. By the same token, the theme of wives' dependency today on policy may, with all of its ramifications, be readily transposed to contemporary race relations. The sheer scale of the race relations project, however, moves the question of standards further to the forefront. Matters of how much, when, and according to whom become more salient as the imbalance and range of rights among conflicting parties are multiplied, and as what has been accomplished so far seeks "credit" against investments in more change. In this section, we are concerned with the nature of these standards and their application, rather than rights-as-chips as such, which here, as elsewhere in the policy state, prevail.

We said that long after the argument between Justices Bradley and Harlan, essential terms have stayed the same. Insofar as standards are concerned the situation has, if anything, become less clear-cut over time. One instinctively hesitates to award the word "standard," let alone "bright line," to the catchphrase "separate but equal" that was the rule from the late nineteenth century until *Brown v. Board* was decided in 1954, although a bright line it was.[42] As a consequence, its inversion in *Brown* would be a line of equal clarity. The Court's unanimous declaration that separate education is "inherently unequal" cleanly divided social conditions between those separated and not separated by race, thereby providing a trump to the plaintiffs at bar and to all those similarly situated. The opinion said it was in light of education's position in American life that segregation "deprives these plaintiffs of the equal protection of the laws."[43] That might have augured a meaningful qualification but it did not. Quickly, in a series of per curiam decisions (unanimous, issued without opinions), the Court upheld holdings by federal judges that extended the separate versus not-separate line beyond education, ordering desegregation of public transportation and recreational facilities.[44]

As with the Thirteenth Amendment Section 2, a sister decision also accompanied *Brown*. *Bolling v. Sharpe* was announced the same day and was likewise unanimously decided. Concerning schools located in the District of Columbia and therefore not covered by the Fourteenth Amendment, *Bolling* was as unequivocal as *Brown* about the facts at bar: "We hold that racial segregation in the public schools of the District of Columbia is a denial of the due process of law guaranteed by the Fifth Amendment to the Constitution."[45] But whereas *Brown* saw the schools of Topeka and the other defendant districts falling below the constitutional standard of "equal" because of the "place [of education] in American life,"[46] *Bolling* was more circumspect, holding that D.C. schools violated the due process clause only after the justices had "scrutinized" them in light of the community's other legitimate goals. "Liberty under law extends to the full range of conduct which the individual is free to pursue," the decision opined, "and it cannot be restricted except for a proper governmental objective."[47]

Of the two, *Brown* was by far the more important precedent for the Court's expanding authority. It still stands today as a high point in policy making by the judiciary. *Bolling* enjoys little prominence on the record until the 1970s. In retrospect, however, the sister case, with an eye to the liberty of others affected, can be seen as the surer harbinger of rights against racial discrimination being chips, across the board. It makes an important if low-key appearance in 1964, in *McLaughlin v. Florida*, which invalidated a state (rather than federal) statute that forbade interracial cohabitation. It is in *McLaughlin*, recalling *Bolling*'s language, that the idea of "rigid scrutiny"—in later cases "strict scrutiny"—takes hold as the standard that must be met by any law discriminating among persons by race if the judiciary is not to rule it constitutionally impermissible.[48] In *McLaughlin*, satisfying such scrutiny entailed the presence of an overriding statutory purpose (later changed to "compelling public interest" in some decisions); subsequent decisions will add the tests of "narrowly tailored" and "least restrictive means."[49] From there, over time, the standard can be seen to spread into a gossamer of additional standards: standards to determine when the standard of strict scrutiny applies, rather than the standard of "rational basis" scrutiny, which is deferential to lawmakers' judgment, or "intermediate" or "heightened" scrutiny, used with policies that discriminate on the basis of some personal characteristic other than race.[50] These second-level standards in turn go on to impose their own standards, for instance, of what public purposes are "compelling," which purposes are "public," and what evidence is sufficient to prove "narrow tailoring."[51]

This intricate web was several decades in the making. It drew pieces from racial conflict arising in various social activities, with the effect of availing parties in disputes over racial discrimination a citation free-for-all, both on and off the Court, often with the same precedents cited on both sides. For example, the "narrow tailoring" standard stems mainly from decisions to promote more minority employment and participation in government contracts. In recent decades, this is a policy area where the Court has become noticeably stinting in allowing racial categories. One decision in this line was *Adarand Constructors v. Pena* in 1995, which invalidated a minority contracting program in the U.S. Department of Transportation.[52] In 2003, in *Grutter v. Bollinger*, a decision upholding an affirmative action plan in student admissions at the University of Michigan Law School, the dissent opposing the plan cites *Adarand* for the proposition that to meet the standard of strict scrutiny respondents must show that their methods "fit" the state's goals "with greater precision than any alternative means."[53] In the same case, the majority opinion supporting the plan, written by Justice O'Connor, cites *Adarand* for having said strict scrutiny must take "relevant differences" in context into account.[54] What Justice O'Connor fails to mention is that her quote from *Adarand* was originally said by way of a concession to dissenters in that case who criticized the majority's failure in that respect. Their criticism was based on still an earlier dissent from an opinion in which the Court *deferred* to President Franklin Roosevelt in support of Japanese internment during World War II.[55]

Such cross-pollination of authorities raises the question of what circumstances qualify one public purpose rather than another as constitutionally compelling to the extent of justifying racial discrimination. In higher education, an answer came in 1978, in *Regents of University of California v. Bakke.*[56] Allan Bakke, a white student who failed to be admitted to the University of California at Davis Medical School, challenged the constitutionality of the admissions committee's favoring black over similarly qualified white applicants, with the purpose of increasing the number of minority students in the entering class. *Bakke* invalidated the committee's formula and ordered Bakke admitted. Going further, Justice Powell's tie-breaking view that became the judgment of the Court holds that affirmative action for the purpose of achieving "diversity," without rigid quotas, would clear the constitutional hurdle, provided that it was "precisely tailored to serve a compelling governmental interest."[57] Powell's definition of diversity chimes with the pragmatic, forward-looking outlook we have identified with the policy motive: "An otherwise qualified medical student with a particular background—whether it be ethnic, geographic, culturally advantaged or disadvantaged—may bring to a professional school of medicine experiences, outlooks, and ideas that enrich the training of its student body and better equip its graduates to render with understanding their vital service to humanity."[58]

In retrospect, a family resemblance can be seen between *Bakke's* "diversity" and *Bolling's* weighing of different legitimate public goals against one another. But what about *Brown*? Was it significantly different? The question is debatable. Although it would strain credulity for us to argue that the decades of disruptive intervention in society that was school integration did not amount to policy, we still contend that when it was decided *Brown* was the purer rights play. The inequality the Court saw inherent in racial separation provided the stronger, less encumbered endowment to the right of racial equality it affirmed, and it promoted the clearer discourse. To be sure, the goal of not-separate supplied only scant direction for what must happen next; still, integration as a goal held its own in situations of all but universal resistance.[59] As integration spread to new compartments of society, it rode the momentum of rights that were authoritatively and fully endorsed, not rights under consideration. This fact found its strongest expression in a string of "disparate impact" decisions, with federal courts giving priority to equal protection over otherwise legitimate public or private policies pursued with contrary racial effects, however unintended.[60]

In this perspective, it also becomes relevant that the Court in *Brown* was not reacting to legislation, or at least not legislation more recent than the Jim Crow statutes of the previous century. On the contrary, the decision flew in the face of long-standing congressional and presidential resolve against both the substance and practical implications of *Brown*'s holding. *Bakke,* on the other hand, like the affirmative action cases it would influence, had its source in the Civil Rights Act of 1964 Section 6, which provided for the withdrawal of federal financial assistance from any institution with programs or activities that "excluded from participation . . . [or] denied the benefits of . . . [or] subjected to discrimination" any person on the basis of race, color or national origin.[61] The thinking and subsequent discourse of the UC Davis Medical School was bathed in rectification: its brief before the Court spoke of "the commitment to relegate the lingering burdens of the past to the past." The timing and thrust of its admission plan were strategic, designed with the aim of preempting any future adverse impact of Section 6 on its programs.[62]

This same mix characterizes the ruling in *Bakke.* The majority against the admissions formula was a composite of justices willing to permit distinctions by race but only as remediation of past injustice, joined by Justice Powell, who embraced diversity as a future goal. Diversity offered a highly textured standard to meet the strict scrutiny test, one that by its nature invited downstream policy making on the part of lawmakers and their advisors immediately on the scene.[63] Among the dissenters were three justices who favored jettisoning strict scrutiny for a more lenient "rational basis" test, plus Justice Thurgood Marshall, who, writing alone, protested the installation of a new standard not tethered to historical injury: "The experience of Negroes in America has been different in kind, not just in degree, from that of other ethnic groups."[64] The shift in orientation—from past to future, from the anchor of "equal protection" to the sally-forth on the frothier seas of diversity—had become, by the time of the Court's next affir-

mative action decisions in higher education, the chartered course of
the lower courts.

From the standpoint of policy making, the multiplicity and shifting
of viewpoints is expected, even encouraged. From the standpoint of
rights, it seems nothing so much as a reenactment of the parable of the
blind men and the elephant. We have seen this already in the case of
Grutter v. Bollinger. But consider *Grutter* alongside the case of *Gratz v.
Bollinger*, decided on the same day, in which the plaintiff challenged
another University of Michigan admissions plan, this one for achieving
diversity in the entering class of the undergraduate college.[65] In the
years since *Bakke*, strict scrutiny's "second prong" of "narrow tailoring" had increased its importance in the Court's jurisprudence.[66]
On that basis the majority disallowed the admissions formula in *Gratz*,
a total-point system that awarded a "decisive" twenty points to all
applicants who were African American, Native American, or His-
panic, on the reasoning that it did not allow for the individual consideration of each applicant.[67] In *Grutter*, on the other hand, it upheld
the law school's approach to diversity, in which race was only a "potential 'plus'" among other characteristics, as being sufficiently narrowly tailored to satisfy the strict scrutiny standard.[68]

In the eyes of its critics, *Grutter* had reached a new watermark in
vaporous judicial reasoning. The Court determined the law school plan
had legitimately sought a "critical mass" of minority students, selected
through "individualized, holistic review" of each application, distinct
from a rigid quota.[69] This required that admissions officials look
beyond grades and test scores to other criteria important to the law
school's educational objectives. So-called soft variables, such as "the
enthusiasm of recommenders, the quality of the undergraduate institution, the quality of the applicant's essay, and the areas and difficulty
of undergraduate course selection," were all brought to bear in assessing
an "applicant's likely contributions to the intellectual and social life of
the institution."[70] That the critics were correct in their assessment
seemed borne out when federal judges attempted to sort out the rights
of the next affirmative action plaintiff before the Court, Abigail Fisher.
Fisher, a white student denied admission to the University of Texas,
challenged a formula that, tracking *Grutter*, supplemented the race-
neutral variable of placing in the top 10 percent of one's high school

graduating class with a "holistic" index factoring in talents, backgrounds, experiences, as well as the self-defined race of each student. The university claimed that this approach was necessary to supply the diversity that could not be achieved by an applicant's high school standing alone.

What ensued was something of a judicial seesaw. Given the change in justices since *Grutter*, it was widely speculated that the "holistic" portion of the Texas plan would be ruled unconstitutional. In what was experienced by Court-watchers as an anticlimax, the decision of the Fifth Circuit, which had supported the university, was vacated by a vote of 7–1. Justice Kennedy's majority opinion said the lower court had deferred to the university's claim of "good faith" without requiring it to bear its burden of proving it had considered alternative and race-neutral methods necessary to satisfy the constitutional requirement of "narrowly tailoring," and it remanded the case for another look. This time, upon remand, the Fifth Circuit determined that the university had, in fact, met its burden, albeit with one of the judges in the earlier majority now dissenting. The rule of nondeferral in *Fisher*, the dissenter wrote, had simply been "sidestepped": "Because the University has not defined its diversity goal in any meaningful way—instead, reflexively reciting the term 'critical mass'—it is altogether impossible to determine whether its use of racial classifications is narrowly tailored."[71]

Whether this seemingly infinite regression of missing definitions would come to an end was uncertain. Whether two anticlimaxes could build to a resting place and rights made of "holistic variables" and "critical masses" would prove a more stable formula than, say, "the child's best interests," was decided by the Supreme Court in 2016, some eight years after the back-and-forth began. The interval provided the majority of 4–3 with the justification needed to punt. The new opinion, again written by Justice Kennedy, observed that even though the university might be able, upon remand, to offer sufficient data on whether "holistic" admission was needed to add the desired diversity, evidence based on the time elapsed could not clarify the rights of a plaintiff who was denied admission only three years into the story.[72] Nor, in the broader scheme of things was the case closed. "Going forward," the opinion avers, "[t]hrough regular evaluation of data and consideration of student experience, the University must tailor its approach in light of changing circumstances, ensuring that race plays no greater role than is necessary to meet its compelling interest."[73]

For good measure, lest lower-court judges who must decide future affirmative action disputes might feel themselves on firmer ground, the Court describes the Texas program, and presumably the standards it might support, as "sui generis."[74]

Labor Policy, Pure and Simple

In the manner of wives and African Americans, employees of America's diverse workplaces were governed for centuries as personal subordinates, overseen by their employers according to a system of legal rules that reduced any rights they might claim to a near vanishing point. These rules, comprising the common law of master and servant, inherited from England and administered and modified slightly to fit American institutions, took legal precedence over all statutes, state or federal, that were "in abrogation" of their provisions. Apart from the rigors and routines of the workplace itself, over which the masters were afforded rights of full control under a general rule of obedience, they dictated the terms of the employment contract—hiring and firing, the method and timing of paying wages, the length of the workday, and what recourse workers, either individually or in combination, might have to affect these conditions without being subject to dismissal or imprisonment. Virtually all rights of the master were trumps. In particular, masters had the right to dismiss workers for any reason, even causes they hadn't known about at the time. In addition, they could enjoin and take legal action against individuals or organizations for interference in the workplace, at whatever stage of remove, and for violation of contract and trespass, under a collection of both ancient and modern doctrines.[75]

In the United States, these rules—this law—were the object of prolonged and violent confrontation between, on the one side, workers engaged in strikes and boycotts against their employers and, on the other, judges who wielded the decisive weapons and had the final say. The struggle reached its climax in the 1930s, with the passage in 1935 of the National Labor Relations Act ("Wagner Act" or NLRA) and, two years later, its upholding as constitutional by the Supreme Court.[76] From then forward, the law of master and servant was disestablished to the extent that a legislature, federal or state, passed a statute to replace any part. In its opinion, *National Labor Relations Board v. Jones & Laughlin Steel,* the Court also disowned the sanctity of common law ordering as it was asserted in the case, thereby opening the full range of legal relations between persons to legislative change. Likewise, in that many subsequent landmark achievements would have been blocked by these anciently entrenched rights, the American policy state as a whole was critically advanced by labor's victory.

In Chapter 4, "Structure in the Policy State," we take up the fuller implications of these events for the question of constitutional boundaries, indeed, for the principle of constitutional boundaries as such. We dwell on them briefly here because they help to explain why employees' rights have a character different from the others we have discussed so far. The shift from rights-as-trumps, enjoyed from time-out-of-mind by employers, to rights-as-chips, now provided to employees, is the same. But by the time of the Wagner Act's passage, labor union leaders and their political allies had made a conscious decision to diminish the historical role the judiciary had, through its oversight of constitutional and common law rights, played in labor disputes and instead to cast the workers' lot with legislation. To this end, they rejected both the Thirteenth Amendment's ban against servitude and Article IV's guarantee of a republican form of government as constitutional anchors for the new order of workplace relations, in favor of a broadened authority for Congress under a reinterpreted commerce clause.[77] On this plan, labor rights would be lodged in a carefully designed labor policy, expressed in national statutes, providing an array of collective, not individual, rights.

Already in 1932, the Norris–La Guardia Act, forbidding federal courts to issue labor injunctions, had signaled the unions' resolve to give orders to judges, not take them: "In the interpretation of this chapter and in determining the jurisdiction and authority of the courts of the United States . . . the public policy of the United States is declared as follows."[78] It remained for the Wagner Act to create the centerpiece National Labor Relations Board ("the Board" or NLRB), a body whose composition and operations implemented its authors' constitutional, or better, nonconstitutional strategy. "Rights of Employees" were spelled out in Section 7 of the Act: to form, join, and assist labor unions; to bargain collectively with their employers through representatives of their own choosing; and to engage in and refrain from activities in order to promote these aims. Section 8 specified a number of unfair labor practices by employers that gave rise to claims that could be made by unions on behalf of their members, adjudicated before administrative law judges appointed by, and advisory to, a three-member Board, appointed by the president. The Board's orders were enforceable by a federal court of appeals, which must treat the agency's findings of fact as conclusive except if unsupported by evidence in its hearings.

What this meant for ordinary employees was that workers' rights against employers would be mediated through membership in a labor union. Drawing on the motive of representation, the statute gave unions that were recognized under the contract the exclusive authority—the right—to represent all of the workers in that bargaining unit in collective actions, at both the industry and the workplace level. Also, in implementing the contract itself, unions had exclusive authority to represent workers in all grievance proceedings, providing only that the contract spelled out this arrangement. Usually this was the case; if not, the statute gave workers the right to represent themselves, as long as a union representative was present. As a consequence, the only legal actionable right normally afforded most workers under a collective-bargaining agreement was to sue the union—not the employer—for failing to provide fair representation. Under this arrangement, workers' rights were treated in law as statutory and contractual, not grounded in any constitutional clause the way that, say, the rights of women and minorities are grounded in the equal protection clause of the Fourteenth Amendment.

By no means did workers' new rights displace rights enjoyed by workers along with other persons under the Constitution or under what remained of common law. However, making the primary residence of American labor policy a statutory scheme, prescribing rules that extended from the shop floor up through the offices of the NLRB, had critical implications for the basic character of employees' rights. First among these was that relations between employers and employees were intricately tangled into scattered pieces of government authority and affected by their distribution. These included not only the several branches and agencies of national government, but state branches and agencies, as well.[79] Put differently, just as the rights-as-chips discussed in earlier sections were countered by the rights-as-chips of other rights holders, including persons inside and outside government, the nonconstitutional route taken by employees and their organizations arrived at the same destination.

To illustrate: many obstacles to workers' rights have been caused by the protean scope of the Constitution's commerce clause, and the fact that both national and state legislatures regulate commerce within their constitutional spheres. Consider a contemporary labor case to parallel *Town of Castle Rock* and *Fisher v. University of Texas* and likewise still good law today, *Chamber of Commerce v. Brown*, decided in 2008.[80] In *Chamber of Commerce* the Court relied on the doctrine of federal preemption, that is, the rule that states may not legislate on matters that conflict with policies enacted by Congress. California sought to enforce a state statute that prevented private employers who received state money—through grants, contracts, property use, or similar means—from spending it to influence the decision of employees "whether to support or oppose a labor organization."[81] The Chamber of Commerce and other employers' organizations, claiming the statute unconstitutionally injured their First Amendment freedom of speech, sued in federal court for an injunction, arguing that Congress had preempted the state provision when it passed the NLRA. The Supreme Court agreed. Reviewing the Act's original text and subsequent amendments, and the justices' own past decisions, it determined the NLRA "forbids" the regulation of such conduct, by either the NLRB or the states, thus striking a "balance of protection, prohibition, and laissez-faire."[82]

"Balance" was a far cry from the position unions had originally expected to command under the NLRA. The Act had listed only unfair actions by employers and said not a word about unfair actions of employees, let alone suggest the two were to be weighed in the balance. Nor had Congress and its union allies at the time anticipated the ricochet effect of a federal preemption doctrine.[83] In fact, the only two precedents which *Chamber of Commerce* cited for its interpretation of the NLRA's purposes had supported the expectation that unions would take over the rights-as-trumps position historically assigned employers. The first of these, *NLRB v. Virginia Electric & Power*, decided in 1941, overruled a decision by a court of appeals reversing an order of the Board that the company disestablish a union it had supported with speeches and bulletins. The Court said such conduct would be deemed noncoercive speech only in the absence of all other hostile conduct, a condition that seldom obtained during a campaign for union recognition.[84] The second, *Thomas v. Collins*, in the process of striking down a Texas statute requiring registration with local authorities prior to commencing organizing activities, averred that freedom of speech was not "inapplicable to business or economic activity."[85]

Another marker of labor's initially strong position is *Republic Aviation Corp. v. NLRB*, a Supreme Court decision in 1943. In it, the Court upheld the NLRB's reinstatement of several employees dismissed by two companies for variously passing out union application cards during lunch hours, wearing buttons with insignia of an as-yet-unrecognized union, and distributing handbills on their own time but on company-owned property. *Republic Aviation* agreed that the Board's "adjustments" had occurred without sufficient factual evidence, which was the single stated limitation on the finality of its decisions, but it still found the employers had been afforded due process. Congress intended to establish "the right of the employees to organize for mutual aid without employer interference"; this intention must be treated as "conclusive," even when it impaired employers' own "undisputed right" to maintain employee discipline.[86] Moreover, the Board had "fairly . . . explicated the theory which moved it to its conclusions," and had, in a previous case, set out the evidence it would regard as proof. Validity of its decisions, therefore, depended "on the rationality between what is proved and what is inferred."[87]

This dispensation was not long lasting. In 1947, precisely to curb such inferences as these, a less labor-friendly Congress passed the Taft-Hartley amendments to the NLRA, also known as the Labor Management Relations Act (LMRA). Alongside the original unfair practices of employers, the amendments now forbid a number of unfair practices by unions. They also enlarged the Board from three to five members and required that all actions before it from now on must be brought at the discretion of a general counsel, appointed by the president for a four-year term and authorized to proceed independently of the Board. Given this new law, a differently constituted Supreme Court in 1956 reversed a virtually unbroken line of pro-union Board decisions and denied a union's right to distribute organizing leaflets in a company parking lot. Now intrusions on employers' property by nonemployees would be an unfair practice unless it could be demonstrated that all other means of communication were not reasonably feasible.[88]

To many commentators at the time, the Court's decision seemed to herald a return to employers' common law rights-as-trumps before the Wagner Act.[89] But the issue of union organizers' access to employers' property over time demonstrates a rotation into the winning position roughly every decade, with "balance" the watchword throughout. In 1968, when employees were given the right to peacefully picket in the parking lot of a private shopping center, Justice Harlan dissented: the Court was setting a "rigid constitutional rule where Congress has struck a delicate balance."[90] In 1976, when employers were allowed to threaten the arrest of organizers for picketing the shopping mall outlets of a target wholesaler, the majority pondered the role of Section 7 in "the present balance."[91] In 1980, when employees were permitted to picket independent insurance agencies as a means of pressuring an insurance carrier, Justice Blackmun joined the majority because he was "reluctant to hold unconstitutional Congress' striking of the delicate balance" between union freedom of speech and the rights of neutral parties against "coerced participation in industrial strife."[92] In 1992, when it was held that employers might lawfully ban picketing in a shopping center parking lot to pressure the anchor retail store, Justice Thomas, for the Court majority, opined that "certainty in this corner of the law" was unlikely to be fostered by an analysis based on balance.[93]

If, as a practical matter, both employees' and employers' rights are chips, winning and losing in turn, then the same must be said about the First Amendment, and for that matter, about Congress's supremacy over legislation passed by the states, regarded as an important structural constitutional accomplishment of the New Deal. However, if at least in principle, "balance" compromises but does not altogether blot out the rights claimed—chips are, after all, not complete nullities—the same cannot be said of labor's nonconstitutional approach as a whole. When union rights under the NLRA have come cheek by jowl with claims arising under other statutes, the results for labor have been even more disadvantageous.

Such a situation, for example, occurred in recent years with regard to the Federal Arbitration Act (FAA), passed by Congress under the name of the U.S. Arbitration Act in 1925, providing judicial enforcement of agreements reached through arbitration proceedings in the same manner as contracts. Expressly aimed at "commerce" and "maritime transactions," the FAA was written to cope with common law judges' reluctance to enforce collective-bargaining agreements and the unions' own distrust of law courts. The statute therefore allowed only very narrow grounds for overturning the appointed arbitrator's award. This still left unions uneasy, suspicious of arbitration's streamlined, inexpensive method of dispute resolution that had an unseemly appeal to employers and state governors.[94] They conceived the passage of the NLRA a decade later as offering a policy of a very different stripe, notably excluding all involvement by third parties.

The unions' attitude began to change as they themselves found arbitration a useful tool for settling grievances. Taft-Hartley's creation of the Federal Mediation Service provided further encouragement, still under the NLRA umbrella. The most important pro-arbitration development, however, arguably waited until the 1960s with the federal judiciary's embrace of mandatory arbitration clauses in collective-bargaining agreements as a means of cutting down the mounting grievance appeals landing on its dockets. In a set of decisions in 1960 known as the *Steelworkers' Trilogy*, the Supreme Court, tracking legal arguments made by the union attorneys and making no mention of the FAA, linked settlements through arbitration with the unions' right under the NLRA to exclusive representation of their members in grievance proceedings to endorse the cheap, fast, nondisruptive arrangement that would dominate labor relations for the next three decades. This policy left the unions' right to exclusive representation of employees unimpaired, while at the same time affirming organized labor's continuing legitimacy in national affairs.[95]

The situation was jolted slightly in 1974, when, permitting an individual employee discharged for allegedly racially discriminatory reasons to personally sue in federal court under Title VII of the 1964 Civil Rights Act, the U.S. Supreme Court unanimously reversed an arbitrator's award. The contract under which the arbitrator ruled provided for "final and binding" arbitration of all disputes involving "race, color, sex, national origin, or ancestry."[96] But the Court rejected the idea that Congress intended collective bargaining to be the only means of settling employee grievances and, further, declared that rights like those under Title VII could not be waived. Again, there was no mention of the FAA. The statutory rights involved were said to arise under the NLRA and Title VII. From the unions' perspective, parallel proceedings under the NLRA and Title VII did not represent a political setback; if anything, they offered a safety valve in circumstances where a divergence between the interests of a local bargaining unit and the member claiming discriminatory discharge was expected to become increasingly common.

It took some years for the unions to discover they were in a policy trap, but in 2008, in a case of alleged discrimination under the 1967 Age Discrimination in Employment Act (ADEA), that trap clamorously sprang shut. There, the issue arose of what happens when, under a collective-bargaining agreement providing for final and binding arbitration of all claims arising from Title VII, the ADEA, the Americans with Disabilities Act, "or any other similar laws, rules, or regulations," a union for one reason or another declines to represent the grievant. Could the grievant then take the claim to federal court herself? In what some argue was blatant disregard of precedent, the Supreme Court, in *14 Penn Plaza LLC v. Pyett,* answered: no, not directly. For the 5–4 majority, Justice Thomas wrote that the exclusive right to represent members' grievances under the NLRA meant either that the union must represent the employee's claim or that it must allow the employee to proceed on his or her own, but in either event the dispute must be decided in arbitration proceedings as provided in the collective-bargaining agreement.[97] The only circumstance in which this rule would not obtain is if the ADEA (or other relevant statute) specifically excluded such grievances from NLRA jurisdiction, which the ADEA (and the others) did not do.

In *Pyett*, the union, a local of the Service Employees International Union, had agreed with the company that the discrimination claim at issue was without merit. As a consequence, it argued, there was no dispute between the two parties under the collective-bargaining agreement and no provision in the NLRA for representation of the employee. But the Court's opinion rested its decision not on the NLRA but on the Federal Arbitration Act, albeit now read in light of the NLRA and its grant to unions of exclusive representation. Reference to "balance" appears only in the dissent: "there are valid policy and textual arguments on both sides . . . [but none] carries sufficient weight to tip the balance between judicial and legislative authority and overturn an interpretation of an Act of Congress that has been settled for many years."[98] Instead the emergent theme is policy. Both the majority and the dissenting opinions refer to policy: the first in its critique of the mistaken "judicial policy" on arbitration in the past, and in Justice Stevens' dissent, to decry the "subversion of precedent to the policy favoring arbitration."[99]

The Court has yet to determine if arbitration, whether under a collectively bargained contract or not, will preclude meaningful recourse to formal litigation. If so, then what was before a statutory right will have been demoted to a contractual one, fully dependent on the arbitration process. Individual suits by union members against an employer for unfair or illegal acts would then hinge on successful prior litigation against the union for having violated its duty of fair representation—either for refusing to represent the grievance or for making an improper defense. Employees not working under a union contract but who agree to arbitration of grievances on their hiring—in the United States today a larger group than unionized employees—will also see actions in court foreclosed. In this setting, Congress becomes paramount. For instance, recent legislation proposed to allow card-check rather than election for union recognition also provides for arbitration of the first contract in the event of impasse, with the effect of short-circuiting both collective bargaining and judicial recourse by employees.[100]

If the position of employees is evaluated within a framework of collective rather than individual rights, then it becomes highly important for organized labor that the exclusivity of union representation under the regimen of arbitrating statutory rights may become as much a burden as a privilege. The normal argument made in cases of member grievances is that the employer has handed out disparate treatment. When ordinary work conditions are at issue, the claim will be that the employer treated or disciplined the grievant with a standard below that of other employees for no demonstrable reason. When the issue concerns statutory claims of race, age, or gender, the complaint is that the employer treated some employees better or worse—paid or advanced them or laid them off—for reason of their personal characteristics. The last situation is inherently divisive among union members and made even more volatile when, as in *Pyett,* the union declines to move the case to arbitration.[101]

Would employees' rights-as-chips in the workplace be more robust if they were afforded constitutional status?[102] Perhaps. As we have seen, and at least until recently not questioned, it has been the Supreme Court's position that rights against racial discrimination could not constitutionally be waived under arbitration provisions.[103] Some opinions have also distinguished collective-bargaining statutes implementing "majoritarian processes" and statutes intended to provide "substantive guarantees."[104] There is considerable irony in the fact that labor movement leaders in the 1930s who lost the argument for situating the rights of trade unionism under the Thirteenth Amendment included in their appeal the amendment's prospective warding-off of government-sponsored schemes of arbitration.[105]

Policy Auras

The movement of rights-as-trumps, deeply entrenched, central to the operations of society, away from their long-standing holders to become rights-as-chips has occasioned seismic events. The tides of policy they set loose virtually guaranteed their continuing influence on institutions beyond the particular settings in which they occur. We designate this effect as "policy auras." Policy auras further expand policy space; borrowing on language in Chapter 4, what were previously structures of constraint become, under their influence, structures of opportunity. So far, we have discussed only changes in rights that began their American passage as trumps. To introduce policy auras, we consider the aura surrounding rights that were already chips at the time the Constitution was written, rights pertaining to commercial activity. The commercial revolution in England was a product of legislation at all levels, reordering rights of England's merchants, bankers, and industrialists as well as of and among the officers of English government. These changes migrated in turn to the American colonies, and by the time of the Revolution were business as usual, chips on this side of the Atlantic, as well.

An important aspect of this trans-Atlantic crossing is that commerce in America took on an even more capacious meaning than it had in England. In the absence of the still-vigorous common law rules surrounding inherited land, which, until the twentieth century, was the foundational principle of English society and government, commerce in the New World spread to embrace the entire subject of private property, subjecting its regulation as a whole to the discretion of the legislature. This fact is signaled in an English statute, An Act for the More Easy Recovery of Debts in His Majesty's Plantations and Colonies in America, passed by Parliament in 1732. In order to enlarge the pool of investment capital, the statute provided that real estate, and the buildings and slaves on it, would from now on be treated the same as chattel (movable property, like farm animals and household contents) for the purpose of satisfying debts. It also ordered judges, upon a creditor's suit, to arrange auctions to raise funds necessary for payment.[106] In other words, decades before the Declaration of Independence, American property was legally, if not yet rhetorically, a commodity, exchangeable like other goods in the marketplace. No less an authority than Justice Story referred to property in America as a kind of substitute money.[107]

At the Constitution's framing, then, property rights, under the aura of commercial policy, were chips. To be sure, at that time and ever since, drawing on the protection formally provided in the Fifth and later the Fourteenth Amendments to the Constitution, they have been invoked to challenge public policies of all kinds. Often described as sacred and inalienable, these very expressions demonstrate the gap between the presumed or normative content of property rights and what we have here called their legal valence. A much-watched U.S. Supreme Court case in 2005 will illustrate the point. *Kelo v. City of New London* decided, by a 5–4 majority, that nine plaintiffs, owners of lots and homes on the Connecticut waterfront, well maintained and with deeds up to a century old, could not legally forestall proceedings of eminent domain undertaken by the city. The city sought possession of their properties for a private industrial park, to be utilized as a future site for a manufacturing plant of a major pharmaceutical company.[108]

The Fifth Amendment provides that no property may be "taken" except for public use and with fair compensation for the owner. The *Kelo* plaintiffs argued that their homes and lots were being acted against unconstitutionally, for private and not public use. The city claimed the industrial park would further the public purpose of economic revival in the depressed metropolitan area. In the Court's decision, "commerce" takes precedence over "property" and "public" over "private," an outcome that should not have been a great surprise to the parties. The federal government entered the business of eminent domain in 1875; since that date, the record is a virtually unbroken one of government success over Fifth Amendment claims. A similar pattern is observable in the states, each of which has similar constitutional provisions. Under these circumstances, the best Justice O'Connor could offer in her *Kelo* dissent was that before the Court's decision "it was possible . . . to imagine unconstitutional transfers from A to B" but not after.[109]

Kelo's aftermath is equally instructive. The manufacturing plant was never built. Within a span of five years following the Court's decision, forty-three states either passed statutes or adopted constitutional amendments that reformed their eminent domain laws to better protect property owners. Also, nine state high courts ruled against the use of eminent domain for economic development purposes; and dozens of projects reliant on eminent domain were discontinued under pressure from citizens' groups with names like "The Castle Coalition." Taking into account states where high courts undertook to limit eminent domain on their own, only three states today remain unreformed. In downtown New London, a single pink house, one of the properties condemned in the original suit, sits as a monument to this change. That said, the legal protections newly put in place against such takings, being chips, have been characterized as "highly varied and uneven."[110] None of them really privileges property rights; all seek to balance the rights of the homeowner against the sovereign's authority to take their property for the public welfare.

Let us next observe the aura of commercial policy at work on another group of rights discussed earlier in this chapter, rights within the family. The Women's Property Acts of the 1830s and 1840s provide an antebellum example. These were acts intended to shield property that a woman brought with her into her marriage against suits by creditors as long as she was alive. Some statutes also allowed her to manage the property during her lifetime and to control its disposition, including through her written will. Without such legislation or judges' rulings to the same effect, the doctrine of coverture would merge her property with that of her husband's, beyond her control and, in circumstance of default on debt, beyond her husband's control as well. Historians disagree about whether the main benefit of these statutes redounded to a wife herself or her husband or father; in any rendering, women's rights were decisively strengthened, if by the discretion of policy makers.

The Women's Property Acts represent an out-of-phase intervention of the law in family relations along the same lines as the commerce-bites-property story in *Kelo*. In addition, we might highlight two other aspects. The first is the circumstance of their passage, which came in years of commercial adversity. The earliest laws appear in the South toward the end of the Jackson administration, when the price of slaves, land, and cotton rose sharply. Statutes in the North enacted during the 1840s were a delayed response to the severe national depression of 1837. The 1848 statute in New York, regarded as the most influential of the group on subsequent developments, came into being while the legal community of that state was in the midst of revising the law of trusts to make it more commercially friendly. Commercial policy generally and the relationship between landowning and debt in particular were familiar legislative subjects, and thus these laws met no resistance from the judiciary comparable to what we saw in the repeated defeat of interspousal torts. In fact, while some judges engaged in interpretive trimming of the Women's Property Acts, others broadened their reach beyond what legislators had provided.[111]

The pragmatic and outward momentum of policy by its nature promotes the crossing of institutional boundaries on behalf of issues for which there was no anticipation and no a priori respect. Policy auras may coincide with social movements or do their own work without grassroots assistance. The passage of the Southern laws noted above occurred removed from overt social pressures. The New York statute was actively pursued by an ongoing women's movement, a commercial-development movement, and a legal codification movement, with these often sharing supporters. Historians have attributed varying levels of influence to each movement for the law that ensued.[112] The significance of policy auras is not that they cause events downstream so much as they establish the preconditions of changes beyond their core project. For example, English and American legislators had long been tasked with addressing problems of uncollected debts and rearranging rights for their resolution—thus the place of Shays' Rebellion as an important impetus to the U.S. Constitution.[113] In this respect, the Women's Property Acts were more of the same.

The policy aura surrounding commercial policy throws light on similar anomalies in the legal history of race relations. Consider two U.S. Supreme Court decisions concerning the sale of private property. First, in its 1917 decision in *Buchanan v. Warley*, the Court struck down a Louisville ordinance that forbade the sale of a home by a person of one race to a person of another race. The ordinance had been carefully drafted to preserve the constitutional rights of existing home-owners and skirt gingerly around the prevailing rule of "separate but equal" as it affected sellers of both races. Nevertheless, the Court held that the ordinance deprived the white owner from alienating— selling—his property at will, contrary to the Fourteenth Amendment. *Buchanan* was able to go its own way from contrary rulings on segregation in public accommodations, schools, transportation, and from laws against mixed-race marriages.[114] The decision, which was unanimous, reflects the aura of commercial policy, as the justices drew on two precedents to support their ruling, dealing with, respectively, the regulation of commodities and stock trading, even though both cases upheld rather than invalidated statutes.[115]

Fast forward to another era, 1947, in a different case of race discrimination, *Shelley v. Kraemer*. Here the Court held it could not legally enforce a racially restrictive covenant in the sale of a house in Saint Louis, Missouri. Restrictive covenants had come into use shortly after

Buchanan v. Warley, precisely in order to circumvent that decision; they were afterwards upheld by the Court on the grounds that the Fourteenth Amendment protected only against discrimination by state—not private—actors. The *Shelley* Court agreed with *Buchanan* that restrictive covenants were not invalid and that they offended neither the buyer's nor the seller's rights to enter private agreements. However, the decision went on to hold that judicial officers, when they acted to enforce such discriminatory instruments, were themselves state actors. Restrictive covenants discriminate on the basis of race, and for judges to enforce them constituted a denial of equal protection of the laws that the Fourteenth Amendment forbade.[116]

In terms of their practical impact, both decisions fell short of expectations, *Buchanan* because of restrictive covenants that followed in its wake, and *Shelley* because judges declined to apply its holding to factual settings unrelated to property transactions. In the light of policy auras, what are otherwise oddities become evidence of the discretion judges, like legislators, can exercise in the interests of favored positions. It is true that the state-action doctrine was expanded by the time of *Shelley* but had harbored none of the explosive implications of that case.[117] The adjudication of private property rights was one of the oldest duties of common law judges. Under the Constitution, this duty had long been performed in the presence of "police powers," legitimating government policies that, in the judges' opinion, were supported by good enough justification to uphold discriminatory laws. In most instances, as with eminent domain, police powers received judicial deference. Those occasions when judges chose to do something different, as in *Buchanan* and *Shelley,* elicited no greater protest from the legal community than the suggestion the justices might, at a later date, wish to reconsider.[118]

Finally, to observe the aura of commercial policy suspended over labor rights, begin where we left off in the last section, with the topic of arbitration. If arbitration means, as it does today, the parties' voluntary submission of disputes to one or more persons appointed to decide on a settlement in lieu of the regular judiciary, the English precedents go back to a ruling by Lord Coke in 1609.[119] Actual statutes providing for commercial arbitration appear in 1698. By the time of the American Revolution, the colonies of Pennsylvania, New York, and

Massachusetts had installed commercial arbitration systems of their own; during the nineteenth century they were a regular fixture of maritime and domestic businesses of all kinds. Throughout this period, methods were constantly fine-tuned for greater efficiency and fairness; the same questions were asked then as in the *Pyett* litigation, including the relationship of arbitration to other rights and of judges to arbitrators.

The first American system of arbitration between employers and employees was put in place in Maryland in 1878, following the great railroad strike of 1877 that crippled the nation. This was soon followed in New York and Pennsylvania. Each statute provided for permanent boards, with authority to both arbitrate and mediate disputes. The national government entered the scene with the Arbitration Act of 1888, the first of three acts designed to settle labor disputes on interstate railroads; largely investigatory and nonbinding, the board it established was never used. The second, the Erdman Act, passed in 1898, provided for the successive steps of mediation; then agreement to choose a three-member board; then the arbitration, its decision binding for a set period and appealable to a federal court. The Act also ordered government officers to actively persuade the parties to come to the table. After a slow start, this procedure gained broad industry acceptance. The Newlands Act, passed in 1913, enlarged the arbitration board to six members and provided for a permanent mediation commissioner who acted in concert with one or two federal officers designated by the president.

It is the Erdman Act that interests us most. In addition to its arbitrations provisions, Section 10 forbade employers to require "yellow dog" contracts, that is, promises, as a condition of employment, verbal or written, not to join a trade union. In *Adair v. United States* in 1908, the Supreme Court struck this provision down as an unconstitutional violation of the employers' right to hire and fire employees at will, a trump protected as both a liberty and property interest under the Fifth Amendment. In the opinion, the Court said it was making no judgment about the constitutionality of the legislation overall. This suggested to some observers—including union leadership—that the justices were extending tacit legitimacy to collective action as such.[120] In any case, the long background of commercial arbitration, using methods similar to those confirmed for labor via a number of judicial adjustments, opened the policy space for government's initial foray into labor arbitration.

It may be helpful at this point to distinguish policy auras, with their source in actual institutions and events, from norms and values with which they might be mistakenly identified. For instance, private property and, for that matter, commerce more generally, are highly ranked values in American culture; put in our language of rights, they are believed to have high valence, protected by name in two constitutional amendments. Therefore, it might be thought that the result in *Adair*, for instance, could be attributed to the railway employer's successful assertion of his property rights, without resort to supplementary notions like auras. But labor leaders of the period, and indeed throughout American history, repeatedly claimed that workers were property owners just like their bosses, that their property was their labor power, and that they were therefore constitutionally entitled to control and dispense their labor according to their own volition. The *Adair* opinion seems to agree: "The right of a person to sell his labor upon such terms as he deems proper is, in its essence, the same as the right of the purchaser of labor to prescribe the conditions upon which he will accept such labor from the person offering to sell it."[121] But these words were to no avail, so long as the employers' rights over the workplace were upheld as trumps at common law.

Labor's argument returns us to the gap between rights as rhetoric and rights as endowment. Policy auras are neither one; rather, they are the historical distillation of past legal change, suspended over the actions of a later time. Let us refer once more to *Adair* for a more contemporary view. The "yellow dog" contract was finally declared illegal under a section of the bundle of authorizations for conducting labor disputes that constituted the Norris–La Guardia Anti-Injunction Act of 1932. The first case decided by the Supreme Court as to what constituted a labor dispute under that Act was *New Negro Alliance v. Sanitary Grocery Co.* in 1938.[122] A large grocery chain sought an injunction against picketing and boycotting by a corporation organized to promote the civic welfare of African Americans. The particular aim of the action was to secure jobs for black employees. The Court, overturning a lower ruling, certified the dispute as one protected under the Norris–La

Guardia Act: "There is no justification in the apparent purposes or the express terms of the Act for limiting its definition of labor disputes and cases arising therefrom by excluding those which arise with respect to discrimination in terms and conditions of employment based upon differences of race or color."[123]

The labor policy aura over *New Negro Alliance,* like the aura of commercial policy over *Buchanan* and *Shelley,* would continue to hover for years. As events turned out, changes in civil rights legislation proper and also in First Amendment law would eventually take over where that decision left off.[124] Nevertheless, it was a significant opening for racial fairness where none had been intended by the policy makers behind Norris–La Guardia. Lest this appear an isolated event, we might return to the demise of the ancient master-servant law and the momentous decision that supported the constitutionality of the new order's centerpiece law, the NLRA. At the close of his opinion in *NLRB v. Jones & Laughlin Steel,* upholding that Act, Chief Justice Hughes responds to the company's claim that an order to pay back wages to an employee fired for union activity was a denial of its right to a jury trial under the Seventh Amendment. Hughes was concise: "The instant case is not a suit at common law or in the nature of such a suit. The proceeding is one unknown to the common law. It is a statutory proceeding. Reinstatement of the employee and payment for time lost are requirements imposed for violation of the statute and are remedies appropriate to its enforcement."[125]

Scholars have frequently connected the "rights revolution" of the 1960s and 1970s to a footnote in a Court decision issued a year after *Jones & Laughlin Steel.*[126] In the perspective of policy auras, what transpired would not have occurred without the wholesale ouster of the common law pursuant to Congress's labor policy.

"Neighborhood of Principles"

So far the only individual rights written into the Constitution's text that we have discussed at any length are protections for private property. We have rested our argument for the coming of the policy state on the removal of rights of personal relations at common law. Constitutional rights are by far the younger of the two. Rules that distribute authority among government entities, their officers, and members of society, and are formally endorsed, intended as permanent, and acknowledged as "fundamental" or "higher" law, do not appear in political history until long after Blackstone's "rights of persons" had governed English society for centuries. Given its focus on the United States, however, our account of changing personal rights has consistently implicated constitutional ones, even as their constitutional status has been sometimes denied (family relations), sometimes minimized (civil rights), sometimes intentionally circumvented (labor relations). Conceptually, there is considerable overlap between the two categories; constitutional rights were historically modeled on private rights. Put differently, rights against government were initially conceived in private-law terms, arrayed against the rights of individual officers, with the consequence that over Anglo-American history constitutional rights have been claimed through identical legal routines.

The development of the policy state also underscores the important differences that stem from the fact that disputes over constitutional rights—actions that determine their specific endowments and distribution in society—uniformly involve the agencies or officers of government as an intrinsic component. This of course does not mean private persons never sue one another for acts alleged to have injured constitutional rights. But in those instances, a question before the court will be whether a particular rule at issue, usually lodged in a federal or state statute or administrative regulation, was devised or executed in a manner incompatible with provisions of the federal Constitution. In other cases, a government agency or one of its officers will be sued directly for having caused an injury to a constitutional right. This structure in turn interrupts the historical pattern whereby rights change from trumps to chips. Generally speaking, rights that entail government agencies or officers have always been vulnerable to greater contingency than private rights, simply by virtue of their institutional locale.

An instructive contrast is found between the regular course of constitutional litigation and the more insulated traditions of informal resolution of private disputes. As we have seen, the latter engage methods that run the gamut from self-help to elaborate systems of arbitration. From the standpoint of policy, the presence of government, either as party to the suit or as a prior actor within the stream of relevant facts, rather than two parties in disagreement about their personal rights, means that constitutional rights are susceptible to activities—including policy activities—occurring elsewhere in the institutions of state. In this sense, it can be argued that virtually every constitutional right is, from the time of its creation, a chip, if only presumptively. We say virtually every right, since there are certain cut-and-dried exceptions—age requirements for office holding, for instance, or the duration of an officer's term—that yield rights-as-trumps not normally subject to give and take.

For the Bill of Rights in particular, this is a something of a paradox. The Constitution was arranged with an acute awareness of how historical tyranny flourished on the schemes of ambitious politicians. The safeguards installed in response offer a fair road map to the anticipated weak spots. The first ten amendments were added because of a want of confidence in the original text. However, if the purpose was to secure guarantees that would be ironclad, once and forever by the magic of writing them down, it was quickly disappointed by experience. Perhaps the most continuous attenuation of rights by impinging policies is seen in the many episodes of compromise with the requirements of national security. The Alien and Sedition Acts, passed within a decade of the adoption of the First Amendment and deviating from what most contemporaries agreed had been its intention, were defended by leading members of the founding generation as the unwritten power of the people "to preserve its own peace."[127] This began an unbroken tradition stretching across time to the "war on terror" of the present day. In the Supreme Court's 2004 decision *Hamdi v. Rumsfeld*, the plaintiff's successful claim to a hearing on his indefinite confinement without access to a lawyer, based on injury to his Fifth Amendment right of due process, was found by the justices to rest in "delicate balance" with "the exigencies of the circumstances . . . [that is,] their uncommon potential to burden the Executive at a time of ongoing military conflict."[128] *Hamdi* is placed among the most important vindications of civil liberties in a half-century; that said, the balance struck included the permissibility of hearsay testimony and a presumption in favor of the government's evidence.

Such adaptability from the start is evidenced as well in the early ex-
cising by several states of protections modeled on the federal scheme—
the grand jury, for instance, and the right against self-incrimination.
Soon after their adoption they were found to be uneconomic, cumbersome, and in any case, dispensable. During Reconstruction it is shown
in the Supreme Court's denial that the rights contained in the Fifth
Amendment were incorporated into the Fourteenth and in the reason
given: the Constitution was ordained by descendants of Englishmen
who inherited the traditions of English law whereas "we should expect
that the new and various experiences of our own situation and system
will mould and shape it into new and not less useful forms."[129] Likewise, in the twentieth century's first decade, at the height of "legal formalism" in American jurisprudence, Justice Oliver Wendell Holmes, in
his majority opinion on a case concerning private water rights, said this:
"All rights tend to declare themselves absolute to their logical extreme.
Yet all in fact are limited by the neighborhood of principles of policy
which are other than those on which the particular right is founded, and
which become strong enough to hold their own when a certain point is
reached."[130]

Holmes's observation marks a crucial turn toward constitutional-
rights-as-chips. Unlike the other examples mentioned, where rights
and interests are assigned new priority to fit unanticipated events, this
last move entails a redefinition of rights as such. From here, they become openly and at all times a question of more or less, their endowment defined in part by whatever "neighborhood of principles of policy"
prevails at the historical juncture in which they are asserted. If one
seeks a particular inspiration for the event, it might be federal railroad
policy. By this time the justices had heard some ninety cases concerning the Interstate Commerce Commission, which was arguably
the leading institutional innovation of its time, its mission "reasonable"
rates and balanced political party membership. Today, the neighborhood
approach is epitomized by the Court's "degrees of scrutiny" analysis,
applied to different constitutional rights in separate policy areas. The
Hamdi opinion's balance of rights rested expressly on the costs-versus-
benefits mandate of *Mathews v. Eldridge*, the Court decision in 1976
that limited hearings the Constitution requires prior to depriving

government benefits and thus locating national security in the lineage of ordinary administrative law.[131]

This leads to a second point. The cost-benefit approach in *Hamdi* is an example of the distance that may be legally traveled across the policy space in determining constitutional rights. The issue is not simply one of area but of depth; not only the "neighborhood" but the infrastructure. Policy, often inadvertently, affects the procedural actions—the meta-chips, so to speak—upon which all constitutional rights depend. To illustrate, let us return full circle, to where we began this chapter, with *Town of Castle Rock v. Gonzales* and Gonzales's original suit under Section 1983 of the United States Code. As we have seen, Section 1983, providing suits for damages and injunctions in federal court for the "deprivation of any rights, privileges, or immunities secured by the Constitution and laws," has, since its origins in the Civil Rights Act of 1871, expanded to become a principal vehicle by which citizens seek to impose liability on state officers, from governors to policemen to museum directors, exempting only judges and legislators, for injury to constitutional rights.[132]

We would hardly be the first to comment on the strong policy thrust behind the growth of Section 1983, nor on its borrowing from private tort law categories that, unlike constitutional ones, presume balanced and shared liability among litigants.[133] Less remarked upon is the extent to which this growth tracks the stages in the expansion of the policy state. In fact, the pattern precedes 1871. Commercial interests, already the principal component of the policy state, were by now accustomed to calling state officers to account in federal court under federal diversity jurisdiction, a doctrine bent into novel shapes for this use.[134] The 1871 Act was intended as a mechanism by which former slaves might seek redress against resisting local officers. The restricted endowment of the Fourteenth Amendment until the period of the New Deal meant that few cases under that legislation were decided in the Supreme Court, but the few that were concerned either commerce or racial discrimination.[135] Lower court cases were limited to the same subject matter. For instance, one turn-of-the-century suit for damages by a parent against an officer of a state-chartered children's protective agency was turned aside on the ground that the custody of children was outside the range of rights which, under the Civil Rights Act, "a state is forbidden to abridge."[136]

The break in the impasse, the Supreme Court's decision opening the door to eventually hearing heretofore excluded rights claims respecting government, was *Hague v. Committee for Industrial Organization* in 1939.[137] *Hague* did for Section 1983 what *Jones&Laughlin Steel* later on did for Congress, severing employment from its historical association with common law and in the process endorsing a statutory basis for actionable constitutional rights generally conceived. The suit challenged the refusal of a city mayor to grant a permit to labor unions to meet in a public park. Justice Roberts, writing for the majority and joined by Justice Black, said that assembly for the purpose of discussing the Wagner Act was a right protected under the privileges and immunities clause of the Fourteenth Amendment and therefore claimable under Section 1983. Justice Stone's concurrence was based on the wider-scope due-process protection; and Justice Hughes's concurrence split the difference. Justice Stone's view became the rule of the case.

The change underway from *Hague* may be suggested by a pair of famous Court decisions on First Amendment religious rights. *Minersville School District v. Gobitis* in 1940 and *West Virginia State Board of Education v. Barnette* in 1943 were suits for injunctions by Jehovah's Witness parents to stop school officers from coercing their children into saluting the American flag in class, something they argued violated their freedom of religious exercise under the First Amendment. In *Gobitis*, the lower court, deciding only months after *Hague*, denied the injunction, distinguished between the freedom of religion claimed and the freedom of speech supported by *Hague*. The Supreme Court affirmed, holding that educational policy is a question best left to legislatures. This was over the dissent of Justice Stone, who based his opinion on his own broader due-process interpretation in *Hague*.[138] Two years later, in *Barnette*, an appeals court, also relying on *Hague*, granted the identical injunction denied in *Gobitis*. Affirming this judgment, Justice Jackson's opinion for the Supreme Court majority, without referring to *Hague* by name, references the dramatic opening-up to "principles" heralded by that case. The Court's duty, he writes, is not limited by "possession of marked competence in the field where the invasion of rights occurs." It must "transplant these rights to a soil in which the *laissez-faire* concept or principle of non-interference has withered at least as to economic affairs and social advancements are increasingly sought through closer integration of society."[139]

For the floodgates to open fully it remained for an extended legal conversation about the relation of "due process" to Section 1983 to occur, and in particular the meaning of the words "color of law" in the 1871 statute. The answer came in *Monroe v. Pape*, decided by the Court in 1961, overriding a state's own determination of whether its officer had acted illegally.[140] After *Monroe*, 1983 suits grew exponentially, within a decade amounting to thousands of cases each year.[141] Again evident is the policy connection, now to the burgeoning agenda of the civil rights movement. The first Supreme Court case to hold police officers immune from damages if they acted in "good faith," in accordance with what they reasonably believed was prevailing law, concerned a "pray-in" in Jackson, Mississippi. That decision was policy straight-up. With the caveat that "the matter is not entirely beyond doubt," the majority opinion bases the holding not on precedent but on principle: a "policeman's lot is not so unhappy that he must choose between being charged with dereliction of duty if he does not arrest when he has probable cause, and being mulcted in damages if he does."[142]

Policy-induced movements forward and back can be seen with regard to a different meta-chip, habeas corpus. When it was inherited from England the writ was limited to use in federal court only by persons in federal custody to question the legal jurisdiction of the officer in charge. In 1833, Congress, to enable federal enforcement of the 1832 tariff against a resisting South Carolina, extended the right to federal officers who might find themselves in state custody; in 1850, the same was provided federal marshals enforcing the Fugitive Slave Act of that year. In 1867, to facilitate Reconstruction, Congress made habeas available to any person "restrained of his or her liberty in violation of the Constitution, or of any treaty or law of the United States," including state prisoners, and in 1883 the Court permitted habeas actions after conviction under a state law. Interspersed, and setting to one side suspensions of the writ during wartime: in 1868 Congress deprived the

Supreme Court appellate habeas jurisdiction, a ban that lasted until 1885; between 1879 and 1915, Congress permitted the Court to hear habeas suits by state prisoners only when state courts lacked jurisdiction. Instability persists into the contemporary period. Specialists on the writ differ as to whether, after 1867, habeas challenges based on substantive as well as jurisdictional rights could be brought, a question finally settled only in the 1950s.[143] During the broader "rights revolution" of the 1960s, the writ expanded again, allowing state prisoners to proceed immediately to federal court, without exhausting available state procedure.[144]

Not long afterward, both Section 1983 and habeas corpus ran headlong into cold policy winds. The first blast was the rule that costs must be balanced against benefits in government programs. This came in 1976, in *Mathews v. Eldridge*, the Section 1983 decision already mentioned, reversing course from a decision in 1970 that had guaranteed the right to a formal hearing before benefits to mothers with dependent children were ended and thought to herald a "due process revolution."[145] In the case of habeas, it was in the next year, 1977, when the Supreme Court expressed its rededication to the priority of state procedure over access to the federal writ. This policy would be strengthened by Congress in the 1996 Antiterrorism and Effective Death Penalty Act. In the same climate, the scope of both actions was curtailed still more by the Court's emphasis on, respectively, "clearly established law" in assessing the liability of government officers sued and the prevention of questions not already settled at law from being raised in habeas proceedings.[146] Notice that for all the turnabout, the one constant is the Court's trump-like position in establishing the rules.

Let us conclude this chapter with a few words about the meta-chip of sovereign immunity. A doctrine inherited from England, sovereign immunity has the effect of shutting down all suits against government itself, state or federal, before they begin, except when the government in question unambiguously consents. Chief Justice Marshall endorsed this principle for the federal government in an opinion in 1824; as it concerned state sovereignty, the issue arose even earlier and was the occasion in 1794 for the passage of the Eleventh Amendment.[147] In 1907, Justice Holmes, true to form, defended sovereign immunity on the practical ground that there can be no legal right against the authority that makes the law on which all rights depend.[148] Implemented to the full, the doctrine would amount to a full abrogation of constitutional government. The circumvention of sovereign immunity is the precise purpose for which suits against officeholders were designed, both anciently and as confirmed in the United States.

At various points in American history, Congress—as putative sovereign branch—has waived sovereign immunity on behalf of the federal government. The first waiver of importance was the Tucker Act, passed in 1887, culminating what had been a mainly ad hoc approach to paying the government's debts through private congressional bills and the occasional special commission. This cumbersome practice continued even as national operations steadily expanded, especially during periods of wartime. However, having assigned itself this steadily inundating jurisdiction, Congress was long reluctant to cede control over this sizeable piece of the federal budget. After experimenting before and during the Civil War with a Court of Claims whose decisions were mainly advisory, Congress finally endowed that body with binding authority over suits concerning tax and debt but not torts, which was (and is) the category encompassing most noncommercial constitutional rights.

The next milestone was in 1946. After defeating dozens of other bills, Congress passed, as part of the Legislative Reorganization Act of that year, the Federal Tort Claims Act (FTCA). Passage was spurred by an air force bomber in 1945 slamming into the Empire State Building in New York City, killing fourteen and seriously injuring many others, most of whom, under then-existing law, had only the dimmest prospects of ever obtaining compensation. The FTCA assigned all federal claims henceforth to the federal courts, who were to assess the liability of government officers "in the same manner and to the same extent as a private individual under like circumstances."[149] One subsection of the Act, however, excluded "any claim arising out of assault, battery, false imprisonment, false arrest, malicious prosecution, abuse of process, libel, slander, misrepresentation, deceit, or interference with contract rights." This exclusion, based on the long-standing idea that the torts named would by definition exceed the "scope of employment," the phrase delimiting the activity for which the officer was accountable, was lifted for law enforcement officers in 1974.

Notice that while individual government officers may now be sued under the FTCA, the government as such, to which "scope of employment" does not apply, is still not liable. More relevant for our purposes, the Act contains a "discretionary function" exception, which applies to any suit "based upon the exercise or performance or the failure to exercise or perform a discretionary function or duty on the part of a federal agency or an employee of the Government, whether or not the discretion involved be abused."[150] No less an authority than the Supreme Court has confirmed that Congress passed this exception "to prevent 'second guessing' of its legislative and administrative decisions grounded in social, economic, and political policy through the medium of an action in tort."[151] Subsequently, the Court explained that the exception included action involving the officer's choices or judgments that are "susceptible to policy analysis."[152]

The protection for public policies in the "discretionary function" exception, sanctioned by both Congress and the Court, must be viewed against the historical facts behind the FTCA, and, for that matter, the Tucker Act, as well. These indicate that the politics behind the FTCA were in large part institutional: in passing the FTCA, Congress was again motivated by fear of losing control of the nation's purse strings, now in the face of executive encroachment through the programs of the New Deal. Put differently, at least without closer scrutiny of the legislative record than is found in existing scholarship, there is no evidence of any narrow interest-group rationale or activity important in the Act's passage. In this perspective, the relaxation of sovereign immunity offers a good example of how government authority over public policy takes legal precedence over the remediation of citizens' rights, quite self-consciously so. Seemingly, a plane crashing into a skyscraper was just the sort of policy-free injury for which Congress was prepared to have responsibility assigned, a sentiment critics of the legislation ever since would likely endorse.[153] If it can be said that *Hague v. CIO* was on the path to constitutional rights becoming a sword in the wars of public policy, the "discretionary function" exception is a marker on the path to public policy becoming a shield against citizens' constitutional rights.[154]

CHAPTER FOUR

Structure in the Policy State

THE Constitution's framers placed provisions to expand policy's domain at the center of an elaborate structure to contain it. They arranged institutions to assure those threatened by the expansion that the national government's newfound powers would be self-limiting. Since that time, policy has challenged the structure of this government more or less continuously. Accommodation has vied with resistance, and the stress of competing purposes has grown ever more pronounced.

This much seems plain: policy's advance unsettles institutional relationships, and constraints loosen as accommodations accumulate. The rules of action have been renegotiated repeatedly, with constitutional principles invoked to guide each adjustment. But with novel applications, principles eventually wear thin. Policy's widening reach has gradually confounded the architecture's rationale, sapping rules of their ordering effect.

Let us begin our analysis with an early assessment of how the policy motive might affect this government's structure, one ventured before the virtues of adaptation were taken for granted. In 1800, James Madison rose to defend resolutions by the Virginia legislature protesting the federal government's Alien and Sedition Acts. In the course of his remarks, Madison described consequences likely to follow the broad authority for policy making claimed by Congress under the Constitution's "general welfare" clause. Congress's intrusion upon the rights of the states on this basis would, he reasoned, "transform the republican system of the United States into a monarchy."

Madison saw two dynamics at work, both of which are now familiar. One was the delegation of power from Congress to the executive:

> Even within the legislative limits properly defined by the constitution, the difficulty of accommodating legal regulations to a country so great in extent, and so various in its circumstances, has been much felt; and has led to occasional investments of power in the executive,

which involve perhaps as large a portion of discretion, as can be deemed consistent with the nature of the executive trust. In proportion as the objects of legislative care might be multiplied, would the time allowed for each be diminished, and the difficulty of providing uniform and particular regulations for all, be increased. From these sources would necessarily ensue, a greater latitude to the agency of that department which is always in existence, and which could best mould regulations of a general nature, so as to suit them to the diversity of particular situations. And it is in this latitude, as a supplement to the deficiency of the laws, that the degree of executive prerogative materially consists.

The other was the transfer of power from local to national administration, or what Madison called the "augmentation of the offices, honors, and emoluments depending on the executive will":

Add to the present legitimate stock, all those of every description which a consolidation of the states would take from them, and turn over to the federal government, and the patronage of the executive would necessarily be as much swelled in this case, as its prerogative would be in the other.[1]

Of special interest to us here are the systemic effects of policy's expansion. Stretching Congress's policy-making authority implicates the states, the presidency, the bureaucracy, and the Congress itself. Accommodations to policy defeat structure by leaving all authority less secure. The federal legislature was not, Madison contends, designed to act beyond its specified spheres of competence; it is, he ventures, unlikely to do so effectively, and more to the point, when it attempts to extend national policy into the jurisdiction of the states, it falls victim to its own inflated ambitions. In this scenario, Congress loses control over the policy state in the very act of creating it.

Skeptics may object to so stark a portrayal, and the point would be well taken. Madison's assessment is methodical to the point of seeming mechanical. The choice between republicanism and monarchy is forced, stubbornly indifferent to other possible outcomes. The complications of political practice are especially hard to ignore. Madison was organizing a national political coalition to oust the sponsors of the Alien and Sedition Acts in upcoming elections. Sounding the alarm with a disquieting prediction was part of this (eventually successful) political strategy. Flash forward to the present, and the case for caution is reinforced by irresolution still found in these arrangements. Encroachments on the states have multiplied exponentially since Madison's time, but the federal system has not succumbed to "consolidation." Our "executive magistrate" is now elevated in stature and provided awesome discretion, but monocracy has yet to materialize. Policy ambitions have led Congress to cede a good deal of control to the executive, but it still holds the purse strings. The structure of American government has stretched every which way, but it has not been replaced.

Whatever the intention of its designers, the Constitution offered dual templates for policy making, each different in its conception of the authority of officeholders. Madison's conjecture assumes their authority has been fully allocated, jurisdiction by jurisdiction and from top to bottom. He does not present the Constitution as a provisional scheme whose actual arrangements are yet to be worked out. In the assessment he offers, discretion has been entrusted to officers and institutions in advance, according to their "nature" and special competencies. The distribution is explicit and exhaustive. Each of the government's interlocking parts is "properly defined" in relation to the others; the work of each is protected in its due "portion" and constrained by surrounding authority. Adhering to the regimen set forth is not easy, but there is no ambiguity purposefully implanted for instrumental manipulation or creative exploration. Such a government, though vigorous in every part, will be threatening to none. The states are safeguarded by the national government because, as Madison might say, its "legal regulations" preclude regulations of "a general nature."

This is the Constitution operating as a containment structure. The containment structure is strong to the extent that the Constitution is concrete and complete, its arrangements transparent, locked down in writing, and legally binding. Policy's domain is set by the text, enclosed in a dense field of other, equally authoritative motives. Rules are grounded in what Madison elsewhere calls "the constitutional rights of the place," and these rights are in the nature of what Chapter 3 called "trumps." They endow officers with claims against policy, allowing them to shut down initiatives that impinge upon their prerogatives. By the vigorous assertion and enforcement of their rights, the Constitution's officers ensure the integrity and supremacy of the framework itself.

Congress's use of the vagaries of the general welfare clause in 1798 tested the containment structure, revealing in the process an alternative that would over time give it increasingly stiff competition. That alternative is the Constitution operating as an opportunity structure. The opportunity structure is implicit, abstract, and entrepreneurial. It renders policy's domain pliable and speculative. Here the rights of institutional actors have the character of what Chapter 3 called "chips," tokens of access to a contest with no particular outcome assured. Incumbents at all levels are at liberty to maximize their policy preferences by leveraging institutional resources and coordinating with others. They approach the Constitution strategically as a matrix of assets to exploit and obstacles to overcome, and possibilities are uncovered catch-as-catch-can through changing calculations of risk and advantage. The opportunity structure turns on contingencies in the struggle for political power. Creativity is on tap, for governing arrangements adjust to whatever policies can be sustained.

America's policy state straddles widening disparities between these two templates. The more creatively it stretches to accommodate change, the more awkwardly it strains to conform to its set design. With the containment structure preserved in writing, novel accommodations generate suspect forms of unsteady authority. Escalating demands for performance weaken the deference accorded to formally assigned duties but without canceling out earlier claims. The different branches of government retain their essential properties amid progressively more elaborate workarounds. As constraints loosen and the formal division of institutional labor erodes, rules regulating institutional interactions cannot but grow more complicated and less decisive. Much depends on tolerance for ambiguity, but there is, by the same token, little that can be taken for granted. A court bent on "reviving" federalism or a Congress intent on freezing the debt limit could arrest this state in its tracks. Short of that, the age-old charge of derangement fuels a permanent siege, with attacks on the legitimacy of current operations facing off against the heightened risks of following through.

America's policy state does not translate every proposal into governmental action, nor does it resolve every problem it addresses. But a survey of developments in the key structural relationships reveals a state that has over time become saturated by the motive it was originally meant to contain. This is structure now shorn of the resources to sort itself out, a framework at cross-purposes in which everyone has come to operate as a policy entrepreneur.[2] Surmounting obstacles is the order of the day, and that has scrambled authority at every turn.

Free-Form Federalism

In the 1970s the Supreme Court began to express concern over the deterioration of the federal structure of American government, and since then, a steady drumbeat of judicial opinion has repelled national encroachments on state institutions. The justices have renewed appeals to Tenth and Eleventh Amendment protections, reasserted an essential connection between local control and republican government, and derided the assumption of a "whatever-it-takes-to-solve-a-national-problem power."[3] If the intended effect has been to shock the system, the Court has repeatedly hit its mark. At issue is not just the impact, sometimes profound, on individual policies under review. More to the point is the threat that this fervent defense of the federal form poses to the practical operations of modern American government. The Court's federalism jurisprudence stands out for our attention precisely for this reason. Judicial agitation for federalism's "revival"— more specifically, the assumption that federalism needs "reviving"— presents the most sustained and aggressive line of resistance to the free-form character of the policy state.

Easy pickings for a revival can be found among the bits and pieces of the containment structure. The Constitution safeguarded the states, first by specifying the powers of the national government, then by building their political interests into the composition of the nation's policy-making institutions, and finally by reserving to them powers not expressly delegated elsewhere. Still, a revival campaign runs up against the proverbial Humpty Dumpty problem: retrieving the remnants of an old form is a lot easier than putting them back together. One challenge is to give the task a convincing rationale. It is not that local control has lost its purchase as a motive of American government; at issue are the other motives on which its appeal has come to rest.

Federalism recommends itself to us for its association with liberty, representation, accountability, equality, democracy, participation, and experimentation, but these values do not impose firm limits on policy, and each can, depending on the policy at issue and the circumstances confronted, be advanced as effectively through national as through local control. The value of federalism has in this way come to draw on its flexibility, variability, and instrumentality in the pursuit of other ends. Put another way, defending state or local authority in its own right verges today on empty formalism.[4]

Federalism was the most novel of the Constitution's institutional arrangements, and not coincidentally, it was also a workaround, a way of surmounting a pressing problem. The states had immediate interests of their own in national policy, but they would only sign on to a safe bet. So federalism empowered the national government to make policy with minimal displacement of the authority of the states to do the same, and it hedged traditional republican commitments to localism without resolving the question of supremacy. Mutually beneficial entanglements followed immediately upon ratification, for example, in the federal government's assumption of the states' Revolutionary War debts, and later, when the states willingly accepted trade-offs like the Sixteenth and Seventeenth Amendments. But prior to the 1970s, and from the time of the framing, the instrumentalism in this partnership was crucially counterbalanced by more stubborn authority, namely, some portion of the traditional, interpersonal rights discussed in Chapter 3. The rights of slaveholders, of employers, of husbands and parents, of white people, all of which were regulated only at state law, gave the federal structure its distinctive moorings. As these rights were cleared away, submitted to national oversight, partly by force, one by one, federal-state relations became, apace, more fluid, less rule-bound, more opportunistic.

These processes can be connected to the standard periodization of the development of federalism.[5] Shifts in structure, each in turn producing a more variable and entangled federal relationship, follow successive resolutions of political contests over rights in personal relations, each displacement opening the field to policy.[6] These contests were not the only factors at work in these transitions, but by all accounts they figured centrally. The period prior to the abolition of slavery has been aptly described as a "states-union" concerned primarily with common defense and commercial expansion.[7] Federalism defined the government's central fault line, and the prospect of states acting collectively in defiance of central authority was a major concern of national policy makers.[8] Nationalizing elites elaborated principles of "dual federalism," asserting constitutional prerogatives for national action within a designated sphere. Their opponents responded with a "compact theory" of federalism, a scheme in which national powers remained provisional and states retained the right to deflect unwanted intrusions at will.[9] The cause of dualism advanced aggressively in these years but backfired repeatedly. Policy initiatives elaborating on seemingly rudimentary aspects of federal jurisdiction—tariff protection, road building, national banking, national apprehension of fugitive slaves—were stymied and countered in the protection of state autonomy.

After slavery's demise, compact theory fell into disfavor. But the legal foundations of dualism were strained as well. The Reconstruction amendments clarified and strengthened national authority. Earlier doubts about the scope of the federal role in promoting commerce—for example, in banking, in industrial protection, in infrastructure—were erased in this period, and commercial policy extended its national profile into resource conservation, scientific agriculture, business regulation, public health, education, and immigration. As the federal relationship became more entangled, the Supreme Court took the lead on behalf of a system of "separate and distinct sovereignties, acting separately and independently of each other, within their respective spheres."[10] It found enduring support for dualism (and substantive limitations on the reach of national policy) in local control over rights in personal relations.[11] The new constitutional amendments were interpreted to exclude federal regulation of "private rights between man and man in society," narrowing the legal opening to intervention in race relations. If such regulation were appropriate, the Court averred, "it is difficult to see where it is to stop."[12] Likewise, the Court resisted federal intrusion into workplace relations and the labor contract: "the evils are all local evils over which the federal government has no legislative control. The relation of employer and employee is a local relation. At common law, it is one of the domestic relations."[13]

The labor barrier fell first. Demand for greater flexibility in the regulation of industrial relations mounted precipitously in the early decades of the twentieth century, and with the advent of the New Deal, labor and working conditions were brought more fully under policy's umbrella. This strained dualism to the breaking point, and in its place, "cooperative federalism" became the dominant theory.[14] In practice, the Court abandoned commerce clause restrictions on the scope of federal regulatory powers, concurrent policy making displaced separate federal and state jurisdictions, and policy partnerships between federal and state governments knit the dual structure together programmatically.[15] A few decades later, with the overthrow of Jim Crow and a concerted assault on patriarchy, the national government assumed a more overtly aggressive posture toward the states. The Civil Rights Act of 1964 and the Voting Rights Act of 1965 ushered in a period of "coercive federalism," sidelining the last of the telltale limits on the reach of national policy. A tidal wave of federal preemption statutes, crossover funding conditions, and sanctions for noncompliance with federal standards overwhelmed the rights of "place."[16]

In the wake of the social revolution, labels describing the arrangements and rearrangements of federal-state relations multiplied, but no general characterization stuck. Political slogans (for example, Lyndon Johnson's "Creative Federalism," Richard Nixon's "New Federalism," Jimmy Carter's "New Partnership") proclaimed the intentions of politicians to adapt the system for their own ends. Scholars deployed a mystifying variety of terms, each of which captured a particular aspect of a fast-changing state of affairs (for example, "picket-fence federalism," "permissive federalism," "integrated federalism," "competitive federalism," "administered federalism," "hyper-interdependence," "devolution," "state resurgence"). Partial and unresolved retreats from the peak of federal coercion recalled the full range of earlier forms (for example, a rollback to cooperative federalism, a revival of dual federalism, a whiff of nullification). But these are now political propositions for which there is no binding law.

The arrangements and practices of contemporary federalism resist labels not only because of their wide variety and disparity but also because each appears caught up in stiff crosscurrents. The states lost autonomy but gained governing capacity. By engaging them more actively in the administration of its programs, the national government fostered more professional, capable, and policy-savvy state governments. State and local authorities developed the means to compete for their policy preferences with the national government and with one another. For its part, the national government has had to grapple with the ballooning costs of its commitments, and it has become more reliant on the states to carry out its policies. It has stiffened its demands with "unfunded mandates" and broadened its reach through preemption statutes.[17]

Hollowed out as a containment structure, federalism flourishes today as an opportunity structure. The form has been liberated for continuous political negotiation across the widening field of policy choice.[18] The rights to be protected by the formal division of responsibilities are harder now to isolate and classify, and the interests to be advanced through it are more varied and contingent. Policy entrepreneurs approach jurisdictional boundaries strategically in pursuit of goals, and the sheer variety of the issues addressed works against any uniform code of procedure. The process of entangling federalism in instrumental pursuits, a process that began with ratification of the Constitution, is now all but complete. Indeed, a common objection to general characterizations of the current structure is that "it depends on the policy area, the policy instruments, and even the skills of the administrator."[19]

"Intergovernmental relations" is the capacious term commonly employed, often by default, to describe these operations.[20] Cleansed of the historical baggage of "federalism" and open-ended about the character of the interactions encompassed, the term aptly describes a relationship that has neither fixed social content nor firm ideological underpinnings. The implied analogy is to foreign affairs, where realist assumptions highlight the overriding significance of calculation and the balance of power. The ordering function assumed by the states in the antebellum period, or by the Court under dual federalism, or by Congress under cooperative federalism is hard to replicate, for the rights that once delimited the field and anchored the rules have been stripped away.

Operations have, as Madison predicted, shifted toward the executive branch, but the management of federalism in the executive is itself dispersed among the bureaus and agencies that administer particular policies and programs. A White House Office of Intergovernmental Affairs was created in 1974 to coordinate interactions with subgovernments and to bring policies affecting them into accord with the president's program. But the managerial capacities of this office were limited by the divergent policy preferences of local authorities, and the alternating priorities of successive administrations worked against efforts to institutionalize these relationships.[21] More significant are the liaison offices maintained at lower levels of the federal bureaucracy. These provide channels of communications for state and local officials on specific matters of program development and operation, and they invite state and local officials to express their interests collectively as well as individually. Organizations like the National Governors Association, the National Association of State Attorneys General, the National League of Cities, and party-based groupings of state officers express the common interests of subgovernments and compete with private-sector lobbies for the attention of policy makers throughout the federal apparatus.

The opening of intergovernmental relations to continuous negotiations among discrete actors in dispersed settings gains additional support from policy instruments that have progressively eased constraints on their interactions. The instrument characteristic of cooperative federalism was the categorical grant. States received federal funds for specific programs according to set formulas, or they applied for and competed to run particular projects under federal guidelines. Conditional spending directed negotiations to the finer points of merit and compliance. Since the 1970s, the use of block grants, revenue sharing, preemption exceptions, and state waivers has become more common.[22] Also notable in recent years is the willingness to negotiate over standards of federal prosecution (on drug-law enforcement, for example) and federal sponsorship of interstate compacts (on Common Core curriculum standards, for example).[23] All in their own way exemplify the displacement of rules by guidelines, or by governance less constrained by structure and more amenable to bargaining and revision. With these devices in hand, federal statutes become less determinative of outcomes, states have more options, and national programs vary more widely from place to place.

Demands for performance encourage this kind of flexibility, and those two values dovetail to create momentum of their own. For example, the use of waivers, which began in the 1960s as a device for setting up state demonstration projects and testing potential alternatives in the design of federal programs, has in recent decades become a device for renegotiating programs state by state and altering policy without resort to statutory changes. During the administrations of Bill Clinton and George W. Bush, entrepreneurial governors leveraged the use of Medicaid waivers to turn assistance to the needy into a program of managed care and to expand coverage to hundreds of thousands of beneficiaries without congressional action.[24] The signature education policy enacted under the Bush administration, "No Child Left Behind," was rescripted by an equally generous distribution of waivers by the Obama administration.[25] The rise of rule by waiver finds Congress torn between its openness to state interests and its suspicion of executive discretion. In the early 2000s, both the House and the Senate contemplated "superwaiver" statutes that would expand and simplify the procedure. One version would remove control from the various program agencies and consolidate the waiver process in a joint interagency board. The board would consider applications submitted by individual states in packages, and the waivers would go into effect automatically within ninety days unless the board objected.[26] Providing "rules" for "waivers" is one of those paradoxical aspirations that riddle the policy state. Interest in institutionalizing the process waned when political resistance to the Affordable Care Act targeted executive dispensation from program rules as a violation of the president's solemn responsibility to faithfully execute the law.[27] Nonetheless, the flexibility offered by waivers can be as valuable to program opponents as to supporters. By using the instrument for their own purposes, they both keep policy in play.[28]

Judicial pushback against the free-form character of contemporary federalism proceeds case by case against these wide-ranging, loosely knit networks of exchange, and with action so thoroughly saturated by the policy motive, it is hard to gauge the scope of the reconfiguration overall. A persistent question of the past forty years has been whether the Court's federalism "revival" adds up to anything more than agitation,[29] and notwithstanding the many inroads that have been cut, there is still reason for skepticism. The political risks of judicial follow-through are substantial, and the alternative aimed at remains cloudy. In an age of wholly contingent interests—when the major social, economic, and political actors switch sides erratically, policy by policy, in the promotion of state or federal power—the Court's restoration capacities would appear limited.[30]

More to our point, after decades of effort, the Court's new rules remain unsteady, their application uneven and their scope continuously refined. The absence of resolve is indicated in the decisions themselves, which have been closely divided, with blocklike resistance that impedes the establishment of precedents. Current opinions air fierce disagreements among the justices about what the essential principle of federalism is and how it relates to the authority of Congress in our more democratic age.[31] With little consensus on that, extrapolations from structure to rules or from rules to operations are bound to remain steeped in controversy. All of this speaks to the altered context for a judicial defense of federalism, to the difference between drawing bright lines to articulate a relationship still freighted with rights and imposing rules on a relationship that has grown progressively more instrumental and policy dependent.

Justice Blackmun flagged the problem at the very beginning of the revival campaign. As the swing vote, he effected an embarrassing flip-flop in the Court's initial attempt to defend the sovereignty of the states against alleged policy overreach through the Commerce Clause. Writing a concurring opinion in *National League of Cities v. Usery* (1976), Blackmun joined in voiding amendments to the Fair Labor Standards Act (FLSA) that applied federal wage and hour regulations to state and city employees. The first major reversal of federal authority under the Commerce Clause since the New Deal, *Usery* distinguished Congress's power over states from its power over private businesses and individuals and declared it essential to the federal structure of the Constitution to protect the states' integral and traditional government functions. Blackmun signed onto the idea that the states' "separate and independent existence" depended on protecting their authority to set terms of employment for their own workers, but he had reservations about making hard and fast rules in these matters, arguing instead for a "balancing approach" that would take into consideration the

importance of compliance with federal standards in the various areas
that come under review. A state's right "to structure employer-employee
relationships" was one thing, but "federal power in areas such as environmental protection" might, Blackmun, suggested, require different
treatment.[32]

Over the next eight years, the Court appeared incapable of offering
further guidance to lower courts as to which state functions were "integral" and in need of protection, and in 1985 Blackmun seized on
another state challenge to the FLSA to call a halt to the effort to sort
things out. Writing for the majority in *Garcia v. San Antonio Metropolitan Transit Authority*, he overturned *Usery*, and in his opinion, he
offered an apt assessment of structure in the policy state. "The attempt to draw the boundaries of state regulatory immunity in terms
of 'traditional governmental function'" was, Blackmun declared,
"unworkable" and bereft of any "organizing principle." Going further,
he asserted that "a rule of state immunity" which "turns on a judicial
appraisal of whether a particular governmental function is 'integral' or
'traditional'" was an affront to "democratic self-governance" and an
invitation "to an unelected federal judiciary to make decisions about
which policies it favors and which ones it dislikes." The only protections for federalism Blackmun found consistent with modern American government were the political safeguards inherent in the structure
of the representative institutions and embedded in the process of policy
making itself.[33]

The Court has pursued several other options in imposing constitutional limitations on policy. It has tried reinforcing state sovereign immunity[34] and curbing national power under Section 5 of the Fourteenth
Amendment.[35] Congress has responded with workarounds, often
falling back on the use of conditional spending to get the job done.[36]
In that regard, the Court's first decision on the Affordable Care Act,
National Federation of Independent Business v. Sebelius (2012), cut to
the heart of the policy state by indicating a willingness to limit the
federal government's use of its spending powers to induce state compliance with national policy priorities.[37] Still, finding a principle that
blocks a certain policy is not, in itself, a revival of federalism. Rules
that remain targeted and fail to cut widely through the thicket of
working relationships do not reorder the federal structure. As Blackmun

implied, these are shadow-boxing exercises, the real effect of which is to draw the Court itself more deeply into policy making.

Consider the regulation of private action under the commerce clause. In *United States v. Lopez* (1995), the Court voided a ban on the possession of firearms imposed by the Gun-Free School Zones Act for failure to demonstrate any connection between the regulation and "a commercial transaction" which, even "in the aggregate, substantially affect(s) interstate commerce."[38] At first, the political branches shrugged off the restriction. Treating *Lopez* as a drafting guide, Congress enacted a revised version of the Act stipulating that the firearm at issue "has moved in or otherwise affects interstate commerce."[39] But the Court doubled down, seeming to foreclose a legislative workaround. In *United States v. Morrison* (2000) it voided the civil damages provision of the Violence Against Women Act, and did so in the face of a legislative record purporting to document the aggregate economic effect of that violence.[40] These early skirmishes opened a broad premise for judicial intervention and, for the moment, shortened the outer reaches of national regulatory authority under the commerce clause.

In the meantime, the Court has proven deft at finding workarounds of its own, so it is still not clear exactly what set of policies the new limits preclude.[41] The lead opinion in the 2012 decision on health-care reform refused to endorse the individual mandate to purchase health insurance as a regulation of interstate commerce. But it upheld the provision as a tax. And previously, in *Gonzales v. Raich* (2005), the Court weakened the line *Morrison* had seemed to strengthen.[42] The Court in *Raich* ruled that the federal Controlled Substances Act preempted a California law authorizing the medical use of marijuana. According to *Raich*, cultivating marijuana within one's home for personal medical use was an "economic" activity, one with substantial effects on interstate commerce and an integral connection to a larger regulatory scheme that fell well within the purview of the commerce clause. The majority found room to evade *Lopez* in the distinction between commercial and noncommercial activity, but in doing so, it relaxed the prior rule, which excluded "attenuated" economic impact, in effect widening the field of choice for Court and Congress alike.[43] The principal dissent lamented this retreat as conceding that the new direction charted by *Lopez* was, after all, "nothing more than a drafting guide":

had Congress "described the relevant crime in *Lopez* as 'transfer or possession of a firearm anywhere in the nation'—thus including commercial and noncommercial activity and clearly encompassing some activity with assuredly substantial effect on interstate commerce . . . we would have sustained its authority to regulate possession of firearms in school zones."[44]

As Blackmun foresaw, it has been difficult to prevent the judicial imposition of constitutional limits on policy making from devolving into policy choices plain and simple. But for judges interested in defending the federal structure, Blackmun's faith in the safeguards embedded within the lawmaking process itself pointed to an alternative, and seemingly less confrontational, strategy. By stipulating rules to be used in statutory review and focusing on questions of means rather than ends, the Court can engage more directly on Congress's own turf. For example, a "clear statement rule" articulated in *Gregory v. Ashcroft* (1991) supported Missouri's constitutional provision of a retirement age for state judges against the federal Age Discrimination in Employment Act.[45] The majority in the case did not mount a *Usery*-like defense of state sovereignty; instead, it found that the statute's application to state judges had not been made sufficiently plain. The clear statement rule does not tell the Congress what the federal-state balance should be or foreclose its manipulation through policy; rather, it advises Congress that the federal relationship cannot be changed by inadvertence, that the intent and scope of the change to be effected by policy needs to be explicit. Similarly, the "anticommandeering" rules articulated in *New York v. United States* (1992)[46] and *Printz v. United States* (1997)[47] did not restrict the scope of federal policy making. Instead, the Court in these cases precluded the federal government from requiring state institutions to carry out its policies and insisted instead that it invest its own resources to achieve its chosen ends.

Rules like these submerge judicial antagonism toward the policy state in a self-styled partnership. The Court weighs in on negotiations over policy by setting more stringent terms for the exercise of recognized powers. Objections ventured in this way appear very much like guidelines for drafting an acceptable policy in the future. Operationally, however, they play upon inherent weaknesses in the legislative process and turn constitutional protections into a test of congressional will and capacity. They value federalism as an obstacle for the legislature to overcome and increase the costs of doing so.[48]

But is there something more to them? Consider the issues presented in *New York*. The state had been party to an effort by the National Governors Association to head off federal preemption legislation in the area of radioactive waste disposal. In deference to the affected states, Congress enacted a policy that incentivized them to develop their own remedies, threatening a federally imposed default solution if they failed. But when New York encountered local resistance to the disposal plan it had adopted under the Act, it sued the federal government for relief, claiming that to compel the state to submit to the federally imposed default violated its Tenth Amendment rights. The Court majority found that the state's active involvement in negotiating a federal regulatory scheme to its liking was not, in itself, conclusive in determining the legitimacy of the scheme. It then elevated a juridical standard over considerations of process and practicality by pulling the hammer from the law's inducement scheme and refusing to allow the federal government the ultimate sanction of directing the state legislature to enact a specific regulation. As the dissent in the case pointed out, the implications were paradoxical. New York had preserved a measure of control for itself by going to Congress to head off the preemption statute initially contemplated. By subsequently protecting New York against a federal statute that had incentivized it to act on its own, the Court exposed the state and its citizens to a more coercive remedy, the unilateral intervention it had initially tried to escape.[49] Perhaps that is what prompted Justice O'Connor, writing for the majority, to articulate a principle to be promoted by a proscription of federal commandeering: whatever the practical consequences, citizens need to know which level of government is responsible for a policy so that they can hold the proper representatives accountable.[50]

Serious pursuit of that overriding purpose would surely be transformative, for it appears to implicate the entire complex of intergovernmental blending that federalism has become. But those prospects remain uncertain, for here too the Court provided a workaround. *Reno v. Condon* (2000) was a rare unanimous decision upholding the Driver's Privacy Protection Act.[51] The Act regulated the sale of personal information about drivers by state motor vehicle departments. The Court did not deny that the regulation compelled state action, nor did it fall back on balancing states' rights against congressional powers, nor did it invoke Congress's power to regulate "the stream of interstate commerce." Instead, the Court made its support for the Act consistent with *New York* and *Printz* with a string of refinements. Though regulations cast upon the states affirmatively, as duties, remained unacceptable, those cast negatively, as prohibitions, might be sustained. Furthermore, though regulations imposed exclusively on state entities were suspect, those which are "generally applicable" to state and private actors were less so. Parsed in this way, the hurdles for Congress to clear appear to dissolve into matters of phrasing.[52]

The one clear product of renewed judicial solicitude for the federal structure has been greater discretion for the Court itself, more options case by case on a wider field of choice. Interceding in this way derides the policy state and clouds its constitutional status while at the same time providing judicial leverage over its continuing operations. Forty years into the revival campaign, the systemic threat of a judicial defense of federalism has yet to materialize, and the persistent skirmishing looks suspiciously like active participation in battles over preferences. In its effort to sort things out and bolster the federal structure, the Court has pulled itself into the same game as the political branches: rules and waivers, and rules *for* waivers. Moving closer in on the business of the legislature, it has, in effect, leveled the field of play.

If federalism is not just an obstacle for Congress to overcome, authority must be something more than a matter of policy. So, as a last case, consider the ringing vindication of federalism in *Shelby County v. Holder* (2013).[53] The issue posed was similar to the one Justice Bradley had addressed in striking down the public accommodations sections of the Civil Rights Act of 1875: How much is enough? When are the programmatic demands of policy satisfied? Specifically, had the Voting Rights Act been effective enough in attaining its objective—protecting the franchise of African Americans in the districts and states where it had proven most vulnerable—to warrant pulling its teeth and healing its breach of structure? For those who objected to the free-wheeling character of contemporary federalism, the Voting Rights Act was long regarded as the most conspicuous violation of form. Still, it took nearly fifty years to assemble a bare majority to provide a remedy, and then only on the Court's unilateral declaration of the policy's success. In Justice Roberts's opinion, the Fifteenth Amendment does not supersede the Tenth for the express purpose of empowering the Congress to protect voting rights against race discrimination, nor does the Tenth preclude national action; rather, the two amendments invite the Court to weigh policy's benefits against the costs to structure and determine whether states' rights still threaten voting rights. Rather than box the Congress out, this reasoning draws the Court into policy's domain.[54] Roberts's resolute defense of the federal structure as an essential feature of American government was in fact built on a second-guess review of the legislature's most recent effort to keep its policy current.[55] Congress, he charged, had not looked closely enough at its own research on voting patterns. If it had read the data as he did (other justices read the numbers differently), it would have concurred that this latest update failed to accord with current conditions and the changing nature of the problem addressed. Maybe another policy would fit the bill. That is containment in a policy state.

The Place of Administration

In his 1933 inaugural address, Franklin Roosevelt assured the American people that their government was up to the challenge of the Great Depression. "Our Constitution is so simple and practical that it is possible always to meet extraordinary needs by changes in emphasis and arrangement without loss of essential form."[56] It was a comforting thought, calming preparation for fateful choices on the horizon, but the "changes in emphasis and arrangement" that accompanied the New Deal did not go down easily, and the "loss of essential form" proved a sticking point. James Landis, a New Deal lawyer and battle-hardened chairman of the Securities and Exchange Commission, offered a less politic appraisal of what the extended negotiations were about: Were the American people prepared to let go of their fetishistic attachment to the notion that there are "only three branches" of government and recognize "the place of the administrative tribunal"?[57]

Speaking in 1938, Landis was witness to a resurgence of three-branch reasoning. Everywhere he looked, he saw a reassertion of jurisdictional claims, claims that threatened the values of flexible response and administrative guidance to which the New Deal had given pride of place in governmental operations. Roscoe Pound, a fierce critic of the New Deal and the nation's leading authority on administrative law, had taken over a recently formed Administrative Law Committee of the American Bar Association (ABA), and the ABA had drafted a plan to uphold private rights by subjecting the new agencies to a strict judicial discipline.[58] Quite different in spirit but no less determined to compartmentalize was the President's Committee on Administrative Management, appointed by Roosevelt himself. It recommended abolishing independent commissions, transferring to the Treasury Department the accounting functions of the independent General Accounting Office, unifying control over the newly expanded executive branch, and subordinating policy guidance by administrators to the president's political agenda.[59] Congress at the time was parrying this drive toward presidentialism and signaling keen interest in the ABA's recommendations. Sensing the squeeze, Landis pushed back, certain that constitutional essentialism would close off the space recently cleared for policy expertise and stifle the efforts of administrators to deal with targeted problems on their own authority.[60]

Administration is an outgrowth of policy, and administrative agencies extend policy making beyond the government's three-branch structure. As long as the three branches kept policy contained, that "hole" in the constitutional design remained self-limiting and the issues surrounding it only intermittently troublesome.[61] "The place of the administrative tribunal" became an absorbing concern when government became more reliant on policy than originally anticipated.[62] Landis had put his finger on the difficulty, but his fear of a stifling response proved as wide of the mark as Roosevelt's faith in a simple change in emphasis. On the one hand, constraints relaxed, the problem-solving ethos extended its hold, and operations in every quarter shifted to accommodate more extensive policy making by administrative experts. On the other hand, the expansion of policy's domain pried open the whole structure of government, and administration assumed its central place in the new state as the premier point of contention.

As with federalism, this shift from containment structure to opportunity structure followed episodically on the overthrow of traditional rights in personal relations. Here, too, policy progressively leveled the field of play, making the activities of the different constitutional principals harder to divide up, sort through, and separate out. As we shall see, the three branches adapted to administrative policy making by reorienting themselves to maximize their options for participation in it. In effect, each made itself part of a more elaborate and far-flung "administrative process." The place of administration has spiraled outward in this way from its bureaucratic core; loosely bound and exposed on all sides, the administrative realm of this policy state grows increasingly indeterminate.[63]

To call the result an "administrative state" or a "bureaucratic state" would suggest other priorities—rules, order, regularity, hierarchy. There is little risk of bureaucratic regimentation in the policy state because there are as many rules to choose from in registering concerns as there are concerned parties. Bureaucrats act strategically, pressing their information advantages or finding protection for their expertise in the swirl of demands competing for their attention, and in that they are no different from anyone else. Administrative accommodations to policy have turned the entire scheme entrepreneurial. Action in all quarters spins around the agencies that policy spawns, eroding the distinction between the government's structure and the designs of those who occupy it.

This administrative spiral has moved through three phases since the New Deal, each in succession straining the government's original design more severely. Call the first "the system of '46." Notwithstanding the persistence of three-branch reasoning, a semblance of Landis's preferred outcome managed to survive this initial shakeout. In the critical action, Congress defeated the reorganization proposals inspired by Roosevelt's Committee on Administrative Management, and Roosevelt vetoed the administrative procedure bill inspired by the ABA. Strict subordination of administrative agencies to one branch or another proved a nonstarter.

The way forward was for each branch to exchange claims of command and control over administrative affairs for a greater share of participation in them. A revised Reorganization Act in 1939, and the creation of the Executive Office of the President (EOP) that followed from it, acknowledged the chief executive's newfound leverage as orchestrator of the nation's expanded policy commitments.[64] Provisions for centralized budgeting and planning joined presidential oversight to technical expertise and tightened the connection between presidential management and agenda setting. At the same time, Congress undercut the pretense of unitary control and reaffirmed the authority conferred on agencies by statute.[65] It retained policy-making functions in agencies outside the executive hierarchy, reserved a "legislative veto" to limit the president's authority to reorganize within it, preserved the independence of its accounting office, and coupled passage of the Reorganization Act with enactment of the Hatch Act, curtailing the politicization of executive branch employees.

Similar accommodations were struck on other fronts once the rush to adapt picked up after World War II. The ABA's initiative culminated in the Administrative Procedure Act (APA) of 1946. The Act extended the protections of due process to interests affected by agency decisions and clarified the role of the courts.[66] It separated administrative adjudication from administrative rule making, mandated courtlike hearings for the former and either "notice and comment" or quasi-adjudicatory procedures for the latter, and it provided the judiciary with a broad scope of review over both. It also acknowledged variations and granted exemptions, most importantly in the area of national security. The compromise lay in the relatively loose standards ultimately prescribed for review—actions unreasonably delayed, "arbitrary" or "capricious," "unsupported by substantial evidence," or "unwarranted by the facts."[67] The impingement on administrative expertise was minimal.

The Reorganization Act of 1939 and the APA protected congressional interests in administration implicitly.[68] But Congress spoke for itself more directly in 1946 through the Legislative Reorganization Act (LRA). Like Roosevelt's proposed reorganization and the original version of the APA, the LRA began as an aggressive bid for administrative control. It originally contemplated direction by Congress though the creation of a congressional budget and the establishment of omnibus policy committees run by the parties. In the end, agreement boiled down to keeping Congress abreast of the action. The Act aimed at "continuous watchfulness" over administration affairs, a goal to be achieved by consolidating the standing committees and clarifying their jurisdiction, by expanding committee staff and research capacities, and by creating a Government Operations Committee with special oversight responsibilities.[69]

The symmetrical, across-the-board character of these adjustments lends the package the weight of a constitutional settlement. The capstone of the new system was the Employment Act of 1946, a measure which motivated the entire operation around an overarching programmatic objective: it was the "continuing policy and responsibility" of the federal government "to foster and promote . . . maximum employment, production, and purchasing power."[70] The Employment Act created a Council of Economic Advisers in the EOP to forecast the performance of the economy. Together with the Bureau of the Budget, the Council would serve to bring agency expenditures into accord with the newly stipulated goal of national policy and coordinate actions by the president and Congress to reach it. Within its ecumenical articulation of the public interest, the Employment Act captured a substantive political agreement, a modicum of consensus eked out of a still uneasy recognition of the interests and newfound rights of workers. Accommodation to the operations of the National Labor Relations Board and accommodation to presidential supervision were integral to that agreement.[71] Perceptions of a pro-labor, anti-business bias in Board proceedings had propelled conservative demands for an APA, and the NLRB had proven the most persistent source of contention in the extended negotiations over the standards to be applied. More broadly, the labor breakthrough had realigned the parties and raised the political stakes of presidential stewardship over the nation's policy priorities. The Employment Act declared these issues resolved. It gave the state an industrial purview, solicited interbranch cooperation in its management, and extended that spirit of joint action in the public interest to the agencies themselves.

The system of '46 was both an affirmation of the Constitution's adaptability and a great leap forward in the development of the policy state. As such, it prefigured much that would follow in later phases of the administrative spiral. Note first the faux formalism. Notwithstanding the persistence of three-branch reasoning and the invocation of constitutional principles to guide each adjustment, separating powers and distinguishing the role of each institution had become more difficult. This was less a structure of constraint than of joint direction and mutual accommodation. Administrators were laced in different lines of control, but reciprocal checks morphed into convergence on a common task. The new system enlarged the administrative process, enlisting into it actors at every site and inviting each to offer guidance of its own. By endowing each with new resources for registering preferences in administrative operations, it recast all of them as policy entrepreneurs.

Equally notable is the system's ersatz Progressivism, its de facto reliance on information, expertise, and management, and its tacit recognition of the power to be wielded on that ground by administrative agencies themselves. Respect for administration as a professionally disciplined activity was implied throughout, but rather than carve out an administrative realm secure in its own jurisdiction and endowed with its own authority, three-branch thinking carved it up in various ways and left discretion to the large and muddy residual. For instance, under the APA, agencies using either rule making or adjudication to operationalize statutes could expect to have their actions subjected to some kind of judicial review, but agencies were free to choose between these two ways of determining policy. Other administrative instruments with important policy implications (for example, guidance documents, technical manuals, policy statements, interpretative rules, circulars, memoranda, or bulletins) received little attention, and even less was given to more explicitly "administrative" work like priority allocation of resources, licensing, permitting, and planning.[72] All told, agencies were given their full share of wiggle room. In effect, the controls imposed by constitutional authorities incorporated administrators along with everyone else into a commodious opportunity structure.[73]

Thirty years after policy breached the rights barrier against intervention in the employment relationship, it broke decisively through the race barrier. Collectively, the social movements associated with the rights revolution of the 1960s and 1970s—minority rights, women's rights, consumers' rights, environmental rights—propelled the administrative spiral into a second phase. More important even than the number of new agencies created to administer the attendant policies was the infusion of additional stakeholders into the policy calculus, for with greater inclusion, prospects dimmed for recapturing any substantive agreement on the public interest. Pressure on administrative procedures mounted precipitously as the authority previously entrusted to agency experts was laid bare.[74] Over the next two decades, the administrative process pushed outward from the agencies at a rapid clip, encircling them in wider sets of concerns and pulling at them from all directions. The three branches shifted their operations simultaneously with similar objectives in view. Each sought to make the agencies more representative and to open them up to outside parties. Securing new opportunities for participation expanded all aspects of administration, but on this round, interventions traded more heavily against regularity in operations. Interbranch cooperation, a keynote of the system of '46, would never be the same.[75]

Begin with the presidency. Like the labor breakthrough, the rights revolution nationalized political issues and jolted old alliances. Compelled to juggle a wider range of competing demands and to refashion coalitions, the presidents of this period sharpened their claims that the Constitution anticipates an executive branch unified under a single head and that the president serves in that role as the tribune of democracy, the sole representative of the people in their entirety. In 1970, President Nixon deployed this newly aggressive posture toward administration to reorganize the Bureau of the Budget into the Office of Management and Budget (OMB). He sought to pull discretion from the agencies and bring action within the executive branch more fully into agreement with his own policy priorities and political coalition.[76] Refocusing the budget bureau on administrative control was an opening salvo in what proved to be a multifront initiative. Nixon replaced interbranch coordination through the EOP with policy development directly within White House councils, he tightened White House control over political appointees in the agencies, he inaugurated centralized assessments of agency regulations, and he opened new channels of White House contact with politically friendly groups interested in policy formulation.[77]

Previewing the performance reviews and "policy czars" of our day, Nixon's innovations were, in the near term, steeped in partisan contention. It was left to Jimmy Carter to lend them the seal of best practice. Carter, too, moved on multiple fronts. The civil service rules were relaxed to provide senior careerists incentives to cooperate more fully in planning and rule making with presidential appointees in the agencies, and administrative rule making was redirected to expand participation by affected interest groups. "Sunset review" was prescribed for rules deemed outdated or ineffective, and new rules were held open to wider public consideration of alternatives. Congress agreed to Carter's request to replace the old Civil Service Commission with an Office of Personnel Management under a single director, one who would oversee staffing with an eye to improving performance (a goal later augmented by an Office of Performance and Personnel Management in OMB). It also agreed to create an Office of Information and Regulatory Policy (later, the Office of Information and Regulatory Affairs, OIRA) as a new division of OMB to oversee agency operations.[78]

White House determination to leverage presidential authority over policy making in the agencies received its most forthright expression in Executive Order 12291, issued by Ronald Reagan in February of 1981.[79] The order transformed OIRA into a central clearinghouse for rule making in executive agencies (not in independent commissions). Under its provisions, the office subjected all "major" rules to a "regulatory impact analysis" using cost-benefit criteria to determine their performance value. OIRA review breaks into administrative processes in the agencies prior to the posting of a proposed rule and again prior to the posting of a final rule, and it can delay, pending changes, those rules that fail to comport with presidentially prescribed standards. Formally, OIRA cannot stop agencies from issuing rules nor can it compel an agency to adopt one, but these distinctions blur in practice. OIRA oversees the exercise of authority that agencies might otherwise derive directly from statutes, and these interventions begin before agencies start consultations on their proposed rules with outside groups under the APA's notice and comment provisions.[80] The office can look deeply into agency operations to monitor findings, research methods, evidentiary standards, and guidance documents.

The policy state turns on calculations of costs and benefits, and OIRA's overhead assessments afford a great opportunity for presidential spin. Nonetheless, the office monitors a vast field of action with limited time and resources. Agencies on the wrong side of the president's priorities can delay initiatives, prevaricate on compliance, or pursue goals through mechanisms other than formal rule making. Moreover, a president accused of abusing OIRA's technocratic analyses to advance particular political interests and ambitions—for example, by targeting agencies on a regulatory "hit list"—would place the whole operation in jeopardy. Bill Clinton, the first Democrat to come to power after Reagan instituted regulatory review, showed how the office might navigate these uncertainties without sacrificing its political utility. He "saved" OIRA by altering it. Issuing his own executive order, he sought to make relationships with the agencies less hostile, to limit the number of regulations subject to review, to open review to qualitative assessments of costs and benefits, and to provide access to a wider array of outside groups.[81] Because OIRA pulls from the agencies authority to determine best practices, it allows presidents to advance their policy agendas by tweaking the standards of good government.[82]

Presidents would not have been able to cultivate this more interventionist stance without congressional indulgence. Carter's reorganization of the civil service and the creation of OIRA both proceeded through statutes, and congressional endorsement of OIRA's activities has alternated over the years with objections to its presidential tilt. Like the president, Congress wants more responsive administration; what it does not want is responsiveness enclosed in the president's orbit. During this second phase of the administrative spiral, Congress answered Nixon's reorganization of the Bureau of the Budget with the Congressional Budget and Impoundment Control Act of 1974, which limited presidential discretion over spending decisions and created a central budget office under congressional authority, free of presidential bias, to coordinate its spending plans with forecasts of economic performance.[83] It responded to Nixon's politicization of the higher civil service with the Inspector General Act of 1978, tightening control over the offices in the departments most directly responsible for investigating administrative compliance and political abuse.[84] It countered the threat of executive command and control by bypassing the regular bureaucracy where it could and providing for policy enforcement directly through the courts,[85] and it enacted a series of measures—for example, the Freedom of Information Act (1966), the Federal Advisory Committee Act (1972), the Privacy Act (1974), the Government in the

Sunshine Act (1976), the Regulatory Flexibility Act (1980)—to make the administrative realm more permeable by, and protective of, private individuals and interest groups.[86] After Reagan's OIRA order, Congress stipulated that the head of that office would be subject to Senate confirmation.

As the constitutionally designated source of national policy, Congress can assert its will in administration most directly through program design. The most serious limitations it faces in this regard are structural, for as Madison noted long ago, the constraints of collective action make it difficult for the institution to dictate agency choices in detail or to alter those details with sufficient regularity as circumstances change. Nevertheless, the Clean Air Act of 1970 signaled a newfound determination to overcome these difficulties, and the legislation of that decade indicated by degrees the potential efficacy of statutory control.[87] The instruments employed were policy specific, varying according to institutional will and political strategy, and some operated at cross-purposes. Among the variations were the imposition of more exacting procedures for gathering information and dealing with outside interests in rule making, limitations on agency choice of regulatory instruments, the imposition of "hammers" or hard deadlines for formulating policy administratively before a default policy takes effect, and of course, appropriations and appropriation riders.[88]

The cornerstone of Congress's drive to compete for control over administration in this second phase was the Legislative Reorganization Act of 1970.[89] There was much in this initiative that elaborated on the institutional interests expressed in 1946: it expanded committee staff, reorganized the Legislative Reference Service into a congressional think tank (the Congressional Research Service), and it directed the General Accounting Office (eventually renamed the Government Accountability Office) to look beyond bookkeeping and agency compliance to "analyze the results" of governmental programs. But the impetus behind the initiative came from a new breed of representative, and the imprint of the rights revolution was clearly evident in their demands. Policy entrepreneurs with freshly minted agendas aimed to break the grip of the committee chairs, many of them from the "Old South," over congressional proceedings. Their demand was a wider distribution of institutional power over policy. A 1973 follow-up, the Subcommittee Bill of Rights, attended to that objective.[90]

The decentralization strategy of the 1970s multiplied the number of leadership positions in Congress and the points at which policy could be negotiated.[91] The proliferation of more powerful subcommittees promised more rigorous lawmaking and agency monitoring, but it also produced a more densely shaded and fragmented field of action. Multiplying points of access to administration makes it more difficult to determine both the institutional and temporal location of authority. Agencies already pulled between political directors in the executive branch and statutory instructions from the enabling Congress faced more intense scrutiny from a wider variety of committees and from individual overseers from later Congresses interested in revisiting implementation decisions. Decentralization relaxed constraints on Congress acting as a whole, facilitating more targeted oversight, but it also blurred the distinction between the institution and its members, expanding options for entrepreneurial interventions on policy interests.[92]

Judicial interventions ramped up as well during this second phase. At the forefront of rights' expansion since the 1950s, the Court headed into the 1970s the most aggressive of the three branches in opening new pathways for their expression. In 1966, the Supreme Court revised its Federal Rules of Civil Procedure to widen an attractive bypass around administrative machinery, making it easier for private parties to pursue statutory remedies directly through class action lawsuits. Congress had passed to the Court the authority to create a federal code during the New Deal. Its promulgation in 1938 was the culmination of efforts by reformers like Roscoe Pound who, though skeptical of the bureaucratic turn, recognized the mounting impediments the common law posed to swift remedial action in court. The code changes in 1966 relaxed, among other things, requirements concerning "good cause" to bring a class suit and barriers to obtaining documents from private parties. This transformed what had been a procedure of modest application into a capacious format for the play of chips. The new rules seriously tested the premises of civil action: the individuals in these class suits asserted their rights passively, often with only an "opt out" option; and even in the biggest settlements, their compensation was often negligible. But the new rules were nonetheless very well suited to the assertion of group rights—for tenants, for passengers, for patients, and for consumers generally—and, in the process, they vastly expanded the involvement of the courts in determining policies in the public interest. The chiplike character of these rights was made more pronounced in the decades that followed these innovations as the business community mounted stiff resistance. The Court, in a partial pullback, pointed to arbitration as the preferred solution to the resolution of these claims.[93]

Even more mercurial were the judiciary's assaults on agency autonomy in this period. Repeatedly the courts pried the administrative process open to judicial scrutiny only to negotiate a partial pullback in deference to agency discretion. Chapter 3 touched on one such wedge. Countering the assumption of agency discretion over eligibility for welfare benefits granted by statute, *Goldberg v. Kelly* (1970) recognized those benefits as a new species of property subject to constitutional rights of due process, and it provided individuals the opportunity for an administrative hearing prior to (as opposed to after) termination.[94] Heady with the spirit of rights abounding, *Goldberg* appeared unconcerned with the practical difficulties agencies faced in managing these new programs. *Mathews v. Eldridge* (1976) acknowledged that dilemma with a partial pullback. Affirming property rights in Social Security as such, *Mathews* invoked a "balancing test" to determine whether a hearing was required before cutting off "statutorily created property." From then on, and, as it happened, in a widening variety of due process claims, the interest of the individual would be weighed against the likelihood that the agency had erred in its procedures and the costs of additional administrative proceedings.[95] The right to be heard had turned into a widely applicable chip.

There was similar push and pull on other fronts. In each instance, the court's initial inclination was to shift the locus of the public interest in administration away from internal sources of purportedly neutral, objective expertise toward fuller collaboration with the outside interests. A series of environmental decisions illustrates the stiffening demands.[96] *Scenic Hudson Preservation Conference v. FPC* (1966) proclaimed "the right of the public" to "receive active and affirmative protection" in administrative decision making.[97] The circuit court in this case rebuked the Federal Power Commission for focusing narrowly on economic considerations in its approval of a site for a hydroelectric power plant and extended standing to groups that based their injury on aesthetic and environmental concerns. Acting next to expand the availability of judicial review, the Supreme Court overturned a decision by the secretary of transportation to route a highway through parkland in Memphis.[98] *Citizens to Preserve Overton Park v. Volpe* (1971) extended the procedural requirements of both the APA and the department's own statutes to address informal adjudication and turned a public record testifying to citizen interest in an alternative administrative choice into a constraint on the secretary's discretion. In *Kennecott Copper Corp. v. EPA* (1972), the D.C. circuit court went further still, finding that the APA's minimal requirements for explaining agency decisions were inadequate to the protection of the public's interests in rule making.[99] And in *Portland Cement Assoc. v. Ruckleshaus* (1973) that court insisted on the presentation of fresh data for any new application of standards, along with disclosure to affected interests of "detailed findings and procedures" for their comment. The court announced that it would brave the risks of "steeping" itself "in technical matters" to keep judicial review from becoming a "meaningless exercise."[100]

This opening to continuous consultation with the public in administrative decision making necessarily entailed adjudicating the question of whether the agencies were sufficiently responsive to the concerns expressed, and that came to look suspiciously like a judicial takeover of agency decision making.[101] *Vermont Yankee Nuclear Power Corp. v. NRDC* (1978) addressed that implication in another partial pullback.[102] In this case, the Supreme Court rebuked the D.C. circuit for setting aside a rule issued by the Atomic Energy Commission regarding environmental hazard in waste disposal and for imposing rule-making procedures on the agency beyond those required by the APA. The justices instructed outside parties interested in administrative rule making that they would henceforth have to "structure their participation so that it is meaningful" and not ask the Court to vacate agency actions merely because factors they deem important "ought to be" considered more seriously. They informed the D.C. circuit court that, in responding to such demands, it had strayed "beyond the judicial province" and imposed upon the agency "its own notion of which procedures are 'best' or most likely to further some vague, undefined public good."[103]

In these varied efforts to balance deference with participation in administrative affairs, the Court was not unaware of the newfound willingness of the elected branches to stir the pot. Increased interest in administration from the president and Congress provided a ready rationale for recalibrating the judicial stance, but the Court did not do so without some initial hesitation. A divided opinion in *Motor Vehicle Manufacturers Association v. State Farm Mutual Auto Insurance Company* (1983) dealt with a new regulation concerning the installation of passive restraints in automobiles which had been adopted during the Carter administration but rescinded by the incoming Reagan administration.[104] Setting aside earlier hints at accommodation, and insisting again on substantive explanations for agency action, the Court overturned the change as "arbitrary and capricious." The majority granted that "an agency's view of what is in the public's interest may change" but insisted that, if it is going to discard a prior decision, it has to supply "a reasoned analysis for the change."[105] The fact that this shift in the agency's position was "related to the election of a new president of a different political party" was of more interest to the dissenters in *State Farm* than the majority. It seemed to them that a change in presidential administration was "a perfectly reasonable basis for an executive agency's reappraisal of the costs and benefits of its programs and regulation."[106] A few months later that view claimed a majority. *Chevron U.S.A. v. Natural Resources Defense Council* (1984) dealt with another rule change associated with the transition from Carter to Reagan, one governing the practice of "bubbling" sources of pollution for the purpose of issuing permits and calculating offsets. *Chevron* endorsed the change, stating that "an agency to which Congress has delegated policymaking responsibilities may, within the limits of that delegation, properly rely upon the incumbent administration's views of wise policy to inform its judgments."[107]

The administrative spiral is now well into a third phase. The conservative reaction against the policy state and the political stalemate that ensued expressed themselves institutionally in an acceleration of the structural free-for-all. The constitutional branches appeared to shed concern with rule regularity altogether. Since its pullback from detailed procedural prescription in *Mathews* and *Vermont Yankee,* the Court has become more ad hoc in its oversight. Decisions on matters of deference to administration appear to be "framed by the circumstances in each case and by the philosophy and experience of the judges."[108] In an empirical survey, William Eskridge Jr. and Lauren Baer put the point more bluntly: "The Supreme Court's deference jurisprudence is a mess."[109] They find that the Court now has a stockpile of deference regimes, each affording administrators a different degree of discretion, and that the Court invokes these doctrines in an unpredictable manner. It does not appear tied to any particular doctrine, not even when controlling for subject matter, and, more often than not, it decides cases without reference to any deference regime at all. Keeping its options open, the Court avoids rigid insistence on what are likely to prove impractical rules.

Chevron had hinted at a renewed determination to sort things out. The decision magnanimously acknowledged the stewardship of the political branches and the impracticality of substituting judicial process for administrative process. It promised deference to clear statutory authority, to reasonable agency interpretations of ambiguous statutory provisions, and to presidential input. Addressing all those contending for control over administrative policy making and setting each in its proper place, it recalled the accommodating spirit of the system of '46 and the prospect of a constitutional settlement of the knotty issues surrounding the operations of America's policy state. But sorting schemes like this are always clearer in the abstract than in the actual choices presented, and consensus on their meaning has proven hard to sustain. When the administration of George W. Bush put environmental policy on OIRA's "hit list" and allowed its interest clientele to stifle EPA findings on climate change, the Court revived the scrutinizing spirit of *State Farm,* challenging the political control of administration that *Chevron* appeared to countenance and demanding that agency experts show more backbone.[110]

As the *Chevron* doctrine bumps up against other Court priorities, settlement moves farther and farther out of reach. When *Chevron* was extended in 2014 against state and local interests to allow the Federal

Communications Commission to interpret the scope of its jurisdiction on its own authority, Chief Justice Roberts, writing in dissent, unloaded a broadside against the central place administration had assumed in modern American government, reiterating the whole litany of complaints that have plagued the coming of the policy state—the erosion of the separation of powers, the functional independence of agencies wielding legislative, judicial, and executive powers, the failure of political oversight, and judicial deference to delegation.[111] In 2015, now writing for the majority in *King v. Burwell*, Roberts set the *Chevron* framework aside and relegated agency discretion in interpreting ambiguous statutes to the margins. Assembling in *Burwell* a majority to save the Affordable Care Act for a second time, the Chief Justice asserted the Court's authority to determine the meaning of the law whenever it thinks that the issue is too significant to be left to an agency. This "major questions" doctrine bears down on administrators with an expansive premise for putting judges back at the center of policy making.[112]

Congressional interventions in this third phase also appear rudderless. Power has shifted to the party caucuses, concentrating resources in the leaders who move bills on the floor. Committee and research staff has been cut back, increasing members' dependence on external sources of information and expertise, much of it provided by private lobbyists. Budgeting, the cornerstone of the cooperative ideal in administrative management in the system of '46 and of the reassertion of congressional authority in 1970s, has become hit or miss. Notwithstanding a shift in authority over budget projections from the OMB to the Congressional Budget Office, the budget procedures Congress outlined for itself in 1974 were never institutionalized. Neutralized as a counter to presidential control by the Reagan Revolution, their implementation has been stymied repeatedly by the absence of consensus. Regularity has given way to budget "showdowns," budget "summits," "omnibus" appropriations, and continuing resolutions that provide ad hoc solutions to emergency situations.[113]

Another tool of the system of '46, the legislative veto, was voided by the Supreme Court in 1983.[114] Congress has generally ignored that firm stand by the Court for a separation of powers, but in the 1990s new expressions of its interest in overcoming these divisions began to drift toward gimmickry. "Corrections Day," introduced with great fanfare by House Speaker Newt Gingrich, acknowledged the challenges Congress faces in writing complicated legislation and the power it relinquishes to agencies and courts to fix obvious "mistakes" and "absurdities" in its handiwork. Confronting the difficulties of providing detailed policy directives in statutes, this initiative set aside time for Congress to participate in the cleanup operations.[115]

The Congressional Review Act of 1996 was more ambitious.[116] Its "report-and-wait" procedures mimic OIRA's function as a central clearinghouse for administrative action. Report-and-wait stops action on new agency rules pending a review by the GAO and the relevant oversight committees. It also allows members to bypass committee review with their own "resolutions of disapproval," and it expedites passage of these resolutions by simple majorities in both houses. By providing more time than the notice and comment procedures of the APA to reconsider administrative regulations and register discontent, the Review Act may facilitate informal negotiations to resolve conflicts prior to putting new rules into effect. As an instrument for nullifying policy changes, however, the device has proven effective only in very special circumstances. Because these resolutions take effect only on the signature of the president or by override of a veto, they add little to Congress's law-making capacities. Passage through both houses is rare. When Congress managed to send two such resolutions regarding EPA regulations to the Obama administration, they received pocket vetoes.[117] The leading case of nullification was the voiding in 2001 of ergonomic standards issued by the Occupational Health and Safety Administration, suggesting that the Review Act may be most effective when reversing regulations imposed by an outgoing administration after a partisan change in the elected branches.[118]

Arguably Congress's most determined intervention in this period concerned not administrative action but its increasingly attractive alternative, class action. A decade-long effort to assert control over this remedy culminated in 2005, when Congress, with newly installed Republican majorities, passed the Class Action Fairness Act. Broadening federal diversity jurisdiction and adding a Consumer Class Action Bill of Rights, the act confirmed the strategic character of contemporary federalism and with it, the chiplike quality of the rights in question. It made it easier for defendants to transfer class action cases out of the states, where "venue shopping" for sympathetic courts was thought to run rampant, and into the federal courts, thought at the time to be less readily swayed by plaintiffs' claims.[119]

The most striking of Congress's recent ideas for liberating the administrative process from set forms has been "negotiated rule making." Whereas the APA required agencies to provide interested parties with notice of its proposed rules and an opportunity to comment on them, the Negotiated Rule Making Act of 1990 encouraged affected interests to participate face-to-face in the drafting process itself.[120] By coordinating with interests and sharing information up front, these negotiations promised to garner consensus, to expedite the rule making process, and to reduce exposure to litigation. Negotiated rule making dispenses with troublesome formalities; it dissolves institutional boundaries, turning private interests into full-fledged representatives and administrators into participants in group deliberations. If there is an institutional model behind the process it is legislative, but the effort to get administrative processes to imitate legislative processes founders precisely on the problem of determining who gets represented in decisions over policy.[121] Enthusiasm for the procedure appears to be waning, apparently because of the practical difficulties encountered.[122]

The Constitution expresses its "essential form" by denying a set place for the most conspicuous feature of modern American government. Structure chases administration in the policy state, and every part of the framework gets caught up in it. The dilution of rights and their proliferation as chips has stripped away the rationale for the containment of policy. By the same token, the growing priority of policy has thrown government into an administrative spiral, each of its three branches propelling the others to keep its options open. None can attain authoritative control, so each reaches for maximum flexibility. Rather than becoming more regular over time, these operations have grown more amorphous, the competing rules mirroring the opportunistic interventions and ad hoc arrangements of policy itself. More rules with less regularity is a developmental paradox, a consequence of jerry-rigging a structure to accommodate more of precisely what it was designed to restrain.

If these arrangements, taken collectively, serve any higher purpose, it is to keep policy in play, and intended or not, that bias against settlement has consequences of its own. The sprawling, multifaceted, indeterminate architecture of administration in the policy state favors interests with the resources to take advantage of it. Once the public interest in administrative management was hollowed out of substance and reduced to so many procedures, opportunities for outside intervention in the formulation of policy multiplied, and the capacity to engage the process at its many points of access began to pay a premium. For president, Congress, Court, and agency, administration in the policy state is all about flexible response, but for their constituents and clients it has become "blood sport."[123] Everyone gets to share in policy's specification, as long as they can power up.

Makeshift Presidentialism

A curious feature of Madison's depiction of the transformation of the American republic into a monarchy was that the chief executive did not need to do anything to bring it about. A Congress determined to stretch its policy-making authority would of its own accord pass to that officer managerial discretion out of all proportion to his limited charge.[124] If presidents were implicated at all in the change, it was passively. Their institutional independence had originally been conceived as an active check on policy overreach by the legislature, the veto power a formidable instrument for containing congressional ambitions. The most conspicuous wrinkle in the containment structure was that presidents might accrue far more expansive opportunities for themselves by withholding that discipline and simply biding their time.

A century after Madison warned of monarchy, a more positive prognosis was on offer. When, in 1898, the Progressive historian Henry Jones Ford surveyed "the rise and growth of American politics," he dismissed the threat of kingship, observing that it had "dwindled away" even in England. He then went on to document wholly unanticipated roles assumed by the American presidency. The American people had seized on the office as "the only organ sufficient for the exercise of their sovereignty."[125] They had recast it as the superior institution for representing the will of the electorate and the spearhead of their irrepressible democracy. The "agency" of the executive had proven itself indispensable in "extricat[ing] public authority from the control of established political interests";[126] its newfound value lay in mobilizing opposition to entrenched governing arrangements and overcoming the constraints of an otherwise preservative structure of authority. These unique, proactive capacities—to concentrate political power electorally, to disentangle the institutions of government from their settled social connections, to initiate change and redirect the whole—would, Ford thought, accelerate the emergence of the office as "the master force in the shaping of public policy."[127] "The greatness of the presidency," he enthused, "was the work of the people breaking through the constitutional form."[128]

Ford conjured an executive-centered democracy dislodging interest and privilege from the constitutional arrangements that protected them; Madison envisioned an executive manager of loosely written statutes on whom every interest and privilege would eventually come to depend. Neither tied these changes, as we have throughout this book, to the overthrow of the private rights that originally undergirded the structure of American government, but those connections will not be hard to draw out. Suffice at this point to note that Madison and Ford both saw a structural transformation in the making and that each captured an essential aspect of the presidency as we know it today. The "modern presidency" mixes unimagined responsibilities for managing interests and the policies that serve them with fulsome promises of programmatic redirection and political transformation. That volatile brew has turned our executive magistrate into the most aggressive of the government's policy entrepreneurs.

The presidency in the policy state badgers the constitutional structure, goading other rule makers with its ever-more-formidable advantages as an instrument of expedience. The dispersion of rights, the weakening of rules, and the priority of policy, all play to its strengths. Incumbents push against rules by expanding the boundaries of mobilization and management; issue by issue, they calculate prospective gains for independence in programmatic action against the risks of reaction. These three elements—mobilization, management, and calculation—converge in an unsteady composite, a makeshift presidentialism. We will consider developments on each front and their impact on one another.

Little in the original framing of the presidency anticipated alliances with those mobilized to upend rights and overhaul the government. The Constitution contemplated management without mobilization. The nation's chief magistrate was charged to maintain order, to enforce the law, to "preserve, protect, and defend" the Constitution. Concern that the election of a new president might prove politically destabilizing was met with provisions for an extended term in office, unlimited reeligibility, and a selection procedure that empowered local elites and shunned interstate cooperation. Nonetheless, it did not take long to figure out that an officer elected nationally and able to exert influence over legislative enactments and their enforcement could serve as a focal point for advocates of change. In a constitution otherwise organized to protect existing authority, political mobilization around the presidency was the key to programmatic action. Opposition movements, beginning with Madison's own, co-opted the office, altering it in ways that would put increasing stress on the structure in which it had been lodged.

In its early phases, this reorientation came principally from presidents who led new parties into control of the national government. The desired direction of programmatic change varied from case to case; what made presidential power expeditious in each instance was a collective determination to overturn the prior course of policy and reorient the nation's agenda. Jefferson and Jackson left a portentous legacy in this regard. They developed instruments of power that lodged presidential action more firmly in its electoral support, and that left all commitments, including their own to strict construction and states' rights, more fully exposed to the policy preferences of future incumbents. One of these innovations, the Twelfth Amendment, cleared away obstacles to political coordination on a national party ticket and thus to mobilization outside the formal institutions of government on a program for national action. Another, the electoral mandate, drew on the national canvas for independent authority for presidential action on professed policy priorities. It was Jackson's assertion that he was elected to support the Constitution as he understood it, and his willingness to counter on that ground a decision of the Supreme Court upholding the constitutionality of the National Bank, that emboldened Lincoln to mobilize political opposition to the Court's defense of slavery in *Dred Scott*.[129]

Jefferson rallied his followers to extricate the federal government from the designs of "the Anglomen"; Jackson, to extricate it from the clutches of bankers and protectionists; Lincoln, to extricate it from a conspiracy to expand slavery. There was, however, little indication that their respective followers were interested in going farther and institutionalizing a presidency-centered government. On the contrary, once the great political leaders of the nineteenth-century presidency had cleared away the governmental arrangements that supported their old adversaries, fellow partisans took care to cabin the mobilizing energy of the office in deliberative institutions that they could control. Congress took charge of Jefferson's nomination to a second term, and in short order, the congressional party caucus was said to be "king." In the aftermath of Jackson's presidency, national conventions of state party delegations assumed control over presidential nominations, and in due course, the leaders of the state organizations were recognized as the "bosses." For the most part, nineteenth-century parties corralled the political independence of the presidency and used it for their own purposes. The president became the titular head of an aggregation of state-based organizations, and the managerial dilemmas that attended the presidential office centered on the distribution of the spoils, quite literally on offering up the offices of the executive branch to the service of local patronage machines.[130]

Arrangements more conducive to presidentialism arose from a loosening of these constraints in the face of novel demands for national policy. The critical development was the emergence of "presidential parties," organizations better able to mobilize wide-ranging interests and the programmatic ambitions of far-flung constituencies. Over time, presidential parties have marginalized the party convention as a deliberative body for candidate selection and collective control. Primary elections for the selection of delegates to the convention facilitated the shift, prompting candidates to contest the presidential nomination by demonstrating their own personal appeal to voters and by creating their own electoral machinery. Sidelining conventions also affected the role of jurisdictional questions in party competition. Jacksonian Democrats had elevated the value of states' rights and enlisted presidential power to counter congressional threats to localism; Whigs and Republicans had inclined toward nationalism but resisted presidential power as an affront to congressional prerogatives. Squaring off in this way, each party had promoted its own view of a rightful, durable structure. Weakening the party convention as an institutional intermediary submerged collective commitments to any particular design for the government. At the same time, it exposed leaders more fully to the nation's most intense "policy demanders."[131] Contenders were thrust into direct engagements with issue activists, interest groups, and campaign benefactors, all of whom tended to prioritize expedient action on behalf of programmatic goals.

Theodore Roosevelt pointed the way in 1912, first by entering the preference primaries in an effort to derail the renomination of incumbent President Taft at the Republican convention, and then, when that failed, by renouncing his old affiliation and assuming leadership of a fledgling Progressive Party. That new organization collected nationally dispersed interests and activists. Civic reformers, corporate reformers, conservationists, women's advocates, social gospelers, settlement workers—all rallied behind Roosevelt's magnetic personality, casting him as the point man for their various programs of social improvement, economic regulation, and welfare provision.[132]

As with the other structural shifts surveyed in this chapter, benchmarks of a more decisive breakout from institutional containment straddle the middle decades of the century when traditional rights in personal relations were decisively overthrown. Franklin Roosevelt, nominated in 1932 on the fourth ballot, departed from usual procedures to accept his endorsement in person at the Democratic convention. Calling that move a symbol of his intentions, he signaled his interest in policy-based mobilization around a presidential party. He announced a New Deal, solicited support for it from progressives in all parties, and warned conservatives in his own ranks that he would part company with anyone who refused to get on board with his program.[133] In subsequent action, he followed through. In 1936 Roosevelt drafted the national platform himself. He also pressured the party into easing its grip on nominations by dropping a rule (protective of the Old South) that had required support from two-thirds of the delegates in favor of a simple majority.[134] He then strengthened his relationship to the labor movement, using its financial resources and organizing muscle to compensate for a falloff in his business support.[135] In 1938, he intervened in the primaries in a (failed) attempt to defeat conservative Democrats who resisted the further advance of his agenda.[136]

The push toward presidential parties accelerated in the wake of the civil rights movement. In the 1970s, it was Richard Nixon who gave symbolic expression to the new form. Determined to exploit fissures opening in loyalty to the Democratic Party among Southern whites and the working class, he separated his reelection drive from the regular machinery of the national Republican Party and ran a personal campaign through his "Committee to Reelect the President."[137] More consequential were new primary rules through which the traditional system of party-controlled convention delegations was finally overtaken by delegates bound to individual candidates, in effect, turning the nomination over to candidate organizations and the enthusiasts mobilized behind them.[138] The presidential party assumed its current, symbiotic character sometime between 1976, when Jimmy Carter was elected in a campaign that stigmatized his own party's priorities, and 1980, when he tried to repair relations with interests in the Democratic coalition in an unsuccessful bid for reelection. Candidates are now driven to mobilize interest activists and acolytes around a self-styled brand, while party regulars try as best they can to limit their risk by throwing support behind whoever appears to be the safest choice.[139] Campaign finance regulations have strengthened the hand of the issue groups arrayed around candidates, making any assertion of control by the party organization more controversial and driving it further into the shadows.[140] The rules governing these relationships are informal and opaque; the convergence of the candidate with the organization, hit or miss.

New forms of executive management developed alongside these new forms of mobilization. Nationally organized and interdependent interests elevated the importance of central direction over patronage distribution, a reorientation that announced itself ostentatiously in a 1901 labor dispute. After long effort, private mediation failed to resolve a coal strike in Pennsylvania. The idea of federal arbitration, discussed in Chapter 3, was still embryonic and focused on railroad disruptions.

This left half of the nation under threat of a fuel famine. Theodore Roosevelt, nine months into an accidental term, grasped the urgency of this situation as a crossroads for his office: "There was no duty whatever laid upon me by the Constitution in the matter, and I had in theory no power to act directly unless the Governor of Pennsylvania, or the Legislature, if it were in session, should notify me that Pennsylvania could not keep order, and request me as commander-in-chief of the army of the United States to intervene and keep order." Not one to wait on others, Roosevelt pulled from the silences of Article II a broad warrant for presidential action beyond set rules: "[The president] is the steward of the people, and the proper attitude for him to take is that he is bound to assume that he has the legal right to do whatever the needs of the people demand, unless the Constitution or the laws explicitly forbid him to do it." Assessing the political risks of proceeding to arbitration on the basis of his "stewardship theory," Roosevelt solicited assurances from local and national authorities that if he could break the impasse, complaints about his methods would go nowhere. He then finessed the chief impediment to negotiations—the refusal of the operators to recognize union representatives in the settlement of contract disputes—by designating the union's voice on his arbitration panel a "sociologist." With agreement on a mechanism to resolve the conflict, labor returned to work.[141]

Roosevelt was not a leader of the labor insurgency, or even a party to it. This was, rather, a pointed demonstration of the presidency's managerial prowess, its ready availability for assuaging conflicts, fostering cooperation, staving off crises, preventing breakdowns, and getting results. Proclaiming himself the sole representative of the people as a whole, Roosevelt turned the presidency toward social outreach, spontaneous engagement with groups in contention, central coordination, and hands-on problem solving. Woodrow Wilson pushed ahead. Reaching across the Constitution's separation of powers and fusing interest management to legislative leadership, he took it upon himself to orchestrate the terms of economic regulation and policy accommodation. Foreshadowing challenges of coordinating management with mobilization, he dampened his party's populist fervor for the Clayton Anti-Trust Act and negotiated a more corporate-friendly addendum, the Federal Trade Commission Act.[142] Another notable maneuver followed the breakdown of White House efforts to head off a national railroad strike on the eve of American involvement in World War I. In this instance, Wilson overcame his long-professed resistance to special-interest legislation, intervened directly on the side of labor, and spearheaded enactment of a bill to grant rail workers an eight-hour day.[143]

The breakthrough moments of mid-century followed this pattern, extending the president's policy reach through progressively deeper engagements in interest management and social adjustment. Franklin Roosevelt and Lyndon Johnson offered political support to the insurgent interests of their day, helping to extricate organized labor and African Americans, respectively, from their legal subordination and to bring them more fully under the umbrella of the policy state. Each was instrumental in reorienting government around a historic redistribution of rights, and each transformed the party system in the process. Neither, however, could afford to ignore the interests of those adversely affected by these transformations. Instead, they tried to arrange a new concert of interests and experimented with novel institutional arrangements that promised ongoing programmatic adjustments. FDR's signature initiative in this regard looked to industrial code-making authorities in the National Recovery Administration; Johnson's to a War on Poverty and the community action agencies of the Office of Economic Opportunity. Sponsoring the incorporation of labor rights and civil rights, these presidents transferred intractable problems from the economy and the society into their own offices and ratcheted up their political responsibilities for interest management and conflict amelioration.

Both code making and community action backfired, leaving their presidential sponsors constitutionally and politically exposed.[144] Having arrayed themselves on the side of expanded rights and newly mobilized interests, these presidents found that outreach and management do not comport especially well with one another. Both objectives serve to elevate the president's profile as "the master force in the shaping of public policy," but each organizes political engagement differently, and together they put policy making in the modern presidency at cross-purposes. By mid-century, the competing imperatives had been institutionalized. The president's proactive stewardship of the nation had been recognized by Congress in the Reorganization Act, overhead responsibility for social and economic affairs had become embedded in the Executive Office of the President, and norms of "neutral competence" and "honest brokerage" lent legitimacy to central direction. At the same time, presidential parties were assuming primary responsibility for the political mobilization of national reform energies and promising routinely to shake things up.

One face of this makeshift presidentialism is populist and transformative. Even when modern presidents are not directly invested in social movements, they are trying to sustain a movement of their own. Mobilization is inherently disruptive; it arrays presidential leadership against entrenched interests and policies. Followers expect the leader to expose the mismatch between received governing arrangements and their reform aspirations and to extricate the government from the commitments that constrain it. The rise of personal organizations singularly devoted to the leader's success heightens these expectations, and the transfer of organization operatives into the offices of the White House lends support for whatever it takes. The other face of this makeshift presidentialism is prudential and pluralist. Notwithstanding the abiding promise of purging the government of interests that constrain programmatic innovation, populism has become a more difficult proposition as the government has incorporated more interests into its policy purview. The president takes charge of an office that is surrounded by institutions designed to find practical policy solutions to the social and economic problems of a widening array of recognized groups. Political leadership on this count is sustained through demonstrable success in improving performance, and every shortfall on that count threatens political disaffection and countermobilization. The political compulsion to mobilize discontent, dislodge vested interests, and redirect policy contends in the modern presidency with the managerial incentives to negotiate productive adjustments and find workable settlements. The incongruity consigns incumbents to a perpetual struggle for credibility.[145]

America's policy state relies on mobilization and management in equal measure. It is hard to keep policy current without a source of political energy sufficient to break through the knots of interests that tend to tie up American institutions and thwart change. It is just as hard to navigate conflicts among interests and improve performance without the orchestrations of a deft manager. Presidents try in various ways to reconcile these tasks, to square expectations of managerial prowess with the political interests arrayed under the presidential party. President Nixon led the way by reorienting the operations of the EOP away from "neutral competence" toward greater political responsiveness to White House priorities.[146] Gerald Ford followed suit, using a new White House Office of Public Liaison to reach out to his political "base" and incorporate its interests more directly in his decision making.[147] Ronald Reagan expanded the use of that office to manage his ties to newly mobilized Christian conservatives. President Obama completed the fusion of management with mobilization by redeploying his electoral machine, Obama for America, as Organizing for Action. Through "OFA," the president could explain his every move to supporters at the grass roots, he could monitor their reactions, and he could solicit their endorsement for his chosen course.[148]

Still, the competing expectations of mobilization and management test even a diehard's faith in the political skills of incumbents. Hitting the sweet spot has become the modern presidency's most elusive promise. Political breakthroughs seldom align with workable policies, and workable policies almost always jeopardize movement enthusiasm. The Reagan Revolution of 1981 enacted the budget priorities of the conservative movement. Congress initially expressed skepticism about Reagan's plan, but the president went public, mobilizing support for setting aside the lawmakers' new budget processes and compelling them to substitute his package for theirs. As it turned out, the president's plan had in fact been based on fabricated projections. With presidential budgeting discredited and the nation in an economic tailspin, managerial responsibility shifted from the White House to the Federal Reserve Board. George H. W. Bush sought to reclaim lost ground. His budget compromise of 1990 produced a credible plan for economic stabilization and debt reduction, but the tax increases he agreed to outraged his administration's movement support. A revolt within the ranks propelled the Bush presidency into a political tailspin. Barack Obama dedicated his presidency to having it both ways: he proposed to "change the trajectory" of the nation, to do for progressives what Reagan had done for conservatives, but he sought to do so in a responsible and ecumenical way, one that recognized that "we are all in this together." In his signature initiative, "Obamacare," he assembled a grand coalition of all the stakeholders in the health-care industry, and he pulled skeptics within his own movement behind a program that proved to be as complicated as it was monumentally ambitious. His assiduous cultivation of interests did not, however, garner the promised consensus, and with movement supporters already anxious over the compromises they had been forced to swallow, the administration had little choice but to cut through the remaining resistance. Like Reagan, Obama gamed the congressional rules and trampled his opposition. A countermobilization carried the president's opponents to power, and when implementation of his new program proved a managerial nightmare, they effectively paralyzed his administration.

Hard as it is, striking an effective balance between mobilization and management is a three-part, not a two-part, calculus. Recall that stewardship theory asserts the president's "legal right" to do anything in the public interest, *except* that which the law and the Constitution explicitly forbids. Those stipulations cloud contemporary affairs. It should come as no surprise by now that the added complications were first addressed in a labor dispute, this one affecting steel production during the military action in Korea.

When, upon a breakdown of contract negotiations, President Truman decided to seize the nation's steel mills, he knew that he was probing the outer reaches of his constitutional authority.[149] But the alternatives that Congress had provided for managing such disputes posed a threat to his political base in the union movement. To move ahead, the president resolved to mobilize the base and assert the public's interest in extraordinary action. His message to the nation clarified the policy imperatives, issued a populist attack on powerful business interests obstructing the path forward, and asserted presidential responsibility for resolving the crisis. Procedures put in place by Congress to help the president manage the economy in wartime had, Truman charged, left the nation at an impasse. The union had acted sensibly, accepting a moderate wage increase in line with workers in other industries, but the owners had demanded in exchange an exorbitant price hike that threatened agreements on other fronts and spelled economic hardship for everyone else. Continued effort to use the tools

Congress had provided would jeopardize the overriding goal of avoiding disruption in the production of a resource vital to the nation's war effort. To meet the emergency, the president proposed to use the aggregate of his powers as chief executive and commander-in-chief to take hold of the steel mills and operate them under government supervision, pending the outcome of renewed contract negotiations and/or further instructions from Congress.[150]

Questions about the scope of presidential power seldom make it to the Supreme Court, and the justices grasped this one as a rare opportunity to speak to its accrued pretentions. The seizure of property offered a ready premise for review, but in keeping with the chiplike character of rights in commercial relations, the controversy focused on how the property was seized, not on whether it could be seized. More notable still, although *Youngstown Sheet and Tube v. Sawyer* (1952)[151] has become the iconic case limiting the power of the modern presidency, the only collective voice heard from the Court came from the three justices in dissent, who gave a full-throated endorsement to Truman's action. A majority of six held the president's seizure unconstitutional, but each weighed in with a separate opinion, as if no single resolution of the issue could be reached.[152]

The lead opinion by Justice Black made a starkly formal case for the separation of powers and drew a sharp line against the assumption of independent policy-making authority by the president. There were three statutes on the books that spoke to the circumstances (at least one might have been construed to contemplate seizure), but Truman, deeming none adequate to his assessment of the situation, had instead substituted his own procedure for those provided him. Finding no warrant for that, and upholding Congress's "exclusive constitutional authority to make laws necessary and proper to carry out the powers vested by the Constitution," Black left little for stewardship to draw from silences.[153]

Justice Frankfurter found the matter "more complicated." He wanted to preserve a measure of flexibility and to remain open to future demands. He acknowledged that congressional "acquiescence" in presidential practices can become a "gloss on 'executive power'" and, eventually, a "part of the structure of our government." What was dispositive for him in this case was the legislative history of the Taft-

Hartley Act of 1947, in which Congress had openly debated seizure as an option for resolving labor disputes but had chosen other remedies. In effect, Frankfurter trimmed the stewardship theory of any pretense that the president could circumvent a law written to avert a course of action he might prefer. "Congress has expressed its will to withhold this power from the President as though it had said so in so many words." This indicated that options not expressly ruled out in the texts of statutes could be foreclosed by the legislative record. As for Truman's invocation of presidential war-making power, Frankfurter was unimpressed, noting wryly that "the country was not at war, in the only constitutional way in which it can be at war."[154]

Justice Jackson, a vigorous proponent of presidential power during the administration of Franklin Roosevelt, penned the opinion that framed the way forward, and more than any other, it caught the entrepreneurial spirit of the emerging policy state. In thinking through limits on presidential power, Jackson rejected "doctrinaire textualism" in favor of a set of guidelines and calculations that judges might employ according to the circumstances. He arrayed constitutional authority for presidential actions on a continuum of three zones: actions consistent with congressional directives were on the strongest ground; murkier were actions taken in the absence of directives or where authority was concurrent and its distribution uncertain; weakest were actions inconsistent with congressional directives. In the case at hand, Jackson found Truman treading on the most vulnerable ground, and he could not find anything in the specifics to convince him that the president's constitutional authority should overcome the strong presumption in such instances in favor of Congress's stipulations.[155] But this schematic rendering of relations among Congress, Court, and president loosened the structure of government and opened opportunities all around. Distinctions were drawn with ample room for judgment calls; the abstract sketch of risks and probabilities did not rule out anything categorically. Truman had taken long odds and lost. Each of the players was advised to calibrate their actions and their justifications accordingly.

Presidential power emerged from these different opinions less constrained by rules than by political calculations of the odds of getting caught. The president's domain was deemed to be less expansive than

TR's claim of a free-ranging mandate to fill any silence with a policy of his own, but how much less is harder to say. At times, it might prove to be as restrictive as Black's rigid textualism, but it is difficult to tell in advance. Presidents were invited to test the boundaries, and they could expect the outcomes to vary. Truman's fate notwithstanding, the field of play is such that presidents will often have the strategic advantage.[156] Congress is a deliberative body, seldom of one mind, preoccupied by the political interests of individual members, prone to delegation, and often inconsistent in its directives. The Court is self-protective, reluctant to engage "political questions" or to provide standing to the complaints of lawmakers. Presidents choose more easily and move more quickly. Like Truman, they mobilize support and stigmatize resistance; they define situations and stand ready to manage them; they convey the urgency of the moment and the dire consequences of inaction. Acquiescence becomes part of the structure.

Calculations of law and politics commingle within the modern presidency to produce more and more novel strategies for gaining leverage at the margins. To keep options open at the outer reaches of Jackson's scheme, presidents have the services of the White House Counsel and the Justice Department's Office of Legal Counsel.[157] When congressional directives from the 1970s began to hem in presidential discretion, lawyers appointed by the Reagan administration recommended the attachment of conditions to the endorsement of legislation. Providing for the publication of these "signing statements," the administration sought, among other things, to create an alternative to the legislative record for judicial reasoning about statutory intent and to imprint legislation with presidential terms and conditions. Used vigorously by George W. Bush, the authority of signing statements received an approving nod from Justice Scalia in *Hamdan v. Rumsfeld* (2006), dissenting from a ruling on the use of military commissions.[158] But the instrument looks suspiciously like a "line item" veto. It certainly blurs the line between protecting presidential prerogatives and circumventing the Constitution's veto process, and that continues to cloud its legal status.[159]

More potent are the resources presidents have developed to extend their policy-making prerogatives in Justice Jackson's middle zone of discretion. Opportunities to reset policy unilaterally through executive orders have grown with the expansion of policy's domain.[160] Calculations of the risks involved vary. Resistance is likely to prove stronger during periods of divided party government than during united party government, but the incentives for presidents would seem to work the other way around. When stiff congressional resistance from partisan opponents threatened to shut down President Obama's agenda, his "we-can't-wait" campaign ramped up the use of executive orders to reformulate policy. Setting policy through memoranda is a variant. The leading expression of that device is the national security directive, originally conceived by the National Security Act of 1947 as an instrument for coordinating foreign relations, national defense, and intelligence.[161] Often secret, these directives have over the years stretched the warrants of the law, encompassing ever-widening notions of what national security entails.[162] The deployment of "policy czars" is another tactic. These appointees, often acting without Senate confirmation or statutory authority, "coordinate, regulate, and otherwise direct outcomes in certain policy areas."[163] Policy czars push the envelope on presidential use of staff support and advisors, broaching the constitutional proscription on presidential creation of agencies. Pulling together programs with separate authorizations to tackle policy problems that the president himself has identified, the czars redirect agency expenditures and governmental priorities, blurring the line between delegated discretion and programmatic redirection. When Congress objected to Obama's use of czars in its emergency budget of 2011, the president issued a signing statement rejecting the alleged encroachment on presidential prerogatives.[164]

The badgering, goading disposition of the modern presidency is another constitutional expression of the systemic reordering of priorities that we call the policy state. The office developed by elevating demands for policy over the government's jurisdictional design. It has leveraged political mobilization against the security of established rights and executive management of interests in conflict against structural constraints. On both counts, its contemporary operations reveal the makeshift character of the transformation that has occurred. America's policy state relies for its operations on the perilous presidentialism of catch-me-if-you-can. It is led by a policy entrepreneur arrayed against the constraints that define the framework of the government, one who is pledged politically to overcome the obstacles in his path and celebrated historically for success in rewriting the rules of the game.

Blockages, Outlets, and Institutional Identities

Innovations that ease institutional blockages facilitate government by policy. Institutional blockages were not, however, incidental to the design of American government; on the contrary, they were integral to its conception of a stable and consensual regime. Persistence in innovation has vastly expanded policy's domain, but that has not squared the old frame with what has become, in effect, an entirely different understanding of how order and regularity are best secured. Headlong pursuit of an improbable strategy for adjustment explains a lot about why reordering tends over the long haul to breed irregularity, why adaptation has become hard to distinguish from dysfunction, and why the basic institutions of American government all appear to be caught up in their own identity crises.

We close out our survey of structure in the policy state with a brief look at three pressure points where the strains of adaptation appear particularly acute. Two of these, the filibuster in the Senate and "regular order" in the House of Representatives, take our discussion to the constitutionally designated engines of policy making. The drive to overcome constraints in the interest of moving policy is evident on both fronts, as are the distortions of institutional identity that have followed from efforts to cut through them. A third point of pressure brings our analysis full circle to the curious position assumed by the Supreme Court in the new regime. Here we link the familiar charge that the Court's identity is threatened by its "politicization" to its concomitant and paradoxical rise to preeminence in a policy state.

Though the institutions of American government were not designed to operate in lockstep, they can at times be found adjusting in tandem to demands for greater responsiveness, and once in a while, they appear to trip over one another to loosen constraints and open possibilities. This was the case during the Obama administration when the president, the Senate, and the Supreme Court confronted blockages in the process of confirming appointments. The president led off with aggressive action during congressional recesses to circumvent minority obstruction of his appointments in the Senate. Notably, the Court had never spoken to the recess appointments clause before, and the emergence of that obscure practice as an important outlet for releasing pressure on the operations of the policy state exposed the absence of clear rules. The unanimous decision in *National Labor Relations Board v. Noel Canning* (2014) opened with a stunning rebuke. It voided three appointments President Obama had made to the National Labor Relations Board using this workaround. Nonetheless, there was considerable discontent among the four concurring justices over the lead opinion, in which Justice Breyer found that the constraints imposed by the text of the clause were "ambiguous." Echoing Justice Frankfurter, and invoking the Court's respect for a long history of acquiescence in considering questions of structure, Breyer took instruction from the practices of the previous seventy-five years. He tempered the ruling against Obama with a broad reading of what the Constitution allowed both to the president in making recess appointments and to the Senate in scheduling pro forma sessions (without business) to preclude them. Breyer's historical analysis yielded the judgment that recesses of three days or less were too short to justify a departure from the constitutionally preferred process of Senate confirmation, but that presidential appointments (during either inter- or intrasession recesses) to fill vacancies (either those that exist at the time of the recess or those that occur during it) were permissible so long as the break was at least ten days long. Under extraordinary circumstances, filling vacancies might even be justified in breaks of shorter duration.[165]

Breyer's concern in *Canning* was to articulate rules commodious enough to keep the Constitution abreast of the demands of the day. But by the time the decision was announced, his careful handiwork had become an anticlimactic addendum to a far more radical response to appointment blockages from the Senate majority leader, Democrat Harry Reid. Reid had invoked the so-called nuclear option: he discarded the storied norms of Senate deference to minority objections, using a point of order to override the Republicans' right of obstruction in presidential appointments.[166] As long as the president's party holds the Senate majority, there is no longer any need to wait for a recess to staff the government with like-minded administrators or judges. Reid reserved the filibuster for nominees to the Supreme Court, but that stipulation fell at the first test.

The constitutional construction of the Senate protected established authority from the impulses of simple majorities. The shield was evident in its designation as a second legislative chamber, one in which each state had equal representation. Early on, that protection received additional, if unexpected, reinforcement when Senate proceedings were reorganized without provision for cutting off debate.[167] The priority this gave to deliberation, consensus, and senatorial rights over majority rule and policy output came over time to distinguish the Senate. But the Senate assumed this identity at a time when demands for national policy were relatively limited, and in early practice, Senate minorities rarely felt the need to invoke their option to filibuster. Through most of the nineteenth century, they demonstrated considerable restraint, routinely allowing votes on measures on which they knew they would lose. Moreover, when filibusters were mounted, they tended to be grand events. Their classic form as personal endurance contests, rhetorical "wars of attrition," revealed the relative intensity of majority and minority preferences over policy and registered the importance of factoring in the fervor with which positions were held when contemplating decisions on particularly controversial matters.[168]

In a government more fully dedicated to policy, however, minority obstruction in the legislature turns more vexing and appears more anomalous. From 1917, when Senate rules were first revised to allow for the imposition of cloture by a two-thirds majority, to Reid's rule-by-declaration in 2013, reforms in the Senate have pushed against minority obstruction and toward majority empowerment. Policy has found three outlets. One is constitutional. The Twentieth Amendment, ratified at the outset of the New Deal, coordinated the executive and legislative calendars and replaced the "short" second session of each Congress with another "long" one. In addition to accommodating an expanded workload, this move sought particular relief from Senate filibusters, which had clustered in the second sessions owing to their tight time constraints. Second is cloture reform. Rule changes in 1959, 1975, 1979, and 1986 lowered the cloture threshold and closed loopholes in the procedure, for example by tightening post-cloture debate. A third outlet has been found in particular substantive set-asides, allowing simple majorities to prevail on especially urgent business. This tack was evident in legislative veto provisions beginning in the 1930s, it appears in the Congressional Review Act, and it was used in tariff and trade agreements when offering the president "fast track" authority. Prior to Reid's move in 2013, the most important of the set-asides were for budget and reconciliation bills. In recent years, that exception has been stretched to facilitate "omnibus" legislation, packages of bills unlikely to pass muster individually, and to allow controversial agenda items (for example, Republican tax cuts and Democratic health-care reform) to move forward in the face of stiff minority resistance.

The press of policy against the limits of time would seem to mark minority obstruction as a doomed remnant of the older order of things. Once invoked, the "nuclear option" becomes more accessible and more tempting. But the Senate's development in this respect has not been all of a piece. Over the course of the twentieth century, obstruction became a more routine and increasingly prominent feature of Senate proceedings.[169] Though the chief motivation for the classic filibuster was overwhelmed by the civil rights revolution, the practice was "institutionalized" alongside the vast expansion of policy's domain that attended that breakthrough. The "sixty-vote Senate," now the baseline premise for conducting ordinary business, allows individual senators to leverage the value of their consent and to force attention to their policy preferences on any matter they consider important.[170] The right of obstruction is a chip played in virtually all regular proceedings. The press of policy against the limits of time has in this way pulled the institution in opposite directions simultaneously. It has driven the majority to assert its prerogatives more forcefully, and to open new pathways for expediting legislative business, and it has empowered senators individually, making them more insistent on personal policy preferences and more protective of their rights.[171] With the advent of the policy state, the Senate finds itself in an identity crisis.

This change in the character of the right of obstruction follows the pattern we have observed throughout the development of the policy state. Its original association with state representation and limits on congressional power has been strained by the nationalization of interests. The pretense that it protects institutional principles—that it defends the priority of deliberation and national consensus or deference to the intensity of preferences—is even more attenuated. Cloture is a method of breaking through resistance. The Senate seeks now to avoid extensive debates, either by cutting them off or by signaling objections in advance of any test so that the institution can move more quickly to other business. One reason the procedure has been associated with rising levels of obstruction is that it makes open contests of reason and will unnecessary and allows members to exercise their rights with little effort. In the rush to policy that followed the civil rights revolution, Majority Leader Mike Mansfield urged his colleagues to act accordingly and to adopt this more policy-centered view of their interests in the practice. As he saw it, senators willing to set aside their policy preferences and withhold a vote for cloture out of institutional loyalty—deference to senatorial norms of free and open debate—were inviting majoritarian reforms that would cut even deeper into the distinctive character of the institution: "a refusal by a substantial body of members to vote for cloture even when such a vote would accord with their position on the substantive issue tends to reduce the Senate to a debating society and it might well precipitate in time a drastic reordering of the constitutional structure of the government."[172]

The Senate is no longer a debating society, but what it presents as an alternative is less clear. Senators assert their rights so as to cultivate their individual reputations as policy entrepreneurs. Paradoxically, these policy ambitions do not make the Senate a more productive legislative body. By exercising their rights and promoting their preferences, individual senators repeatedly paralyze the institution, at times leaving it unable to perform its most basic functions (appropriating money for basic services; confirming staff for administration). Conflicts that the Senate once absorbed, processed, and contained internally, are now directed inside out, the institution disembodied by members who gain more through self-branding and self-advertising than through collective action. Each maintains a personal organization which prioritizes the policy motives of outsiders—constituent groups, lobbyists, and contributors—and each enlists media and public relations services to carve out a distinctive identity on the national political landscape. The normalization of obstruction invites the executive branch and the judiciary to bypass the legislature and open alternative paths to policy.[173]

Under these circumstances, the office of the majority leader has become an increasingly important outlet for Senate action. Unlike the minority, which might hope to score political points from evidence of the institution's incompetence, the majority leader wants to move his party's agenda forward and will at least consider the Senate's reputation as a responsible steward of national affairs. The office was relatively insignificant until the New Deal, when it gained greater control over proceedings on the floor through the right of first recognition.[174] With the rights revolution producing more homogeneity and cohesion in party caucuses, the policy motive of the majority leader has been strengthened, and the office has risen in stature and resources. Though committee staff has been cut back elsewhere in recent years, the majority leader's "war room" has been expanded with new capacities for messaging, coordination, and negotiation,[175] and as the Reid rule of 2013 indicates, the incentive to advance the common ends of the party caucus against senatorial rights is correspondingly enhanced. Much depends on the size of the majority coalition, its critical agenda items, the political disposition of the president, and the strength of the threat that the minority will bring all other business to a screeching halt, so rules are improvised to maximize flexibility in moving particular items of interest.

The policy motive confronts senatorial rights in the construction of these rules. The primary meeting ground is the majority leader's "unanimous consent agreement" (UCA), the rule that sets the terms for Senate consideration of an issue. Cobbled together case by case, UCAs trade procedural regularity for the immediate prospect of getting something done. Important legislation will often require several UCAs, one for each phase of the bill's consideration.[176] Each is a separate negotiation, a procedure designed at once to take account of senators' policy concerns and to limit the prospects of minority obstruction on the floor. UCAs put senators' rights-as-chips on full display. They are "individualized," "customized," and "complex."[177] The business of the Senate is expedited in this way, by subordinating rules to the demands of the policy in play. The institution operates issue by issue, each agenda item handled discretely in accordance with its own special procedure.

The "common law" of our legislative assemblies, often referred to as "regular order," consists of the expectations of rank-and-file representatives of reliable rules of procedure. These claims have been undermined in recent years by the same factors that press against the government's containment structure more generally. With rights less effective as a way of governing and with heightened demands for policy, institutional arrangements turn into resources to exploit and obstacles to overcome. To be sure, the baseline of regular order in Congress has been shifting all along, pacing increased demands for policy. Turning attention to the House of Representatives, regular order looked very different before the 1890s, when minority obstruction was as common as in the Senate, than it did after the strong speakership took hold and the majority party caucus extended its control over the development of policy.[178]

Notably, however, the last time Congress was able to restore credible rules of procedure in the wake of a major change in rights was in the post–New Deal period. As we have seen, in the system of '46, Congress reorganized itself to work within the limits of the industrial policy that liberal legislators demanded and that conservative legislators could abide. The pressure point in that system was the power of the committee chairs, which restrained progress on other fronts, like civil rights and the liberal reform agenda of the Democratic Study Group.[179] Since the civil rights breakthrough of the 1960s and congressional reforms of the 1970s, regular order in the legislature has proven more elusive.

The reforms of the 1970s broke the power of the committee chairs by decentralizing and centralizing operations simultaneously. The first move was expressed in the aforementioned Subcommittee Bill of Rights; the second, in authorizing the Speaker of the House to appoint the majority on the Rules Committee and to work around the jurisdictional claims of the substantive standing committees through control of the bill referral process. The pressure point in the post-reform House shifted from the committees to the floor. Using their newfound influence, the rank and file pursued their policy preferences by piling amendments onto bills under floor consideration, often forcing fellow partisans into embarrassing votes in the process. The enhanced powers of the Speaker offered relief from these pressures through the use of "special" or "restrictive" rules to govern floor proceedings. The rise of special rules in the House parallels the rise of policy-specific UCAs in the Senate. Under the system of '46, members could expect "closed" rules (barring amendments) to appropriations bills and "open" rules (entertaining all germane amendments) for the great bulk of their business. In today's House, as throughout this policy state, nearly all rules are special rules.[180]

The system of '46 drew on a limited but substantive policy consensus. In contrast, the reforms that followed upon the rights revolution relied almost exclusively on procedure to manage contending ambitions and burgeoning agendas. Procedure, however, proved a poor match for these pressures. The difficulties faced by the Democratic majority in the House in reestablishing a semblance of regular order in the wake of those reforms reflected the wider incorporation of interests within the majority caucus, but those differences paled next to the options and ambitions percolating through the minority. Republicans won control of the House in the 1994 elections with promises to restore regular order, but their leader, Newt Gingrich, quickly scrapped that ambition out of acute sensitivity to the urgency of now. The "Gingrich Revolution" repealed much of the Subcommittee Bill of Rights, it further enhanced the prerogatives of the Speaker, and it cut the minority further out of the legislative process. Regular order gave way in these years to new devices for achieving results faster: "self-executing rules," which carry amendments without a vote on them; congressional task forces, which (not unlike the president's policy czars) cut across committee jurisdictions in search of novel solutions to new problems; committee bypass through more active policy making by floor leaders and their staffs; policy summits, which cut the rank and file out the process of negotiating major programmatic changes in favor of emergency deals hammered out between congressional leaders and the president.[181] The House has a reputation for being more effective than the Senate in clearing blockages to collective action, but ever since the rank-and-file revolt against Gingrich, the institution has been torn between the perennial promise of restoring some semblance of regularity and the mounting pressures to move policy.[182] Resentment of the power of the Speaker has magnified the difficulties of maintaining order, testing at once the policy-making capacities of the House and its identity as the backbone of representative government.

Contemporary complaints about "congressional dysfunction" tend to look at these matters a bit differently. The major concern of the day is with evidence of legislative "gridlock," with the failure to produce and support policy expeditiously. Political scientists disagree about the nature, scope, and significance of this problem,[183] but their debates obscure a fundamental point. Legislative "gridlock" is an anxiety of the policy state, a counterpart to the executive ethos of "we can't wait." Both express the priority of policy and the mounting frustration with the structural obstacles in its path. Charges of dysfunction and gridlock are none-too-subtle indictments of the Constitution's own prescription for dealing with dissensus, which is a generous distribution of rights to block collective action and protect existing authority.[184] The drive to open new pathways to policy exacerbates this predicament, for it meets the pressing demands of the day by sacrificing the integrity of deliberative processes, and it sets the representative institutions themselves at odds with their own standards of legitimacy. If the decline of "regular order" in the House is a worry, it is because the concept still seems definitional, the idea inextricably linked to what institutions are supposed to be and what we expect them to provide.

Concern over congressional dysfunction is one of the great paradoxes of America's policy state, but it is not the most profound. That distinction must be reserved for the position of the Supreme Court in contemporary American government. An institution designed to ensure that policy conforms to the law is sure to find itself uniquely exposed, and its identity sorely tested, by developments that bend the law in service to policy. And yet the Court in the policy state cuts a stronger profile than ever before in its history; its power has never been more widely acknowledged. This paradox brings us back to fundamentals, and directs attention to an issue we have found lurking behind every particular. On one side are the essential properties of courts as institutions ready to hear the legal claims of individuals and to uphold their rights against infringement by others; on the other side is the historical diffusion of those claims and associated changes in the character of rights. The rapidly expanding field of choice enhances the Court's institutional position, but it also makes it more difficult for the institution to set itself apart from policy conflicts and protect the integrity of its mission. Policy entrepreneurs are willing to risk judicial intervention in their proliferating disputes, but the price they extract is to erode the distinction between policy and law. As that erosion becomes more apparent, it exposes the entrepreneurial character of judicial action itself.

In the Court's first decade, Chief Justice John Jay took precautions to avoid judicial entanglement in policy questions. Fearful of embroiling the Court in political disputes, he rebuffed President Washington's efforts to enlist his help in assessing the propriety of proposed governmental actions.[185] In its second decade, Chief Justice John Marshall followed suit. In both *Marbury v. Madison* (1803), asserting the Court's authority to rule on the constitutionality of legislation, and *Stuart v. Laird* (1803), upholding the abolition of new judgeships through repeal of the Judiciary Act of 1801, he carefully avoided a political confrontation over the programmatic changes underway in the elected branches of the federal government.[186] The prudent course for the Court in its early years lay on the side of disengagement from politics. The separation of powers provided the institution a measure of security and protected its authority to rule on "cases and controversies" on appeal.

Nonetheless, these structural boundaries and distinctions are notoriously hard to uphold, and the incongruities of policy and law have always been extremely discordant. For most of American history, the favored method for releasing the pressure on this point was a direct political assault on the assumption of judicial independence and the binding authority of courts. Between Jefferson's campaign to impeach politically recalcitrant justices and Franklin Roosevelt's Court-packing scheme, politicians empowered to enact sweeping programmatic change repeatedly rejected the final authority of the Court to determine the lawful range of their actions. Jackson ignored Court rulings and acted on his own authority. Reconstruction Republicans preempted judicial obstruction of their designs by manipulating the jurisdiction and the size of the bench. In the Progressive Era, when judges themselves began to urge more "realistic" strategies for interpreting the law, movement enthusiasts campaigned for the recall of judicial decisions. For newly empowered groups with policy agendas to promote, there was always "altogether too much power in the bench"; "the people and not the judges [were] entitled to say what their Constitution means."[187]

The Court's acquiescence to the New Deal did not remove the pressure on this point, but it did open onto a structural inversion. By mid-century, the Court had shed its resistance to the assertion of new rights and had placed itself at the forefront of efforts to remove the remaining obstacles to their full realization. When faced with a rising tide of resistance to its newfound concern with race segregation, the Court doubled down on its authority. *Cooper v. Aaron* (1958) dismissed state and local efforts to "nullify" *Brown* with a stunning declaration of judicial supremacy.[188] The justices harkened back to *Marbury* for support of their claim, but there was no hiding the programmatic extension of their power. Not only did the Court declare its ruling in *Brown* the supreme law of the land, binding on all state officers and preempting all laws to the contrary, it also positioned itself at the forefront of the social transformation of the day, demanding reform and pushing recalcitrant policy makers to the point of confrontation.

Cooper v. Aaron did not clear blockages of its own accord. That awaited legislative follow through. In the near term, political responses to the Court's supremacy claims reprised the full range of traditional renunciations, beginning with a political campaign for judicial impeachment.[189] But by deploying its self-declared supremacy in the service of expanding rights, the Court was foreclosing the state's traditional governing strategies. It was nationalizing the issues that the early American state had dealt with through localism and exclusion, it was turning itself into a magnet for relatively disadvantaged groups in society seeking redress, and it was opening legislative assemblies to the interests of those groups.[190] In time, as the pathways were cleared and more of these rights were recognized, the political value of the Court's supremacy claim began to register in the other branches. With more rights in play, judges had more options in adjudicating the conflicts presented to them and in determining what was entailed by each. The inclusion of new claimants made it more difficult for any to assert trumps and left the Court awash in choices that the political branches were often eager to avoid. That made judicial supremacy appear less like a threat to policy than another outlet for it.

This willing deference to the Court's supremacy did not come without strings. It has been sustained by more intense scrutiny of the Court's decision making methods. In the political branches, there is heightened awareness of the implications of different approaches to the law. In a developmental analysis of political confrontations with judicial power, Stephen Engel describes a gradual waning of the old political impulse to cabin and neutralize the Court's power, and a simultaneous broadening of interest in "harnessing" judicial discretion for policy ends. He finds that harnessing strategies finally achieved dominance in the immediate aftermath of the rights revolution, during the Nixon, Carter, and Reagan administrations. This has been a double-edged process: it has preserved judicial supremacy by relegating jurisdiction stripping initiatives to the realm of symbolic politics, and it has transformed judicial selection from an ordinary matter of patronage into a valuable tool for keeping policy in play.[191] The institutionalization of ideological screening for judicial appointments and the expansion of litmus tests through to the lowest levels of the federal judiciary extends political control over enhanced judicial power. It provides a new outlet for policy negotiation and eases pressure on elected politicians who face an increasingly diverse set of claimants on their own policy-making authority.

The political harnessing of judicial power has one additional advantage for the elected representatives of the policy state: it facilitates the political mobilization of policy-minded constituents and turns control over the judiciary into a campaign issue. Inter-branch respect for the Court's role as a protector of rights has come to rest on this shaky ground of politicization from within and without. Deference to its supremacy claims comes from the same actors who are subjecting its makeup to more intense political interrogation. In the early months of 2016, with a presidential election campaign shifting into high gear, the Senate sharpened this point with an odd assertion of its own rights. It sidelined the president's nominee to the Court pending the outcome of the national canvas. At issue in blocking this appointment was a Democratic incumbent demanding that a Republican majority act on a nominee who would likely change the ideological complexion of the Court. By denying the president his authority to appoint in the final year of his term and by disavowing any obligation of its own to provide a hearing or a vote, the Senate majority indicated that the nominee's judicial qualifications and credentials were beside the point and that no argument on behalf of other officers' rights or constitutional procedures would overcome its programmatic concerns. Furthermore, by pointing to the election as the appropriate outlet for resolving the impasse and by inviting partisans on both sides to turn the appointment into a campaign issue, the Senate majority effectively transferred authority out of institutions altogether, acknowledging that law, policy, and politics have become one and the same. The Republican nominee for the presidency, Donald Trump, took the cue. He offered a slate of potential judicial nominees vetted by conservative advocacy groups as an inducement to the party faithful to support his campaign, and he added public statements pledging to apply litmus tests in selecting nominees.

To enlist the Court so directly as an extension of the policy motive is to throw its institutional identity into question, and when Court decisions air the deep political divisions over the meaning of the law, the problem is compounded. These issues are no longer episodic and transient; they are engrained features of institutional politics in the policy state. According to Chief Justice John Roberts, they are central dangers facing the Court today.[192] Roberts has repeatedly vowed to try harder to negotiate differences among the justices and to broaden consensus on the law through more determined deliberation. But the Court is an integral part of the system, and the difficulties it faces in maintaining its integrity reflect evolving relationships within and between the branches. The process of selecting justices for a policy state rewards subtle efforts at self-branding, so that over time justices come to personify different approaches to the interpretative arts, to project different political sensibilities regarding the presumptively irresolvable dilemmas of containment and opportunity, and to stake out just so many reasoned positions on the widening field of choice. It remains to be seen whether a Court constituted in this way can achieve a broader consensus, or more important, what consensus will add up to when it is hammered out among learned luminaries with high profile reputations to promote and protect. Their challenge is not unique. We have found something similar at virtually every institutional locale.

CHAPTER FIVE

Politics in the Policy State

POLICY is a solvent. It attacks blockages, erodes boundaries, dissolves distinctions. As policy expands its reach, it renders authority more homogeneous, more policy-like in all its aspects. Thus far we have been concerned with documenting this change. We have tracked policy's newfound dominance through adaptations of rights and structure, seemingly the least policy-like features of American government, and we have described a governmental transformation hitherto acknowledged only in bits and pieces. We have found the character of the policy state in the proliferation of rights, with rights holders more exposed to practical adjustment and less reliable as constraints on policy, and we have found it in the relaxation of the Constitution's divisions, making government and law harder to disentangle from policy. In this chapter, we delve more deeply into the murky result. Although the alchemy we have described affects American government in its entirety, there is more to this new state than a washed-out version of the original.

Consider a solution of a different hue. The policy state is an etymological cousin of the police state, but the difference is stark; there is no mistaking one for the other. The policy state developed in America alongside political parties that competed for popular support, social movements that demanded equal citizenship for those excluded, and progressive reformers who smoothed the way for constitutional adjustment. Each of these was implicated in the periodic turmoil surrounding rights and structure. But each also tied the loosening of constraints to democratic aspirations, and, in general, policy's expanded domain coincided with the rise of a more inclusive polity. Democracy was never a master plan, but it has long been the policy state's most compelling rationale. As an ongoing project, a wellspring of collective action, an inexhaustible motive for political and institutional reform, it would appear to have been the perfect complement.

A police state provides little recourse against peremptory decisions, overbearing agents, or self-executing commands. Democracies, on the other hand, insist on retaining popular control over the new powers they pass to government. Policy's expansion accelerates democracy's drive to hold government accountable. Therein lies the rub. The mutually reinforcing relationship between democracy and policy that spurred the development of a new state in America has turned in on itself as government and policy have become increasingly synonymous. The polity at large is now riddled with the insecurities of policy. Political volatility in election results makes individual policies harder to sustain, and political gridlock in institutional interactions impedes policy adaptations. Impediments to action at the center once served to safeguard government stability, insulating national action from gyrations in the public mood. But with demands now more wide-ranging and urgent, gridlock and volatility feed off one another. Frustration is more easily ignited and resistance more easily mobilized; the political exigencies of the moment loom larger for all, and overreach breeds overreaction.

Approaching these concerns from the perspective of the policy state's formation, we see them as parts of a syndrome of codependency. Throughout this book, we have taken note of strains building on the authority of American institutions as they are mandated to solve more diverse and complex problems. Open now to all the issues once handled by exclusion, these institutions have not only been overrun by competing claimants; they have also become more alike in what they have to offer. Responding to democracy's demands within a widening policy space has, as a practical matter, shifted the burden of accountability off rights and structure and onto policy itself. This means that barriers to change and backstops to conflict are weaker, and that it is more difficult for government to respond coherently to the different expectations it generates. Politics draws out the competing standards of legitimacy that policy has submerged. It exposes a system of authority at cross-purposes, prone to spin governing motives to suit the needs of the moment. Perpetually out of kilter, the policy state undermines the conditions for its successful operation.

Earlier we mentioned a policy trap. That sense of entrapment can be found lurking behind a host of political issues that preoccupy contemporary observers. It is evident, for example, in writings about citizen responsibility and attention overload, about information asymmetry and the absence of transparency, about "deliberative" democracy and elite "nudges," about venue shopping and issue cycling, about drive-by media and the eclipse of the public interest, about judicial activism and "the counter-majoritarian difficulty," about partisan polarization and flagging faith in government itself. Policy's expanded domain fuels issues like these, while government's de facto reliance on policy also makes them harder to resolve.

Our approach to the political dilemmas now entrenched in the policy state begins by turning back the clock. We follow cues from the intellectuals of the early twentieth century who confronted engrained barriers to the new policies they saw as necessary in a democracy rapidly changing on virtually every front. These early "Progressives" found American government caught in a trap of a different kind, ensnarled by received thinking about rights and structure. They imagined a new state free of those self-denying strictures and more harmonious in its operations. There is no more apt guide to the current predicament than the template for reordering that they offered.

American Progressives often worked in tandem with mobilized workers, women, and farmers in promoting reform.[1] But it is their reasoning about the workings of American government and how best to overcome the built-in inhibitions of innovative action that deserves attention here. "We no longer believe," Frank Goodnow wrote in 1916, "that good social organization can be secured merely by stressing our rights. The emphasis is being laid more and more on social duties."[2] Reformers turned from rights to duties, both to narrow the claims of private actors against policy and to distribute rights more widely through policy. Having little patience with exclusive guarantees drawn from time out of mind, they extended rights proactively in support of newly perceived social obligations. Mary Parker Follett put it this way: "Particularist rights are ruled out as everything particularist is ruled out. . . . The whole truth of the matter is that our only concern with 'rights' is not to protect them but to create them. Our efforts are to be bent not upon guarding the rights which Heaven has showered upon us, but in creating all the rights we shall ever have."[3]

Constitutional structure would be repurposed along similar lines. Woodrow Wilson struck a chord with reformers in 1885 when he described the framers' approach to institutional design as a "grievous mistake."[4] Progressives were skeptical of a government that protected separate jurisdictions, divided authority, and checked the popular will to change things. The aim, Herbert Croly declared, should be "representative men exercising discretionary power," not "principles of right which subordinated all officials to definite and binding restrictions."[5] Progressives approached structure with an eye to ways in which a greater concert of powers might be orchestrated for greater efficiency in action.[6] Reforms that blended what the Constitution separated, that unified its operations and integrated the work of policy making, received their certificate of "good government."

Easing the restrictions of rights and structure went hand in hand with support for new forms of empowerment. The reformers' deep suspicion of party power is especially notable in view of the party polarization of today. Progressives were convinced by their own experience that partisan competition and electoral division were unstable foundations on which to rest policy's accomplishments. Once-potent vehicles for policy making, parties appeared now dangerously out of step with demands everywhere for programmatic action; still anchored locally, party democracy had grown predatory and mindlessly myopic in its approach to government. Confident that the people would sustain the public interest by their own volition, Progressives resolved to open government to their will. To that end, they endorsed a "direct democracy" that included formal instruments of popular rule—initiative, referendum, recall, direct election of senators, and candidate-selection primaries. They also invented informal ones—information clearinghouses and civic-minded publicity, nonpartisan journalism and public opinion surveys, voluntarism and group association. Through all these, Progressives sought to break the monopoly that parties held over the mediation of popular will and to expose officeholders to "the people who want programs accomplished."[7]

Equally prominent in the Progressive scheme for empowerment was the cultivation of alternative forms of elite guidance, in particular, science and professional expertise. They proposed to hold governmental action to standards of objectivity, to experimental research, and to observable fact.[8] Privileging knowledge as the legitimate basis for state action served at once to justify initiatives that relaxed fixed contraints and to clear ground for consensual problem solving. Science and expertise offered a presumptively neutral medium though which actors in separate institutional locations could deliberate and coordinate on new courses of action. A young Walter Lippmann described science in just this way: it was "a substitute for authority" and "the discipline of democracy." Policy advanced by science and expertise would, Lippmann thought, change the political culture, creating a nation in which "people can live forward in the midst of complexity, and treat life not as something given but as something to be shaped."[9] Enlightened managers would serve a nation disenchanted with clergymen and custom, with judges and rule by superior right.

However strong the tension between scientific management and popular rule, Progressives believed that they could have it both ways. Aware of the importance of building consensus, they sought to produce greater public cohesion. Their case for the policy state came to rest on faith in what John Dewey called "like-mindedness,"[10] common understandings among citizens and the elevation of reason over brute force and raw emotion. The necessary values could be secured either by limiting the relevant public to persons thought most likely to share them or by disseminating them more broadly. These were white, middle-class Protestants anxious about a changing national population. Progressives understood how cultural diversity could complicate the smooth operations of activist government, and it was still permissible in their day to talk seriously about who was "fit" for democracy. Some were quick to enlist the latest science in that discussion;[11] others put their faith in the schoolhouse. "The best way to popularize scientific administration and enable the democracy to consider highly educated officials as representative," Croly wrote, "is to popularize higher education."[12] Progressives promoted universal secondary education, they built universities and graduate schools, and they circulated the "Wisconsin Idea" of the university as a center of collaboration on the public's business. They sought to link their new state more closely to a receptive and engaged citizenry.

Here in rough outline was an ingenious political formula for the subordination of state form to state formation, for prioritizing performance and adjusting the arrangements of government accordingly. Different elements of the formula could be reworked to keep the new state poised for action, moving forward, always in the making. For a long time, the great appeal of the scheme obscured inherent problems. Now we deal with the pitfalls.

Policy Science

The guidance of experts is vital to the policy state, not only for sorting options and working through technical questions but also for purposes of assuring the public on the soundness of actions taken. The marriage of science and democracy, however, has always been difficult, and for those most determined to make the relationship work, the issues have not gotten any easier.[13] Lippmann's appeal to science as "a substitute for authority" elided the difficulties. Science and expertise are cultivated in enclosed, self-regulating communities, in bounded systems of authority not wholly unlike those Lippmann thought they would replace.[14] When government enlists science directly in setting policy, it compromises the autonomy on which experts rest their credibility. Beyond that, it further obscures the location of state authority. Policy science does not sit comfortably within boundaries, and the politics of expertise works to erode them. It is here that the spinning begins.

Neither side in the partnership can countenance loss of control to the other. The elaborate safeguards provided by institutions like the National Academies of Science, Engineering and Medicine, the National Science Foundation, and the National Institutes of Health are the pride of the policy state. By the same token, the government's investments in science and expertise now extend far beyond its own precincts. Government contracts and grants cover a large portion of the budgets of American universities and private research laboratories, government agendas determine the direction of much research, and government draws widely on that repository of academic know-how for direction and advice. President Eisenhower's now-famous farewell address outlined the various risks that attend this blending: the "government grant" that "substitutes for intellectual curiosity," the "unwarranted influence" of a "military-industrial complex," the "danger

that public policy could itself become captive of a scientific technological elite."[15]

The authority of science in governmental affairs has grown more
controversial over time. Highly visible clashes like those over AIDS
research, for example, over stem cell research, over climate change, and
genetically modified food expose deep and widening fissures in the
assumptions behind the policy state's development. But the conflicts
that make headlines obscure even deeper strains beneath. Consider the
difficulty encountered in recent years in resolving questions about who
gets to define science and what science requires in setting public policy.
As the regulatory advances of the 1970s turned politically contentious,
the positions staked out revealed how far things had strayed from the
assumptions of the Progressive era. The judiciary, the branch the Progressives thought to be most resistant to their formula, began making
forceful demands of its own for better science. As we have seen, judges
required administrators to widen the evidentiary and disciplinary bases
of their research and take a broader range of social impacts into account. Another target of Progressive suspicion, corporate business, demanded better science as well. Partly in reaction to the pressure from
the courts to widen science's purview, business wanted research claims
more strictly separated from policy considerations through the imposition of independent review of agency findings.[16] Seeing their
authority under assault, the agencies—sometimes under instruction
from Congress, sometimes acting on their own—sought outside scientists to shore up their standing. Expert advisory panels would strengthen
their arguments in court and counter industry demands. Agencies
adopting this course could also expect to exert some control over the
composition of the review boards and to retain some discretion in
acting on the advice tendered.

When agency managers submit their methods and findings to outsiders with unimpeachable credentials in relevant fields, they risk
getting cornered. Experts checking experts is a hallowed ritual in the
advancement of science, but civil servants work under pressure from
principals with high expectations and short time horizons. Charged
with arriving expeditiously at results, they must decide whether the
science is good enough to act upon. Scientists on their advisory panels,

on the other hand, have no policy-making responsibility. They may have professional and academic concerns foremost in their minds, or they may come to the work of advising with their own political biases. When they lecture the agency on just how difficult it is to say anything with certainty, or when they use their open meetings to offer aggrieved parties yet another hearing, the system begins to spin. Rather than "substitute" for authority, they unravel it.

Sheila Jasanoff, an astute critic of the standard of objectivity in policy choice and a sympathetic analyst of what it takes to make these relationships work, describes a process of legitimation that relies less on science than on "boundary work" and "negotiation."[17] Savvy agency officials turn to these tactics to avoid entrapment. Much depends on the understandings that administrators hammer out to define the scope of the advisory board's review and to determine when in the policy-making process the review will occur. Often more important is the recruitment of panel members who are relatively more sympathetic to the agency's mission, less hunkered down in their narrow fields of specialty, and more open to interdisciplinary perspectives. It would appear that politics stops the unraveling of policy science, not the other way around, and that the politics involved is itself none too steady.

Agency managers are not the only ones prompted to think about the importance of boundary work. For every administrator who calculates when the science is good enough to act on, there is a private interest adversely affected by the impending policy choice whose answer is "never." In this way, the political assault on boundaries goes deep into the protections surrounding the scientific community's authority. Business interests sponsor their own research and employ their own scientists, generating what Thomas McGarity and Wendy Wagner call "bent science," basic research with all the trappings of best practice but conducted with particular policy ends always in view. Bent science exploits the scientific community's openness, flooding journals with objections by "peers" who are threatened by findings, harassing and exhausting unaffiliated researchers in hopes of derailing publication. The Information Quality Act (IQA) passed by Congress in 2001 assists in this gambit by directing the Office of Management and Budget to set guidelines for hearing private challenges to the reliability of all information used in agency decisions.[18] Setting the authority of science against itself, the IQA completes the circle. With the boundaries broken down, the spinning accelerates.

Social science lends itself more readily to policy applications than does laboratory science; it also speaks more directly to the economic and social quandaries of the policy state. If, as Lippmann asserted, science is "the discipline of democracy," economists are its sternest taskmasters. That point was made in grim detail on the eve of the New Deal when a Committee on Technocracy at Columbia University reported findings showing that gains from increased productivity were bound to generate a permanent worker surplus, with economic abundance for all short-circuited by "technological unemployment."[19] For those hoping to weld science to democracy, this was an inauspicious finding. The New Dealers wasted little time outflanking those technocrats by injecting political economy with a heavy dose of working-class realism. They propelled the policy state forward on a compact with organized labor, on production and price controls for farmers and pensions for older workers. Eventually they released an "economic bill of rights," promising ongoing investments in human resources and the provision of essential services for all.[20] It was not until 1939 that one of the government's professional economists, Lauchlin Currie, was transferred to the White House as a presidential adviser.[21] It was not until 1946 that professional economists were assigned a lookout specifically reserved for them as a Council of Economic Advisers. By then the task was to manage the spreading commitments of a new state, to strike a balance among them through fiscal policy.[22]

Economists now assure policy makers of the long-term social benefits to be gained from steady adherence to sound strategies for growth and caution them of the lags and social dislocations produced by the mismatch of existing skills with best-practice innovations. The political economy of the policy state has become, to borrow a phrase from two contemporary economists, a "race between education and technology."[23] The state banks on the experts' formulas for increasing economic productivity and for realizing social gains from organizational efficiency, innovation, and trade, but alas, adhering to that regimen consigns an anxious workforce to a perpetual state of retraining. The race is a policy leapfrog, promoting economic growth dependent on pulling workers forward from behind.

In recent years this policy nexus has become the premier testing ground of the capacity of governmental institutions to rise above the social conflicts they are now called on to resolve. Can they carry through with elaborate program packages that will maximize social benefits and minimize social costs? That is what the authority of experts promised, but it is becoming a heavier lift. In the 1970s American business started fighting harder to compete globally, graduation rates from high school and college began to sag, students began to find themselves less well prepared for the job market, and inequality began to rise. Both Republican and Democratic administrations tried to hold to the recommended course. Notwithstanding important differences in emphasis, both supported trade agreements that projected growth in productivity over the long haul, and both promised to train students and workers for the new demands of the global marketplace. But this modicum of policy consensus at the top, aided as it was by a general agreement among the experts, faced an increasingly unruly political base, and the entire operation has grown wobbly. Social dislocations have made it harder to sell the electorate on the prospective benefits of trade, and education reform tends to spin over disagreements about local control, private school options, and how to measure progress. Unions, weakened by trade agreements, resist more trade agreements, but they are also less effective in promoting more generous social investments. Teachers' unions, still strong at the local level, often resist experimentation with promising innovations in schooling. With the interests of those most affected by their prescriptions in revolt, the economists' discipline appears to be buckling.

Hard as it is to sustain long-range, multifaceted courses of action, it does help the policy state to have an expert consensus at its back. The consensus among economists about the virtues of free trade has long set the standard, but it increasingly looks like an outlier, and it is itself showing signs of strain.[24] This is due to the difficulty of sustaining the full range of national priorities while at the same time dropping national boundaries. Economist Jeffrey Sachs, a leading dissenter in the ranks, has rejected proposals like the Trans-Pacific Partnership and the Trans-Atlantic Free Trade Agreement as "investor protection agreements" that work around and undercut other state regulations. As Sachs sees it, globalization has in practice all but canceled out "the sovereign right to pursue the national interest in the face of investor interest." Precepts like "open trade" and "open investment" have, he charges, been hijacked by political procedures that distort the full range of values that economists now seek to advance: "goals are not processes . . . the goals should be goals of job creation in the signatory countries, good living conditions for workers, environmental protection . . . and distributive policies to help those who would be losers in what is otherwise potentially a winning hand for all the countries involved."[25]

When experts air their disagreements publicly, common ground for action gets shaky, and when government is called on to juggle a wider range of interests with the experts at loggerheads, the policy trap opens wide. One gauge of change in the authority of experts may be found in the development of the nation's "think tanks." At mid-century these institutions still played an important role in promoting and ratifying the methodologies of best practice and "good government." But with the policy breakthroughs of the 1960s and 1970s, a new generation of experts arose to challenge that style of state service.[26] Each think tank developed its own political slant on policy. With the creation of the Heritage Foundation (1973), the Cato Institute (1977), and the Center for Budget and Policy Priorities (1981), policy expertise and political intelligence were redirected away from the Progressive model. Relying for funding less on government contracts and foundation grants than on corporate and individual donors, the new think tanks had less patience with the cause of delivering to government neutral, purportedly objective services. Correspondingly, this sector has become less effective in fostering public confidence in the government's choices.

The new think tanks do not temper competing priorities; they express them. These former purveyors of ideas for cooperation and for finding common ground are now directly engaged in promoting conflict over the nation's agenda. Position taking, issue advocacy, and political marketing are integral parts of the job description, so that, like everyone else, experts too have become policy entrepreneurs. For the politicians who inhabit the institutions where policy is made, expertise delivered in this new format is often more readily accessible than that provided by university luminaries. The new think tanks provide "ammunition for policy makers" who need "public justification for their already preferred policy choices."[27] They stand ready to staff the government with mid-level political overseers during politically friendly administrations, and those experts can return to their think-tank positions during unfriendly administrations to challenge policies pursued by the incumbents. Policy conflicts among the experts do little to ease doubts about the knowledge basis of the choices made; more often than not, they fuel them. As the voices bestowing legitimacy on the larger enterprise grow weaker and their intramural exchanges become more embattled, the policy state faces a more skeptical public with less to claim for itself.

The divisions that fractured the parastate in the 1970s were not restricted to labor or social welfare policy, or to any particular line of political cleavage.[28] The telltale pattern of development may be observed in disputes over nuclear power. The leading history of the politics of expertise in this area closes with remarks delivered in 1972 by the chairman of the Atomic Energy Commission in response to mounting opposition to his agency's plans. Reaching for a lifeline, he latched on to the Progressives' old formula: "We must create today a 'participating citizen' who will have to become something of a 'super citizen,' one who is educated in the fullest sense of the word to understand and evaluate the facts of life and the web of complexities into which we have been woven."[29] But that assessment, as the author of this study points out, missed the mark. The problem confronting the AEC in the 1970s was not that the citizens following the debate failed to see experts as their representatives or were insufficiently educated to absorb what the experts offered them. Political resistance was grounded in the very different perspectives presented. Disputes were "joined by a host of institutions with resources to engage expertise of their own and fight to a war of attrition."[30] The Progressives had envisioned an educated populace marching forward arm in arm with public-minded experts; but in the policy state, the experts and their legions of enlightened followers tend to scatter over the field.

In all these ways, the policy state has begun to consume its most vital resource. Policy science has been this state's answer to the collapse of that other "natural" order of things, lodged in legally enforced personal hierarchies. Evidence-based action offered an anchor of another kind, and it is no exaggeration to say that modern American government would be lost without it. Defenders of the policy state profess their faith accordingly: "I believe in science" is, once again, a political rallying cry.[31] But as a boundary-crossing enterprise, policy science is as much an extension of this state as it is a stabilizer. As it has grown more interdisciplinary, dialogic, contestable, and open-ended, consensus is more difficult to achieve, and conclusions reached are less secure. Contending experts are useful in drawing out the complexity of issues presented for governmental action, but that does little for institutional resolve. When faith in experts wears thin, a doubtful public turns to other Progressive nostrums.

The Direct Approach

Direct democracy is less enthusiastic than policy science about government institutions and their many intermediaries. It rejects boundaries and filters as a matter of principle. In its purest guises, it calls on the people to pursue their preferred policy choices in clipped instructions to government to follow a specified course. Insofar as the development of the policy state has always pushed against established authority, this is a test of all limits. The direct approach stiffens demands for performance while stripping the state of its last claims to deference.

When the Progressives championed popular reversal of judicial decisions, legislating by referenda, and direct primaries, they were, at the same time, cultivating institutional authority in other forms. Direct democracy put courts, legislatures, and parties on notice, but programmatic government expanded through the bodies those institutions once contained and controlled. Blending populism with statism, Progressives promoted executive management, a neutral civil service, and administrative discretion as superior instruments for representing the public interest. That approach ran into serious trouble in the 1970s when the initiative and referenda were taken up in a new wave of popular discontent. In 1978, California's Proposition 13 delivered a rude shock to government by instigating a rolling tax revolt and propelling a conservative insurgency to national prominence. The same forms of direct action that once cleared a path for the Progressives' state building now mobilized against their former creation. Since then, politics in the policy state has grown more unsettled and increasingly convoluted. Not only has direct action rendered government more tentative, its decisions less conclusive, and its options more extreme; it has also intensified the scramble on all sides for end runs and policy workarounds.

Notwithstanding its rejection of institutional filters, more or less on principle, the direct approach has brought little clarity on the locus of authority. Its shortfalls in that regard are legion.[32] Direct action is a poor substitute for regular government, for its interventions are targeted and sporadic. Set aside for a moment the argument that unmediated rule by the people becomes less practical as policy becomes more esoteric and every single policy interdependent with others in its implications; the signal effect of the direct approach is the one we have been tracking all along: it disperses policy making responsibility and renders authority in all its forms less dependable.

Looked at closely, these modes of action are themselves seldom "direct." They require political and legal strategy, and they rely on organization, mobilization, and financing. Far from elevating the priorities of the "people," the direct approach has become another arena of combat for issue activists and special interests. In California, for instance, official election booklets explaining ballot propositions run on for hundreds of pages, taxing the attention spans of all but the most determined policy demanders. Furthermore, the direct approach creates its own kind of spin, a version of what some have called "rule by nobody."[33] It allows voters to revisit and reconsider government's policies, but their decisions invariably cycle back through the institutions of government where the issues are reconsidered again and aggrieved parties get another crack at them. Issues cycle the other way as well. Policies that fail to gain sufficient support in the state legislature do not necessarily die, for they can be referred out to the ballot box ready offstage. This also means that when legislators prefer to avoid a difficult issue, they can pass it off to the people who elected them and avoid responsibility for the outcome.

The national government remains relatively insulated from these procedures. In the late 1970s, the National Taxpayers Union spearheaded a movement for a constitutional convention to mandate a balanced federal budget, a cause that quickly gained the endorsement of twenty-nine of the thirty-four states necessary. In the past decade, conservative advocacy groups have made another run at a "convention of the states," this time closing in on the threshold and promising to clear it.[34] These brushes with direct rule are a vivid reminder of how the process for amendments set out in Article V protects established authority. With the policy state now in place, however, the high bar set by the Constitution for challenging received arrangements does not protect against activism so much as it preempts demands to dampen it down. The same can be said for proposals to apply local modes of direct action nationally. Back in 1912, Theodore Roosevelt championed popular recall of presidents who had lost the confidence of the nation; Jack Kemp, a leading proponent of tax cuts during the Reagan Revolution and a vice presidential candidate in 1996, promoted the idea of national policy referenda. Neither proposal gained traction.[35]

The proposals of Roosevelt and Kemp do, however, speak to the broader point: the rise of the policy state chafes against institutional boundaries, continually calling into question the relative insulation of federal authority. Forging closer connections to the public is an ongoing legitimation project, one that requires ever-more energy and, over time, compounds the difficulty of reconciling the demand for policy access with basic institutional operations. The tie to public opinion at large has been taken over by the polling industry and given a life of its own. Politics in the policy state runs on a perpetual referendum on governmental performance, affording politicians more or less leverage according to their approval ratings or the popularity of their proposals. Bolder experiments in direct democracy have appeared from time to time at the other end of the federal policy pipeline. The national government's call for "maximum feasible participation" by communities engaged in the antipoverty programs of the 1960s proved a formula for institutional confrontation, but participatory bureaucracy and stakeholder democracy have a long history in American public administration. They were featured in the organization of farm cooperatives, for example, and in procedures for determining union representation in the workplace. They have reappeared recently in experiments with negotiated rule making.

The rejection of filters and the demand for direct access implicate the federal government even more thoroughly in contemporary battles over "transparency." The "right to know," the quintessential claim against boundaries, is now the front line in the march to hold this state accountable. Progressives were notorious "muckrakers." They appreciated the value of information exposure in contesting established authority. Chief Forester Gifford Pinchot became a hero of the Progressive movement by defying a presidentially imposed gag order and publicizing alleged policy abuses in the management of public lands.[36] For the most part, however, Progressives deployed information sharing and publicity as strategies to advance programmatic government. Pinchot was defending his programs against skeptics who threatened to roll them back. The New York Bureau of Municipal Research, one of the early information clearinghouses, brought a million New Yorkers to a 1911 budget exhibition to publicize what an efficient and well-equipped government might accomplish.[37] The point man in important early advances for publicity, information sharing, and transparency was Louis Brandeis, Woodrow Wilson's adviser on regulatory policy. A Supreme Court justice during the New Deal, Brandeis conducted a backstairs campaign to prod the government into publishing a *Federal Register* of all government rules and regulations, presaging the "notice and comment" process for rule making in the Administrative Procedure Act (APA).[38] Successive versions of the Freedom of Information Act (FOIA) (1966, 1974, 1976) began as amendments to the APA.

For Brandeis, publicity, direct access, and transparency did not extend far beyond other Progressive plans for participatory bureaucracy and stakeholder democracy, bringing in the interests most concerned. Today's "culture of transparency" is a bit different.[39] It is less about "the people who want programs accomplished" than a wariness of programmatic government per se. It is less sanguine about cooperative exchanges and more sensitive to the implications of discrete policy decisions for the wider polity. It actively resists the authority of the new state, most especially for its fusion of public and private and its ties to special interests. Today's demands for transparency have turned in upon core principles that built the policy state: that programmatic government can be counted on to operate in service to the public, that government's information advantages can be safely entrusted to its own experts, that internal checks and balances work to protect the people at large. With more interests included, with more discretion over the decisions that affect them, and with the locations of those decisions more widely dispersed, the notion that the institutions of the federal government are self-monitoring has lost much of its purchase.

Statutory provisions for greater transparency offer a policy response to these policy-generated problems. More than anything else, however, these statutes reveal a democracy at odds with itself, that is to say, a public putting greater demands on a government in which it places less confidence. The people become a counterforce, with the right to know set up against policy makers as the last refuge for the public interest. When the demand for transparency is applied to the interests the government regulates, it can be crafted to achieve programmatic objectives; when applied internally, government finds itself chasing credibility at the expense of its own integrity. Freedom of information and open meeting laws rely on journalists, watchdog groups, and whistle-blowers to monitor the policy process and detect its irregularities. The idea is to expose the cozy relationships that develop between government agencies and special interests, but once again, the antidote employed reflects and abets the dissolution of boundaries. By stripping away deference and leveling authority, these laws extend that disaggregation of authority with a grudging recognition of their own.

During the 1950s, American pluralists welcomed the fluid, porous relations between government and interest groups that were already characteristic of the policy state. Confident that the democratic bona fides of the emergent system were safeguarded by "rules of the game," they were nonetheless aware that rule-governed behavior could not be taken for granted, and they saw clearly how the new "governmental process" might lose its bearings. Their worries about access and about potential "deficiencies in the means of communication" were heightened by the mid-century political climate.[40] The Cold War was fueling a battle over transparency. At the very time the pluralists were writing about intelligible rules, group access, voluntarism, and rights of participation, Congress was grappling with a chill on information sharing and challenging President Eisenhower to tear down the "paper curtain" of governmental secrecy.[41] Needless to say, the curtain was composed of the civil servants and executive-branch managers the Progressives saw as reliable stewards of the public interest.

National security is a problem that all states face. It sets a pragmatic outer limit on the right to know. In meeting this challenge, arguably the most critical test of the state's authority, faith in the integrity of governmental service and the public-regarding intentions of the best and the brightest pay a premium. There is, however, unmistakable evidence that faith of that sort is dissipating. The democratic deficit in security matters has been made worse in recent decades by the politicization of the bureaucracy that has accompanied the dominance of the policy motive. The political pressures on civil servants, real enough in their own right, fuel wide political speculation about their actions and their integrity. Claims about the existence of weapons of mass destruction in Iraq is one instance in which the faith in intelligence was tested by perceived political interest; another is the charge of Russian interference in the 2016 election. One Iowa voter captured the current mood of distrust at its darkest: "The way it is nowadays, unless I see positive proof, it's all a lie."[42]

As government gives itself over to policy without end, the right to know becomes more urgent. Like other rights in the policy state, however, this one is definitely a chip, and given the problem-solving rationale of the whole operation, it is routinely countered. Even where they shine brightest, rules of openness are spottily enforced. The Federal Advisory Committee Act (FACA) (1972) and the Government in the Sunshine Act (1976) weigh in against closed-door meetings, secrecy in the choice of outside policy consultants, and undocumented policy discussions. Still, President Clinton lodged the public interest elsewhere. He gave the classic policy-overcomes-rights argument to critics who demanded to know about what was going on in closed-door meetings of his Task Force on National Health Care Reform: "we would never . . . get anything done." Likewise, Vice President Cheney countered the right to know and defended the anonymity of outside advisers to President Bush's National Energy Policy Development Group: "we had the right to consult with whomever we chose—and no obligation to tell the press or Congress or anybody else whom we were talking to. If citizens who come to the White House to offer advice have to worry about lawsuits or being called before congressional committees, it would pretty severely curtail the counsel a president and vice president would receive."[43]

In an age when presidents insist they, and not Congress, are best situated to represent the people as a whole, neither Clinton nor Cheney can be brushed aside on this score. The judiciary proved more sympathetic to Cheney's tactics than to Clinton's, but in both instances, litigation over the secrecy issues stretched on long after the policy discussions concluded. The leading case on FACA, *Public Citizen v. Department of Justice* (1989), spoke directly to the character of these rules. Public Citizen challenged the government's use of the American Bar Association's Standing Committee on the Federal Judiciary as a confidential vetting service on judicial appointments. While the Court granted, over opposition, Public Citizen's right to sue, it cautioned against reading the FACA too literally: "We cannot believe that [the act] was intended to cover every formal and informal consultation between the President or an Executive agency and a group rendering advice." Moreover, to insist on a literal interpretation of the Act "would present formidable constitutional difficulties."[44] *Public Citizen* gave the right to know a hearing, but it left the proposition uncertain.

The cornerstone of the transparency regime, the Freedom of Information Act, is also notable for its chiplike qualities. To defend the public interest in information sharing, the federal government employs about four thousand "access professionals" to collect, sift through, and redact material for the "requester community." The statute authorizing these "gatekeepers" allows for nine categories of exemption, including information touching on national security, foreign policy, trade secrets, personal privacy, law enforcement, financial regulations, and whatever else might be specifically exempted by statute.[45] The circularity in that last stipulation is interesting, acting as an invitation to interest groups to lobby for new exemptions of their own.[46] The categorical exemptions are expandable in their own way. The Critical Infrastructure Information Act (2002) instructs access professionals to withhold sensitive but unclassified information that might harm interstate commerce, national economic security, or public health.[47]

Nor is information transparency per se without its perversities. The FOIA links back to our discussion of policy science, demanding transparency in that regard. During the Clinton administration, the Environmental Protection Agency (EPA) acquired data from a study by Harvard University and the American Cancer Society on the health effects of soot pollution, and it used that study in strengthening national air quality standards. The EPA, however, refused, on grounds of privacy, to give the data, which contained identifiable persons, to the interests regulated. The refusal prompted the Republican Congress to amend FOIA to provide to citizens access to "all data" produced by studies supported by the federal government. Such wide access was necessary, it was argued, so that affected parties could refute "junk science." But since denying researchers protection for the confidentiality of their subjects would also hamper study of many sensitive and controversial policy questions, the OMB drew up interpretative guidelines preserving some of the more important protections. Congress returned the favor, passing the above-mentioned Information Quality Act, instructing the OMB again to hear all challenges to the reliability of scientific information.[48]

The right to know navigates the increasingly opaque boundaries between public and private without lending them greater clarity. Consider the boundary between inside government and outside. The erosion of that distinction is evident in the increased resort to privatization and "contracting out." Using private service providers to do the public's business is not just an index of flagging faith in government institutions, but also a workaround of rules for greater transparency. There is blurring inside the government as well, for with the collapse of deference, citizen oversight of government has become the responsibility of everyone in government service. Leakers and whistle-blowers, government insiders acting as citizen watchdogs, brave gag orders, classifications, security clearances, and organizational norms of cohort and teamwork to expose questionable activity on behalf of the public.

The Code of Ethics for Government Service enacted unanimously by Congress in 1980 invites direct action of this kind. It extends the oversight function to all insiders by putting "loyalty to the highest moral principles above loyalty to persons, party or Government department."[49] Along with the various whistle-blower protection acts (1978, 1989, 1994), the Inspector General Act (1978), the installation of agency "hotlines," the Merit Systems Protection Board, the Government Accountability Office, and the Government Accountability Project (an outside watchdog group), the code acknowledges the end of probity by default. Successive revisions of these procedures also suggest that in-house accommodation for whistle-blowers remains a work in progress. The new procedures afforded are better at dealing with blatant corruption than with gray areas where policy is governed by discretion—by guidelines—and when embarrassment, not criminality, is at stake. For public-minded civil servants seeking policy redress through direct action, much still depends on appeals to partisan opposition within the legislature.[50]

Not surprisingly, these waters turn treacherous with national security policy. Between Daniel Ellsberg's release of the Pentagon Papers in 1971 and Edward Snowden's disclosure of metadata surveillance of citizens and foreign governments in 2013, the distinction between patriotism and treason when applied to personal intervention by insiders has become harder to draw. Snowden, a government contractor for the National Security Agency (NSA) with a prior history at the CIA, walked that line. For the NSA, preventing terrorism was a public interest that far outweighed any right to know about operations in detail. The NSA read the Patriot Act of 2001 to authorize the bulk collection of data regardless of relevance to a specific investigation, a course thought to be sanctioned by all the normal channels of oversight. The intelligence committees of the Congress were privy to this activity, as were the fifteen federal judges on the secret Foreign Intelligence Surveillance Court (some of the judges later claimed that they had been misled by NSA presentations). There is a difference of opinion over how seriously Snowden considered the avenues of grievance open to him, but one constitutional scholar concludes that Snowden had no effective appeal to superiors: "the inspector general surely would have responded that there was no basis for disclosing [the surveillance policy]."[51]

Snowden's disclosures went beyond evidence that the government was abusing its policy mandate for surveillance, so his motives are yet to be fully established. But he apparently convinced himself that American citizens had a right to know about the government's abuse of its policy mandate, and he sought recourse through the only pathway he saw. He stole the evidence, leaked the program to the press, fled the country, and sought guest asylum in an authoritarian regime. Breaking the law is not a right, even a "chip," as we have used the term. A "public interest" claim for illegal actions must be lodged elsewhere, presumably in the court of public opinion. Nonetheless, on this occasion, direct action sent the government spinning around on its own standards. President Obama, erstwhile champion of greater transparency, reacted with new resolve to clamp down on leakers and the journalists who reported their revelations.[52] In a different quarter, Snowden's disclosures sparked outcries to redress the imbalance between policy interests and private rights. The Privacy and Civil Liberties Oversight Board issued a scathing critique of the NSA's actions. In 2015, Congress passed the USA Freedom Act, which modified the surveillance program in ways that its supporters claim is more protective of individual rights. Civil liberties groups disagree. We score the USA Freedom Act a small victory for Snowden and a ringing reaffirmation of the policy state.

Ganging Up

Whatever their shortcomings, direct access, transparency, science, and expertise are assets bidding for policy's legitimacy. Another buzzword of modern American politics, *polarization,* is more ominous. There are no prospective benefits to mitigate the perverse effects of polarization on the legitimacy of the policy state. For the most part, polarization has been of concern because it distorts and confounds policy. It has been fingered as the culprit behind gridlock, drift, overreach, and overreaction. These effects would not have surprised Progressive reformers. Progressivism was in no small measure a reaction against the policy-stifling polarization of American politics in the late nineteenth century. Reformers sought to shift American politics off its partisan foundations and into governing arrangements that were less combative and more conducive to collective problem solving. As it happened, the great expansion of the policy state in the middle decades of the last century occurred with polarization at a relatively low ebb. The step-up that began in the century's final decades came as a nightmarish déjà vu, all the more alarming because government had, in the meantime, become steadily more dedicated to policy.

As it interests us here, polarization refers to any two groups of political actors—any combination of legislators, party leaders or activists, voters—who take sharply opposing positions on one or more political issues. Put differently, under conditions of polarization there are fewer members than would be normal in the population of interest who locate themselves mid-way between extremes; under complete polarization there are none. The proportion of issues over which these distinctly opposing positions face off constitutes the extent of polarization at any given point in time.

There is little agreement on a single cause for the dramatic increase in polarization in recent years.[53] But it seems to us no accident that it followed upon developments that moved the policy state toward its full expansion, and it has continued to intensify under the same momentum. Many of the partial explanations—the collapse of the "(Democratic) solid south," the collapse of the Cold War consensus, the wave of immigration that began in the 1960s, the onset of "culture wars," the rise of income inequality—have connections to new struggles over national policy. Something similar might be said of the structural changes that accompanied these events—greater centralization of power in Congress, a proliferation of primaries, loosening of campaign finance regulations, electoral redistricting. To argue that politics has polarized around policies risks straining at truism, but we are not reaching for a single or principal explanation. No doubt there are other important causes less directly related to policy, the decline of newspapers, perhaps, or the rise of media echo chambers. Perverse effects, however, in the interaction between policy and polarization run in both directions.

A rather modest claim is sufficient for our purposes: the expansion of the policy space at the national level, encompassing potentially all issues of economy and society, is an important enabler of polarization today, and likely also one of its several causes. Legally speaking, by the 1930s the policy space in American government was open to all areas of activity not expressly foreclosed by protections like those in the Bill of Rights. We have argued that even those rights, and those at common law and in state and federal statutes, were well along in the process of shedding their historical character as "trumps" and proliferating as "chips." We have also noted how "the system of '46" sustained a modicum of agreement on the incorporation of labor's claims into national policy decisions. But there remained a conspicuous outlier in the post–New Deal settlement: the right of equality between black and white races under law. A public goal enshrined in the Civil War amendments and on the prospective legislative agenda since Reconstruction, the project remained virtually moribund, sealed off from national initiative by the institutions of Jim Crow and by their continued acceptance by political institutions outside the South. Finally, the reclamation project spearheaded by the civil rights movement and marked symbolically in 1954 by the decision of *Brown v. Board of Education*, had, by the 1970s, produced a stream of anti-discrimination legislation that extended from elementary to higher education, public accommodations, housing, and employment, and would soon include discrimination by age and gender.

The heightened tensions associated with the enforcement of these laws added to disruption during the period that included inner-city riots, campus unrest, and opposition to the Vietnam War. All told, the political system experienced this epoch as a slow-rolling earthquake. The use of the word *polarization* to describe the public's response was not long in coming. Arthur Miller and his coauthors, investigating attitudes in the 1972 presidential campaign, found an unusual division that arrayed voters from left to right ideologically, based on their level of support and opposition to policies aimed at addressing these unsettling events.[54] Among possible determinants of candidate choice, a voter's placement on this spectrum was second only to political party membership. Democratic Party voters were divided in a similar pattern, from left and right, among themselves. At around this same time, studies of roll-call behavior in both houses of Congress revealed a steady rise in votes cast along party lines, with Democratic and Republican members increasingly taking on colorations of "liberal" and "conservative," respectively. The pattern continues today, according to some measures accounting for more than 90 percent of all congressional roll calls.[55] Organizationally, as we have seen, the change has been accompanied by a shift in power to the Speaker of the House and the Senate majority leader and a circle of chosen lieutenants, with the associated decline in the importance of seniority in committee assignments, a smaller role for committees and their chairs in drafting and moving legislation through the chambers, and a redistribution of staff resources.

Whether polarization is understood as two parties divided by their members' positions on policy issues or a division of policy positions brought about by the strength of party discipline, the phenomenon presents several historical ironies for America's policy state. The most profound is the division itself. The policy state is built on a presumption of consensus, on what John Dewey referred to as "like-mindedness." The idea that public problems have rational solutions, that they should be addressed scientifically and with an eye toward fine-tuning down the line, requires for their successful implementation a measure of agreement on goals and a continuity of support over time. The diversity of backgrounds and interests encompassed by democracy in America has always presented a special challenge to the discovery of a nationally cohesive public interest, but polarization in the context of a fully developed policy state poses more than a challenge. It is more an existential threat, potentially denying authority to every significant state action. For the sheer perversity of its effects, this is the sharpest prong in the policy trap.

In a parliamentary system like the British, which allows a party or coalition to assume control across a government boasting a neutral and well-insulated bureaucracy, the problem of consensus on policy is more tractable, at least between prime ministers. In the American system, with its staggered elections and staggered tenure of both elected and nonelected offices, its separated branches frequently under divided party control, and its tradition of judicial review, the need for broad accord on underlying principles is all the more essential. By that standard, an exemplary misfire of this new state in action is, again, the Patient Protection and Affordable Care Act. A sweeping social commitment enacted in 2010 without a single Republican vote, "Obamacare" was more than just another instance of authority drained by the priority of results. Democrats seized the opportunity to advance the oldest unredeemed promise on the progressives' policy agenda, but with Republicans ganged up solidly against them, their policy victory eviscerated the premise of common political ground at the foundation of America's policy state. From its inception, the Affordable Care Act (ACA) was subject to widespread, multilevel campaign pledges of repeal and scores of lawsuits, with plaintiffs that included individuals and groups, twenty-eight states, one United States senator, and the House of Representatives. Supporters gained a massive program of vital social services but traded equally vital political power to fine-tune it later. Conservatives gained a choice target for political mobilization, driving ideological divisions deeper.

It may be argued that this sparring has always occurred over important national policies, beginning with the first programs for public works, say, and the tariff. These early examples, however, occurred in a setting where most activities of daily life were regulated not by policies but by rights—relationships and obligations that were centuries old, implemented and, on the rare occasion when necessary, locally enforced. In that system, distrust of the national government's motives and competence was mollified by vaunted limits on its authority. No less a policy entrepreneur than Alexander Hamilton consoled a nation anxious about the new federal government with assurances that "the strong propensity of the human heart would find powerful auxiliaries" in the regulation of objects closer-by, that "the cement of society" was found in local institutions.[56] In the run up to the New Deal, reformers worried about whether a harmonious community could be transferred to the nation at large.[57] Dewey, himself no advocate of tradition or formality, warned that a mismatch between activity at the national level and a "great community" without commensurate scale and competence might prove counterproductive for all concerned.[58]

The development of the policy state has put Dewey's thesis to the test, for it has rendered all politics national.[59] Virtually no sphere of action is free of incursions by federal policies and their attendant vicissitudes. This includes areas like education and crime—connected with rights indirectly, through the family in the first case and property rights in the second, and perhaps for those reasons historically governed as local concerns. National programs once tailored to individual constituencies have been inundated with universal add-ons. For instance, agricultural price supports under the Agricultural Adjustment Act and related statutes, once the epitome of "distributive" policy, were ended in 1996; agricultural policy is now better typified by Food Stamps, School Lunches, Wildlife and Wetlands Programs, and the like.

The shift to the center can be seen in several statistics. For instance, at the start of the twentieth century, total government spending amounted to 7 percent of GDP. Of this, over half, or 4 percent of the total, was state and local. After a spike during World War I, the federal share of this total rose to half. This division remained until 1940, when federal spending surged again, to more than 10 percent of GDP, surpassing state and local spending. After World War II, federal spending settled at nearly twice that of state and local governments, a ratio that has gone up and down ever since. In 2010 federal spending was roughly two-and-a-half times greater than state and local spending.[60] It is worth observing as well that defense spending in 1960 accounted for almost 10 percent of GDP, whereas in 2010 the figure was under 6 percent. Moreover, the state spending amount includes support for federal programs, most prominently Medicaid.

Spending figures cannot convey the full impact of an expanding policy state on the changes we discussed in Chapters 3 and 4. Nevertheless, they support the general account. Thus, it is notable that, despite the pressure of entitlement costs and variation in budget priorities from administration to administration, federal expenditure on discretionary nondefense spending over the last half century has grown in real terms (adjusted for inflation). A report comparing spending patterns through the first term of George W. Bush shows that under Lyndon Johnson, nondefense discretionary spending grew 34.2 percent in real terms; under Richard Nixon it grew 22.5 percent; and under Jimmy Carter it grew 7.6 percent. During Ronald Reagan's first term the amount was reduced—the only reduction in this series—by 9.7 percent, and in his second term it grew 0.2 percent, only to be eclipsed again by growth of 13.9 percent under George H. W. Bush. Under Bill Clinton's two terms the figures were 0.7 and 14.4 percent growth, respectively. Under George W. Bush it had grown by 25.3 percent by 2005.[61] Note also that this expansion in nondefense spending is *cumulative* and does not reflect the emergency spending in the wake of the financial crisis of 2008 or new costs associated with Obamacare.

Another indicator of the shift in politics associated with the rise of the policy state is the relative influence of national and local factors on congressional elections, something for which there has been calculation for the period since 1954. After declining in the 1960s from previous levels, the national component of contested House elections in presidential years began to rebound in the 1970s. By 2000 national factors proved more important than local, a trend that continued upward. The same picture is observable in midterm elections, with national factors overwhelming local ones in 2006.[62] Moreover, it appears that the growing prominence of national considerations in congressional elections was driven less by stronger attachments to one's own party than by perceptions of the opposition. "Negative partisanship" today describes a voters' feelings that on issues of social and cultural importance—especially matters concerning race, women, and religion—the opposing party caters to constituencies with policy preferences fundamentally at odds with their own values.[63]

In other words, the cushion for consensus once provided by decentralization has been displaced by changes stretching across an immense span of social and political change. Our claim is not that the policy state is, by some gradual and circuitous route, responsible for the result. It is, rather, that the federal government's response to these changes elevated the significance of national policy in areas where there was once deference to states and localities, and, with particular regard to polarization, that national policy has turned into a lightning rod, concentrating social divisions that before this were scattered and submerged. A glance at the subject matters shifted into the national policy arena in the 1970s suggests why this period of policy expansion crossed a threshold into political dissensus, and how the specific ideological cast of polarization today may be similarly explained.

We return here to the observation that each stage of the policy state's advance has been associated with eliminating common law rights that earlier served as limits on its development. These rights had protected close-held privileges over subordinates, and their removal had deep cultural resonance. At each stage, a new settlement of sorts was projected onto the political system: first, in the solidly Democratic Jim Crow South; second, in the social spending and welfare coalition of the New Deal; and, third, in the national commitment to rectify civil rights, in race and then generally. In this light, the development of the policy state presents a social world pulled apart, with polarization drawing out the "winners" in these contests and stacking them up against "losers" serially dislodged from their once "rightful" place. Add to this the relocation of religion into the national arena, a subject that since the founding was within the scope of permissible policy making but contained in the states by the First Amendment. Religion—connected to health policy, employment policy, education policy—now lines up in an era of elite secularism as one more disturbing aftershock to "losers."

With long-submerged conflicts pulled into the center, the policy state has refashioned old limits into a national political divide and, to that extent, has been an enabler of polarization. Barbara Sinclair, a seasoned observer of Congress, has analyzed the current culture of Capitol Hill as partaking of the atmosphere of "armed camps."[64] In addition to the centralized leadership structure and the militant party divisions discussed earlier, Sinclair's image highlights the no-man's land between enemies, with few members available as allies for prospective defectors. This tendency of policy-making elites to, so to speak, gang up, we propose, may be connected to the diminished prominence of state and local affairs. In its early years, Congress was frequently composed of members who rotated back and forth between service in the House or Senate (sometimes both) and offices like state governor or judge.[65] But even as that practice gave way to more focused congressional careers, members held the status of "local heroes" for their special accomplishments at home, beyond the regular service expected for reelection. The relative insulation of local decision making afforded national representatives room to maneuver around and across divisions at the center. Many of those with the local political security to resist the national pressure to gang up became key players in the expansion of the policy state, a dynamic that would narrow still further the room for all members to maneuver in the future.

Consider once again the late nineteenth century. By the numbers, that era was highly polarized. But it was also true at that time that such battles, for instance, over women's suffrage and utility regulation, issues that had yet to be transplanted to the national arena, offered members leverage against party leadership in Washington. One famous example is Robert La Follette. In 1890 La Follette, after serving three unexceptionable terms, lost reelection to Congress. David Thelen, his biographer, describes how, in 1896, after he had been defeated twice in his bid to become Republican nominee for governor, La Follette began looking for issues to promote his candidacy for 1898. In 1897 he decided to advocate a program with which voters could associate him, one that fitted his own ambitions and style of popular politics. He took his new ideology directly from the reformers who had been battling political establishments in towns and cities across Wisconsin and the nation. The obvious popularity of these grassroots reformers converted Robert M. La Follette into an insurgent progressive.[66]

Elected governor in 1900, La Follette championed state control of railroad rates and an end to private utility monopolies, both at that time state, not federal issues. Upon his return to Washington as a U.S. senator, the Republican leadership demonstrated its opinion of "Fighting Bob" by appointing him chair of the Committee to Investigate the Condition of the Potomac River Front, a body that had never met. Yet, despite a well-organized Stalwart faction in Wisconsin, his popularity at home allowed him to support child labor, social security, women's suffrage, and other bills, bucking his party on each.

Another illustration is Fiorello La Guardia. Son of an Italian father and a Jewish-Austrian mother, La Guardia worked his way through law school as an interpreter on Ellis Island and became active in immigrant causes. As a young lawyer, he represented New York City shirtwaist workers in the great 1909 strike. Following the disastrous Triangle Shirt-Waist fire of 1911, he was a leader in the movement for workers' safety that resulted in the New York Factory Investigating Commission, the broadest investigation into factory working conditions to that point in history. By now well known, La Guardia in 1916 became the first Republican to win election to the House in a Tammany stronghold. In Congress, where he would serve until he became New York City mayor in 1932, he supported the full range of Progressive Party causes and gave his name to the historic Norris–La Guardia Act, outlawing the labor injunction. Like La Follette, he faced continual hostility from Republican leaders. Throughout his career he was kept off all important House committees; in 1924 he was expelled from the caucus.

For the period following World War II, Senator William Fulbright shows local heroism at work in supporting liberalism among Southern Democrats. The longest-serving chair in the history of the Senate Foreign Relations Committee, he was also a high-minded, internationalist dissenter from his party colleagues. For instance, in 1953 he provided the single vote against funding the Permanent Subcommittee on Investigations chaired by Joseph McCarthy; in 1961 he objected in advance to President Kennedy's invasion of the Bay of Pigs; later he led the congressional campaign against Lyndon Johnson's war policies. The independence he enjoyed rested in his home state, where he was repeatedly rewarded for his aggressive stance against racial integration of any kind, above and beyond what was politically required. Fulbright was one among the few border state senators who signed the Southern Manifesto to reverse *Brown v. Board of Education*; he filibustered against the Civil Rights Act of 1964 and opposed the Voting Rights Act of 1965 and the Fair Housing Act of 1968. For good measure, during his tenure he opposed a number of bills in support of Hawaiian statehood. Fulbright's brand of liberal reform, regionally rooted in reaction, lost its ground over the course of his career. In 1974 he was defeated in a Democratic primary.

Examples are by no means limited to figures of this stature. Moving forward in time: beginning in 1977, Anthony Beilenson represented a coveted House district on the west side of Los Angeles where Republicans need not apply. He had achieved statewide acclaim in 1967 when, as a freshman state senator, he authored and deftly managed the successful passage of California's first liberalized abortion law. At the time, abortion had yet to become a national issue. In the twenty years in Congress that followed, Beilenson often broke with fellow Democrats on issues of taxing and spending; for instance, he opposed the Clinton tax hike of 1993. In a turn of fortune, he was forced in 1992 to move to a newly drawn and less predictable district rather than fight a primary challenge by Henry Waxman, another House Democrat with powerful party allies. In 1999, Beilenson retired, publicly declaring that the political process in Washington had become "ideological and often mindless."[67]

Finally, Walter Jones of North Carolina, an exception who proves the rule of vanishing local heroes: In a 2015 ranking of members of Congress who vote against their party, Jones placed number one among House Republicans. Best known for naming "freedom fries," a conservative who twice introduced legislation to allow ministers to endorse candidates from their pulpits, Jones arrived in Washington as part of Speaker Newt Gingrich's "Contract with America" patrol, and he was the first Republican to represent his eastern North Carolina district since Reconstruction. As with the others discussed, his reputation preceded him. As a state senator, Jones led a highly publicized campaign to tighten state laws on lobbying and on the finance of state elections. Thus the exception: these subjects are among the few still not controlled by the national policy state. They become fewer and farther between.

Stepping back, it is useful to take stock. Our conjecture is that these and other congressmen in the past gained independence from their party's arm-twisting to conform by championing local, not-yet-nationalized, causes. But it is also true that only Jones, and for a few years Beilenson, would have faced the level of pressure to gang up that is routine in the Congress of today. As already suggested, from the Gilded Age into the first two decades of the twentieth century, Congress was also polarized by party. But virtually all observers of the time are in agreement on the absence of ideology and even of excessive partisanship. Reviewing this literature and examining the data herself, Frances Lee has described the two parties of that era as "long coalitions competing for power and distributive gains," and she argues that major legislation, like the tariff and taxes, was organized by the local-level logic of patronage and pork.[68] Perhaps more to the point, the political parties of that time were not well equipped to exert muscle directly in the districts, nor to wield financial and informational tools available today for keeping existing members on the team.[69]

The squeeze on the local safe-zones that once supported national mavericks stems from still another feature of the policy state, which is the primacy of information. Information has become a major weapon in the arsenal of polarized party leaders. Information has been important to legislators everywhere, leaders and nonleaders, as long as there has been policy of any kind, and as our discussion of access and transparency has already shown, this need has only increased as they decide more and more complex issues. The Congressional Research Service (CRS), begun in 1914 as a unit of the Library of Congress at the urging of then-Progressive Senator Robert La Follette, was modeled on similar agencies in Wisconsin and New York. Since then its staff has processed several million requests from Congress for information, both on legislation and on matters of concern to constituents. Earlier we discussed how an older-style foundation, dedicated to nonpartisan public causes, sometimes specialized in areas like education or child welfare, has given way to think-tank competition and ideologically charged expertise. As members get their information through these newer channels, preferred or managed by leadership, the CRS has found itself in receipt of twice as many constituent-related requests than those related to legislation.[70]

Speaker Nancy Pelosi's statement in 2010 about Obamacare—and also its public reception—neatly captures the synergy between polarization and the policy state. "We have to pass the bill so that you can find out what is in it, away from the fog of the controversy." This was picked up and ridiculed by the conservative side of the media echo chamber as "you have to pass the bill before you can read it," suggesting that Pelosi was speaking to fellow legislators who had little or no knowledge of the bill's details but should go ahead and pass it anyway. In fact, she was talking to the National Association of Counties (NACo), a seventy-five-year-old nonpartisan good-government lobby of the old style, representing some thirty thousand county governments, advocating for issues like tax transparency and against unfunded federal mandates.[71] An unimposing presence in the world of the Heritage Foundation, there is no record that NACo took a position on the Affordable Care Act, yet alone received marching orders from the Speaker. Still, the ridicule hit its mark. The passage of complex bills now plays out as a parody of progressivism.

No doubt, the ACA's twenty-seven hundred pages did go unread by many members of Congress who voted on it, just as the same can be said with fair certainty of the text of the 13,675 bills introduced in that same session, the 601 that were voted on, and the 385 enacted. To pick one: the National Defense Authorization Act of 2015, more than sixteen hundred pages long, was made public and given to House members for perusal thirty-six hours before the scheduled vote. Representative James Moran of Virginia, member of the House Appropriations Subcommittee for Defense, asked whether he had read the bill before voting for it, answered, "Of course not. Are you kidding?" Minority Leader Hoyer, on the other hand, was quoted as saying he had an "outline of exactly what it does," and Speaker Boehner assured questioners that he was aware of "what was in that bill," having been "through most every part of it" as it was put together.[72] Since 2006 bills named Read the Bills Acts (RTBA) have been introduced several times in the House and Senate by both Democrats and Republicans, providing such rules as mandatory availability of all legislation at least seventy-two hours before scheduled votes.

A close husbanding of details and the need to act quickly on multifaceted, cobbled-together legislation, before there are many defections from the team, is consistent with the inherent complexity of policy making. This problem is reinforced by the nationalization of congressional elections and compounded by the insecurity of the majority in each chamber from one election to the next. The situation is circular. To the extent that members might seek out coalitions with representatives from the opposing camp, leadership control of information about policy details makes the garnering of knowledge more costly; at the same time, the team approach makes any deviance, even on minor provisions, more risky for one's own reelection down the line. A recent study of "legislating in the dark" has found that members from marginal districts are more distrustful of the information they receive from party leaders than those who have less to lose by any single vote; for the most part, the marginals succumb to leadership strategies.[73]

In explaining this breakdown, it is hard to gauge the relative contribution of ideological division in the public, the changing nature of political careers, reduced staffing budgets, and the sheer scope of today's legislative agenda. However explained, it becomes difficult for representatives chosen individually in districts to do their designated job.

Get with the Program

In 2016 the Supreme Court decided *Whole Woman's Health v. Hellerstedt*, striking down as unconstitutional a Texas law requiring, among other things, that abortion clinics have a physician on staff with admitting privileges at a nearby hospital and also meet the standards required by Texas law for ambulatory surgical centers.[74] The decision came as close to bestowing trump status on the right of women seeking abortions as any ruling since *Roe v. Wade* four decades earlier. In balancing costs against benefits as the judiciary requires when legislators undertake to affect "fundamental" rights, the 5–3 majority held that neither of the Texas provisions "offers medical benefits sufficient to justify the burdens upon access that each imposes. Each places a substantial obstacle in the path of women seeking a pre-viability abortion, each constitutes an undue burden on abortion access . . . and each violates the Federal Constitution."[75] Justice Ginsburg, concurring, stated the matter more conclusively: "Targeted Regulation of Abortion Providers laws like H. B. 2 that 'do little or nothing for health, but rather strew impediments to abortion,' *Planned Parenthood of Wis.*, 806 F. 3d, at 921, cannot survive judicial inspection."[76]

Justice Thomas's dissent goes to an opposite extreme. Decrying what he perceives as the majority's reliance on an "abortion exception" to certain established legal rules, he opines, "Ultimately, this case shows why the Court never should have bent the rules for favored rights in the first place. Our law is now so riddled with special exceptions for special rights that our decisions deliver neither predictability nor the promise of a judiciary bound by the rule of law." Without drawing the same categorical distinction between rights and policy that we do, he does differentiate a right from other benefits of which one can choose a little or a lot: "A law either infringes a constitutional right, or not; there is no room for the judiciary to invent tolerable degrees of encroachment. Unless the Court abides by one set of rules to adjudicate constitutional rights, it will continue reducing constitutional law to policy-driven value judgments until the last shreds of its legitimacy disappear."[77]

We focus on these opinions not for their outcomes; they are in any case vulnerable to the next presidential election. Rather, they are important because they typify debate ongoing inside the policy state as well as among critical observers. In this respect as others, the judicial branch has become increasingly indistinguishable from the rest. The alternatives posed are these. On the one side, embraced by Justice Ginsburg, get with the program: after so many decades of back-and-forth, it is time to shut down further bickering and move on; concede that rights are "chips" and that a choice among them needs to be made, at least for the time being and in the circumstances at hand. Get over it. On the other side, the position consistent with Justice Thomas's opinion and commentators who agree with him would reduce developments of the past eighty years to, at best, a failed experiment, at worst, to a prolonged assault against the Constitution, an illegal evacuation of its fundamental principles in order to make way for "policy-driven value judgments."

In *Whole Woman's Health* the justices were arguing about their own authority. Within the American policy pyramid, however, they must also pass final judgments on the actions of other government officers. In the same 2015 term, they voted 4–4 in a second case, *United States v. Texas*.[78] The tie meant that the decision of the Fifth Circuit Court of Appeals on the legality of President Obama's immigration program—Deferred Action for Parents of Americans and Lawful Permanent Residents (DAPA)—remained the legal rule. Under the statutory authority given the secretary of homeland security, DAPA granted deferred deportation status to immigrants without legal documentation who are parents of children under sixteen years of age and are citizens of the United States. This executive action, the placement of individuals at the bottom of the list of those to be prosecuted for violating the immigration laws, also conferred "lawful presence," required for work permits and work-related public benefits like Social Security and Medicare. Texas sought an injunction in federal district court staying DAPA's implementation, claiming the program would injure the state financially: under existing state law, Texas is required to provide subsidized drivers licenses to all persons with lawful residence.

The district court issued the injunction; the Fifth Circuit affirmed.[79] Again, what interests us about this case is not the outcome nor, in this instance, the judges' view of their authority. We are concerned with the arguments of the parties, both of them government agencies, regarding their own authority, specifically with respect to the activity of rule making. In its original case, the United States offered several reasons why an injunction should not be granted. By the time the matter reached the Supreme Court, these included, first, that the State of Texas as lead plaintiff lacked standing to bring the suit; second, that the dispute fell outside the "cases and controversies" provision of Article III and would be more appropriately settled through political rather than judicial processes; and finally, that Congress had authorized the secretary of homeland security to provide deferred deportation status at her discretion in enforcing the immigration laws, thereby exempting the plan from the notice-and-comment provision of the Administrative Procedures Act (APA).[80]

Recall that the APA, extending due process protections to persons affected by the decisions of administrative agencies, was one part of the system of '46, which, for its symmetry and comprehensiveness, had achieved the symbolism of a constitutional settlement. Four decades later, the Supreme Court in its *Chevron* decision reaffirmed the institutional division of labor laid out, adding, as it were, an amendment to the effect that unless Congress had indicated otherwise, the judiciary would defer to an agency's own construction of the statute it administered.[81] Among the more recent decisions upsetting that status quo, *United States v. Texas* stands out. The APA's notice-and-comment provision expressly exempts "general statements of policy" and, more broadly, the enforcement of existing rules. General statements of policy merely "advise the public prospectively of the manner in which the agency proposes to exercise a discretionary power"; they create no new rights and have no binding affect.[82] Texas argued that the president's program did not fall within these exceptions. While the secretary had lawful discretion to bestow deferred deportation status on immigrants as an individual matter, she could not under existing statutes do so with regard to many millions of people. Nor could she circumvent Congress's detailed provisions for which alien persons might be permitted to work in this country and how persons might derive lawful immigration classification from the immigration of their children. DAPA was not a "general statement of policy" but was "a significant and immediate change in immigration law and policy" and therefore illegal.[83]

In its brief to the Supreme Court for removal of the stay, the United States did not refrain from using the word "policy" in connection with DAPA. On the contrary, it stressed its significance on the stated policy basis of humanitarianism, denying any departure in the meaning of the Texas suit. The secretary of homeland security had received Congress's express instruction to utilize deferred deportation actions in the process of enforcing the immigration laws. Since 1960, the government had done this on twenty occasions, involving groups of individuals numbering up to, in the case of Nigerian unrest in 1987, between 150,000 and 200,000 refugees. Similarly, since the 1970s it has been the government's practice to extend work permits to aliens allowed to remain, and, in the Farm Labor Contractor Registration Act Amendments of 1974, Congress implicitly sanctioned this practice. In 2012, Congress passed Deferred Action for Childhood Arrivals (DACA), providing a two-year renewable freedom from deportation and a work permit to persons who entered before their sixteenth birthday and before June 2007. According to the government, not only was DAPA not new; it was not really policy in a fixed sense but merely, as it called itself, "Guidance." It was a tentative determination about how existing policy discretion should be exercised, and as such, exempt from APA notice and comment.[84]

The parties' arguments do not end there; many more statutes were cited as relevant by both sides. Texas presented evidence from DACA to show that applications were approved "reflexively," with no discretion involved; in effect, the so-called guidance was binding. The United States argued that the secretary was, in issuing rules, merely delegating her own lawful discretionary authority, with the good result that "the public need not guess about the idiosyncratic behavior of individual agents." Not to allow senior officials this practice, to insist instead on time-consuming notice-and-comment procedures, would "undermine their ability to control the Executive branch."[85] We need not belabor the exchange to demonstrate the complexity facing any decision about when policies might impose accountability on other policies, or on policies that are merely policies about how other policies should be exercised, all channeled through a maze of expressed and implied provisions in numerous and varied statutes. In these circumstances, where the rule of law has no independent solid landing place, political determination begins to seem a welcome refuge.

Were these views isolated, focused on the particular facts of individual court disputes, they would be of only passing interest. On the contrary, as we have suggested, they represent positions held by persons who have thought deeply about the issues and are well situated to be influential moving forward. The detail that surrounds the execution of policy is not the stuff of party platforms. Historically, as we have seen, this is strictly "inside baseball," usually at the initiative of the executive. Today, for instance, in a long line of presidential advisers including Frank Goodnow, Louis Brownlow, and James Landis, stands the prolific Harvard Law professor and former head of the Office of Information and Regulatory Affairs (OIRA) in the Obama administration, Cass Sunstein. As it happens, in 2015, recently out of government, Professor Sunstein wrote an essay on the subject of notice and comment, referring to President Obama's immigration policy as an example of the procedure's disadvantages.[86] Sunstein's discussion rests on a contrast between an "epistemic" approach to notice and comment, one that uses knowledge gained from that procedure to instruct agents and test out proposals, and a formalistic, "rule-of-law" approach. He favors the former.

From an epistemic viewpoint, according to Sunstein, it makes better sense for judges to require notice-and-comment when an agency's policy statement is "legally binding," that is, when it creates enforceable rights and obligations, than when it is "practically binding," that is, when the statement prescribes no "fixed and firm" rules but only noncommittal or tentative ones. That said, he agrees that such a standard would likely run afoul of the much-criticized, not always enforced, but still-alive *Vermont Yankee* doctrine that teaches courts may not dictate rules to regulatory agencies.[87] Therefore, Sunstein falls back on the distinction between policy statements that impose new conduct and penalties versus those, like the decision not to prosecute and deport, that do not. He suggests that upholding this distinction is largely a matter of drafting and phrasing: agencies should take care that their guidance avoids words like *shall* and *will* and includes reference to making discretionary decisions on a "case-by-case" basis. What if it can be shown that virtually all cases are decided the same way? No matter. "(Every professor has had the experience of grading a large set of examinations, every one of which receives a passing grade.)"[88]

Eschewing formality, the epistemic approach bears a close relationship to the forward-looking, information-dependent, fine-tune-as-you-go nature of policy as we have defined it; Sunstein's own proposal, of course, is a new policy, albeit about "policy statements." It is also, incidentally, a defense of President Obama's program, but the prospect on offer is by no means confined to that, or to notice-and-comment, or to the APA. In a more recent publication, the same professor-adviser has argued for the epistemic advantages of extending authority to the executive branch as a whole: "Solution of national problems requires access to a great deal of information, much of it highly technical. Of the three branches of the national government, the executive is the most knowledgeable, and by a very large measure, not only in foreign affairs but in the domestic domain as well." According to Sunstein, the information gap between the executive and Congress is increasing; in the case of the judiciary, the gap is exacerbated by the "grotesquely distorting prism of litigation" so that judges do not know what they do not know.[89]

As a different critic of excessive reliance on the rule of law might have put it, this is progressivism on stilts.[90] Sunstein finds support for executive superiority and its "immense knowledge" in the nature of contemporary rule making itself. Were the task of administration mainly defined with respect to what has gone before, "what the law is," then the principles of predictability and even-handedness recommend the judiciary as interpreter of the final meaning of unclear rules. But when, as is the case more often than not, rules are genuinely ambiguous, when the application of rules involves an assessment of the consequences of this or another definition, then agency expertise, and justification for doctrines like *Chevron* and more recently *Auer v. Robbins* (1997), prescribing judicial deference to agency interpretation of its own rules, comes into their own.[91] As for Congress, Sunstein finds members uninformed, preoccupied by reelection, and reliant on talking points, briefing papers, and "simple heuristics, typically rooted in the ideas of trusted others, many of which are interest groups."[92]

Sustaining priorities is a task without end. Sunstein eyes the pressure points, offering reasoned strategies for avoiding blockages and getting on with the business at hand. He characterizes his views as "normal science in public law," but his proposals are not ventured in an ideological vacuum.[93] They are expressed against an avalanche of commentary, some directly from the Court, leveled against the place of administrative agencies in government and, in particular, their allegedly anomalous role in the Constitution's design for the separation of powers. This in turn is closely connected to a distrust of the executive branch on the part of both left- and right-leaning thinkers, in the case of the former in foreign policy and the latter in domestic affairs. Most recently, indeed, the comparison has been drawn, at length and with considerable erudition, between the contemporary administrative state and the reign of James I.[94] Other perspectives range from "originalist"—the framers took steps to restrain the executive before he could abuse power—to wariness of decisions like *Chevron* and *Auer* for blurring of the line between agencies' legitimate interpretation and unconstitutional lawmaking.[95]

Progressives are not the only ones promoting new methods of path clearance. Calls to get with the program occur on both sides of the ideological divide. Compare, for instance, a book written by Jack Goldsmith, another government insider who served as legal adviser to the General Counsel of the Department of Defense and then as United States Assistant Attorney General for the Office of Legal Counsel during the administration of George W. Bush. Goldsmith's starting point is the close resemblance of President Obama's national security policies to those of President Bush, despite the changeover in party control and the stiff criticisms Obama leveled during his first presidential campaign against Bush administration overreach. The highlight of Goldsmith's argument is an arresting image, what he calls a "presidential synopticon," a kind of episteme in the round, where innumerable eyes watch the presidential office in a "dizzying and often painful swirl of investigations, lawsuits, reviews, reports, and accusations . . . that forces the government to recalibrate its counterterrorism policies and accountability mechanisms constantly based on ever-changing information and ever-changing political and legal constraints."[96]

In Goldsmith's telling, the Obama counterterrorism policy ended up looking a lot like Bush's because neither could deny the policy's priority and because it passed day by day through the same—one might say immense—refiner's fire. As in Sunstein's analysis, the rule of law has a part to play, but here it becomes mainly "lawfare," the strategic use of constitutional and statutory law to badger and corner and shape executive action, until abuses of law become "baselines of opprobrium" for the next emergency.[97] According to Goldsmith, by the time Obama took office, the presidential synopticon had served to smooth out the most offensive aspects of Bush's program, and the new incumbent quickly learned to appreciate the rationale and advantages of the tools left at his disposal. This is not to say that participants themselves were happy with the new equilibrium: each pointed to biases, leaking, excessive secrecy, obstructionism, stridency, and underhandedness of the other. Yet together this was "all very healthy for the presidency and for national security." He calls the effect Madisonian, "a harmonious system of mutual frustration undergirding a surprising national consensus—a consensus always fruitfully under pressure from various quarters."[98]

Goldsmith does not claim that the presidential synopticon produces optimal policy. He freely admits it does not. What it does is justify and accommodate a ratcheting up of policy's demands. It is to be recommended for its capacity to stretch the boundaries of appropriate governmental behavior and executive branch behavior in particular. It draws on much the same material as the Progressives' extensive parastate: expertise, journalism, transparency, public opinion. These are resources that policy advocates have always cultivated. They overcome resistance to doing more by doing it right and doing it smart. Controversial actions are normalized, and everyone, even usually implacable foes, buys in.

Game Change?

"Everybody talks about the weather, but nobody does anything about it." Said in a lecture by Mark Twain in 1897, this comment may well have harbored a bit of irony. It was made at a time when an important group of Americans was just beginning to believe that there was no problem, social or economic, that they could not solve with the help of a better government. In that same year, Oliver Wendell Holmes published his guide to better government, "The Path of the Law."[99]

Twain's remark comes to mind as we bring this work to a close. We might say parenthetically that, as it pertains to the policy state itself, Twain was wrong. No item on the public agenda today is pursued with more urgency or intellect than our changing weather or better epitomizes the dissolution of boundaries between places and disciplines, or the bright future through science, hoped for throughout the last century. In spirit, however, as it applies to us, the authors of *The Policy State*, the remark has a certain bite. After having labored to uncover and report on this state of our union, we offer no proposal to fix it.

It is not as if remedies are in short supply. On the contrary. They can be found today in all political colorations, each an urgent call to action. That seems to us reason enough to pause, to separate description from prescription and consider more broadly what we are up against. We are not indifferent to the issues we have raised. Far from it. But after poking into every corner and prodding at every seam, we see no ready response to what we have found. What we have presented instead should stand as a stiff test for any prescription out there, which is the paradox of the American state's formation.

We have described a state trapped by its problem-solving instincts. Adaptations that have steadily fortified its policy-making capacities have reworked institutions to the point that no one can say for sure what is left to other motives, what underpins rights, representation, localism, limits, or law besides policy. The effect is, in equal parts, encompassing, dissipating, and disorienting. The priority of policy has landed us in a tough spot with no obvious way out.

Tough because the development of a policy state in America has generated a set of problems unlikely to be solved by more policy. Policy is, by its nature, targeted, but the imbalances produced by its widening application are systemic. Adjustments to policy have had a circular effect on American government because they work through a Constitution that makes an elaborate display of limits. Change is widely seen as the genius of the Constitution, but that creative spirit of innovation drives the system to wit's end. A monument to pragmatism, the new American state dispels the myths of pragmatism: that problem solving can proceed with impunity, that the institutions of government are infinitely adaptable. There is certainly nothing to prevent new uses of policy to address the distortions of rights and structures that policy brings about, but they make it ever harder to sustain the pretense that rights and structures are *not* policy, with all of the contingency policy entails. To put it another way, the more thoroughly we compromise on rights and structures to fit policy making, the more we exacerbate the melee.

Sometimes the best advice for coping in a tough spot is acceptance. Yes, the chase may have turned circular—solutions may wind up biting back—but people learn to live with difficult situations all the time.

Accordingly, the first question to consider is whether Americans cannot simply recognize the predicament for what it is and put things in a more optimistic perspective. There is plenty to do; things might not be as bad as they seem; they could be a lot worse. The changing balance of motives may render authority increasingly opaque, but at least it juggles a broad range of competing benefits. From this angle, any sense of distortion or disorientation or dissipation introduced into modern American government by the priority of policy can be treated as a kind of a cultural affliction, a historical hangover, an unnecessary attachment to rights and structures that were never perfect in any case.

Realism of this sort appeals to the intellect: we really have no choice but to carry on. Politics, however, is not therapy, and the American polity is unlikely to take to this cure any time soon. The necessary reduction in cognitive dissonance would entail, at a minimum, tossing out the textbooks. If our analysis is correct, the new primer on American government would have to strike the words "under law" and substitute "under guidelines"; it would need to explain that rights are chips, that structure is opportunity, that rules are interests, and that the Constitution itself is a disembodied set of principles with scant binding effect.

Might such a revision prove acceptable? Speculation here will not be gratuitous. Consider the stiff blowback that greeted Judge Richard Posner, one of the most celebrated realists on the federal bench, when he shared his decades of experience with the legal community: "I see absolutely no value to a judge of spending decades, years, months, weeks, days, hours, minutes, or seconds studying the Constitution, the history of its enactment, its amendments, and its implementation."[100] This was a frank assessment of the game change that has already transpired, and a designated guardian of the Constitution cannot take such a position comfortably. The comment ignited considerable controversy, indicating in no uncertain terms that candor is heresy and realism about the Constitution a nonstarter politically. Posner beat a quick retreat, refining his position in a way that leaves our predicament unresolved: "The Framers of the Constitution were very intelligent and experienced, but they could no more foresee the conditions of the 21st century than we can foresee the conditions of the 23rd. . . . The choice for the modern judge is: dismiss the bulk of the Constitution as nonjusticable because it doesn't address modern problems, or decide many constitutional cases by broad interpretation of the Constitution's vague provisions, recognizing that interpretation so understood is not what we usually understand by the word."[101]

Holding out hope for additional adjustment, some investigators push further into the weeds. There are, to repeat, an endless variety of these ventures: a balanced budget amendment, an equal rights amendment, campaign finance reform, Electoral College reform, congressional redistricting, more power to the states, a tighter APA, a more participatory bureaucracy, more extensive use of fast-track authority for the president, renewed investment in committee staff for Congress. Nothing we have said should discourage such efforts, each considered on its own merits. Curatives of this sort, it must be said, particularize the problems of the policy state and come at its imbalances from different directions. They fail the test of not being more of the same. Recalibrating here and remediating there, they invariably raise new questions elsewhere in the arrangement. It is one thing to reshuffle the cards in hopes of a better deal; quite another to change the game.

Systemic approaches that recognize there are no magic bullets are more in keeping with our assessment. These set out precepts for fundamental reordering, principles around which a large reform package might be made to cohere. By our reckoning, however, the most attractive of these programs are also those that developments in the policy state have put farthest out of reach. "Deliberative democracy" is one. Putting citizenship first, this idea aims to build political communities capable of constructive decision making in complex settings based on common bonds. Even if we count Goldsmith's refining synopticon a surrogate, the evidence we mount shows the political currents running strongly in the opposite direction, with the advantages of ganging up squeezing out prospects for enlightened engagement. A different model, "juridical democracy," gestures more directly to rights and to the rule of law, promising to strengthen procedures particularly hard hit by policy. This approach, in the form of a more conservative tilt on the Supreme Court, might well be in the offing. But like deliberative democracy, juridical democracy is attractive because it so precisely keys off what it is up against. We suspect that once limits on problem solving begin to pinch, we will find ourselves remembering every end run, every workaround, every refinement through which policy has found its way.

To describe the policy state is to confront the predicament in full. Recent years have witnessed broadside assaults condemning modern American government as a betrayal of first principles. We see political development differently. The policy state is not a mistake, nor is it outside the American tradition. It is, first and foremost, a solution, or a composite of solutions; it was an essential part of the American success story, of "The American Century." The project of restoring first principles fails to account for the ratification of the Constitution itself with the aim of more effective policy making. The plea for a return to limits—to stronger rights and sturdier structure—glosses over the social exclusions that stood behind them and held them up. The past impugns the legitimacy of the policy state far removed from the realities of late-eighteenth-century America. Rights were trumps when some people did not have them; structure was a more dependable constraint when it locked certain issues out. Recovering that lost ground is neither possible nor desirable.

Progressivism began with the bold formula for adapting the Constitution to twentieth-century demands. It remains a capacious rationale for further accommodation. This is advanced, however, amid every sign that the outlook is losing its grip on the American public. Overly refined rules, hard to sustain, let alone enforce, are only one source of lost faith in the state that policy built. Each of progressivism's prescriptions is under assault. The authority of experts groans under the weight of too many commitments; scientists with policy concerns recently felt compelled to organize a nationwide march in defense of their cause. Education is short on standards. Poor performance in social remediation lends a hollow ring for repeats. The polarization of our parties is a lot of what these reformers promised to overcome. Progressivism is now locked in the Democratic Party, a party unified by its defense of the policy state, and it has lost the critical capacity to communicate with those disillusioned by its shortfalls.

The question of the day: Is there a game change imminent in current national politics? As we write, the players to watch are those who feel boxed out by the debates, the prescriptions, and the guidance generated from within. A century ago, Progressivism drew on the energy of organized labor to break through received arrangements of authority. The same holds for progressivism's opponents today, energized by frustrations gestating out of doors. The presidential campaign of 2016 offered a glimpse of what the insurgency might look like. Its leader, Donald Trump, was "not a policy guy."[102] He did not rest his case on plans vetted by experts. His appeal was less programmatic than visceral and populist. Forging a new coalition of the disaffected, Trump seized control of the Republican Party and altered the conservatives' critique. His forthright repudiation of "the establishment" rallied national enthusiasm for a "great disruption." A man of independent means and no political experience, he declared the system rigged, corrosive, and corrupt. He promised to "drain the swamp." He rose to power on the collapse of faith in the institutions and practices on which progressives have pegged their hopes.

For the moment, the policy state reveals itself as elites across the spectrum closing ranks against the attack. Claiming for themselves treasured norms of sound judgment and responsible decision making, leading lights from inside government, the media, the universities, the expertocracy, have renounced the interloper as unfit, erratic, and a danger to national security. Many conservatives who previously spearheaded the phalanx against the status quo have expressed qualms about the insurgent or defected outright. Trump's victory threatens to break up the progressive-conservative divide that has dominated party politics since the Reagan Revolution. But what are the prospects for a post-policy state of the populist variety? Is that any more likely to come to pass than the more deliberative or juridical alternatives discussed earlier? Might we expect established elites to harry the Trump people, to hound them for details, demand they adopt more familiar styles of political combat? Even during the presidential campaign, enthusiasm for the new populism was tempered by the thought that Trump would ultimately have to surround himself with sober and knowledgeable advisors. The post-election transition sent mixed signals on that score. The new administration appointed strategically placed disruptors alongside veterans of investment banks, major corporations, and the armed services.

One thing seems certain. The Trump presidency has accelerated a crisis of authority that has been building for decades. This crisis is a product not of this policy or that, or of one type of policy or another, but of the priority of policy itself. This has been the change beneath our feet, the solution that has dissolved the foundations it sought only to improve. The Trump movement seems no less interested in results than its adversaries, and the contest between them shows every sign of extending the pattern of development brought to light in this book. Pivoting off the policy state, the combatants push hard against the few rules and norms still in play.

Notes

Acknowledgments

Index

Notes

1. PUBLIC POLICY AND STATE FORMATION

1. The last and most comprehensive effort along these lines remains Theodore Lowi, *The End of Liberalism* (New York: Norton, 1969). Other suggestive treatments include James Q. Wilson, "American Politics, Then & Now," in *"American Politics Then & Now" and Other Essays* (Washington, D.C.: American Enterprise Institute, 2010), 3–18; Hugh Heclo, "Sixties Civics," in *The Great Society and the High Tide of Liberalism*, ed. Sidney Milkis and Jerry Mileur (Amherst: University of Massachusetts Press, 2005), 63–83; Jacob Hacker and Paul Pierson, "After the 'Master Theory': Downs, Schattschneider, and the Rebirth of Policy-Focused Analysis," *Perspectives on Politics* 12 (2014): 643–662.

2. Final revisions on this manuscript were completed in January and February 2017, just after the consolidation of Republican control of the federal government and with the Trump administration just taking shape.

3. The term *post-policy politics* appears, for example, in "Social Security, Republicans, and Post- Policy Politics," MaddowBlog, MSNBC, October 10, 2013, http://www.msnbc.com/rachel-maddow-show/social-security-republicans -and-post-p; and Paul Krugman, "The Crazies and the Con Man," *New York Times*, October 12, 2015.

4. Zeke Miller, "Obama Says He Wants to 'Get Stuff Done,'" *Time*, November 5, 2014.

5. "Obama on Executive Actions: 'I've Got a Pen and I've Got a Phone,'" CBS DC, January 14, 2014, http://washington.cbslocal.com/2014/01/14/Obama -on-executive-actions.

6. On the "we-can't-wait" campaign, see Richard Wolfe, "Obama Uses Executive Power to Get Past Congress," *USA Today*, October, 27, 2011. After the Republican takeover of the House in 2010, this became a recurrent theme of the Obama presidency, reiterated in his 2014 State of the Union address. Obama has been called to account for the expectation raised by his agitation for action. David Remnick reports Obama's response to a heckler demanding immediate, unilateral action to stop the deportation of immigrants: "If, in fact, I could solve all these problems without passing laws in Congress, then I would do so, but we're also a nation of laws"; see "Going the Distance: On and Off the Road with Barack Obama," *New Yorker*, January 27, 2014, 48–49.

7. Remarks by the President on the Supreme Court Decision in U.S. v. Texas, White House, Office of the Press Secretary, June 23, 2016.

8. John Samples, *The Struggle to Limit Government* (Washington, D.C.: Cato Institute, 2010).

9. National Federation of Independent Business v. Sebelius, 132 S. Ct. 2566 (2012), at 2650.

10. Interview, *Face the Nation*, July 21, 2013; Ezra Klein, "Why Democrats and Republicans Don't Understand Each Other," *Vox*, September 14, 2014,

http://www.vox.com/2014/9/15/6131919/democrats-and-republicans-are
-really-different.

11. "In the present crisis, government is not the solution to our problem;
government is the problem"; see Ronald Reagan, "Inaugural Address," January 20, 1981, Gerhard Peters and John Wooley, eds., *The American Presidency Project*, http://www.presidency.ucsb.edu/ws/index.php?pid=43130&st
=&sti=.

12. George W. Bush, *Decision Points* (New York: Crown, 2010), 440.

13. For a recent reassertion of this connection between the Constitution and
the nation—of the Constitution as inextricably linked to the very idea of
being American—see Laurence Tribe, "America's Constitutional Narra-
tive," *Daedalus* 141 (2012): 18–19.

14. Aaron Wildavsky defines *policy analysis* as "an activity creating problems
that can be solved" or "creating and crafting problems worth solving"; see
his *Speaking Truth to Power: The Art and Craft of Policy Analysis* (Boston:
Little Brown, 1979), 17, 389.

15. For instance, Philip Hamburger, *Is Administrative Law Unlawful?*
(Chicago: University of Chicago Press, 2014); Daniel Ernst, *Tocqueville's
Nightmare: The Administrative State Emerges in America, 1900–1940*
(Oxford: Oxford University Press, 2014).

16. William Eskridge Jr. and John Ferejohn, *A Republic of Statutes: The New
American Constitution* (New Haven, CT: Yale University Press, 2010).

17. Bruce Ackerman, *We the People: Transformations* (Cambridge, MA: Harvard University Press, 1998).

18. Steven Calabresi and Christopher Yoo, *The Unitary Executive: Presidential Power from Washington to Bush* (New Haven, CT: Yale University
Press, 2008).

19. This is not to ignore constitutional scholarship that is close in spirit to our
own. For a sampling, see Mark Tushnet, "Constitutional Hardball," *John
Marshall Law Review* 37 (2004): 523–553; Edward Rubin, *Beyond Camelot:
Rethinking Politics and Law for the Modern State* (Princeton, NJ: Princeton
University Press, 2005); Richard Pildes, "Romanticizing Democracy, Po-
litical Fragmentation, and the Decline of American Government," *Yale
Law Journal* 124 (2014): 804–852.

20. E. E. Schattschneider, *Politics, Pressures, and the Tariff* (New York: Prentice Hall, 1935); Theodore Lowi, *Arenas of Power* (New York: Norton, 2008).

21. Paul Pierson, "When Effect Becomes Cause: Policy Feedback and Political
Change," *World Politics* 45 (1993): 595–628.

22. Paul Pierson, "Increasing Returns, Path Dependence, and the Study of Pol-
itics," *American Political Science Review* 94 (2000): 251–267. See also Eric
Patashnik, *Reforms at Risk: What Happens after Major Policy Changes Are
Enacted* (Princeton, NJ: Princeton University Press, 2008).

23. Jacob Hacker, *The Divided Welfare State: The Battle over Public and
Private Social Benefits in the United States* (New York: Cambridge Uni-
versity Press, 2002); Marie Gottschalk, *The Shadow Welfare State: Labor,
Business and the Politics of Health Care in the United States* (Ithaca, NY:
Cornell University Press, 2000).

24. Joanna Grisinger, *The Unwieldy State: Administrative Politics since the New Deal* (New York: Cambridge University Press, 2012).

25. John Dewey, *The Public and Its Problems* (New York: Henry Holt, 1927).

26. On the relationship between liberalism and the art of demolition, see Karen Orren, *Belated Feudalism* (New York: Cambridge University Press, 1992), 40–45.

27. But note the upending of what were thought to be the sturdiest of the iron triangles during the regulatory revolution of the 1980s. Martha Derthick and Paul Quirk, *The Politics of Deregulation* (Washington, D.C.: Brookings Institution, 1985). See also the complications of capture theory outlined by Daniel Carpenter and David Moss, "Introduction," in *Preventing Regulatory Capture: Special Interest Influence and How to Limit It*, ed. Daniel Carpenter and David Moss (New York: Cambridge University Press, 2014), 1–22.

28. But see work on the persistent manipulation of the social security program, allegedly the untouchable third rail of American government: Alan Jacobs, "Policymaking as Political Constraint: Institutional Development in the U.S. Social Security Program," in *Explaining Institutional Change: Ambiguity, Agency and Power*, ed. James Mahoney and Kathleen Thelen (New York: Cambridge University Press, 2010), 94–131; Daniel Beland, "Ideas and Institutional Change in Social Security: Conversion, Layering, and Policy Drift," *Social Science Quarterly* 88 (2007): 20–38.

29. Frank Baumgartner and Bryan Jones, *Agendas and Instability in American Politics* (Chicago: University of Chicago Press, 2009).

30. On issue networks, see Hugh Heclo, "Issue Networks and the Executive Establishment," in *The New American Political System*, ed. Anthony King (Washington, D.C.: American Enterprise Institute, 1978), 87–125; on "windows" and "streams," see John Kingdon, *Agendas, Alternatives, and Public Policies* (Boston: Little, Brown, 1984).

31. James Mahoney and Kathleen Thelen, "A Theory of Gradual Institutional Change," in *Explaining Institutional Change*, 1–37.

32. Jacob Hacker, "Privatizing Risk without Privatizing the Welfare State: The Hidden Politics of Social Policy Retrenchment in the United States," *American Political Science Review* 98 (2005): 243–260.

33. William Novak, "The Myth of the Weak American State," *American Historical Review* 113 (2008): 752–772.

34. Richard John, *Spreading the News: The American Postal System from Franklin to Morse* (Cambridge, MA: Harvard University Press, 1995); Brian Balogh, *A Government Out of Sight: The Mystery of National Authority in Nineteenth-Century America* (Cambridge: Cambridge University Press, 2009).

35. Jerry Mashaw, *The Administrative Constitution: The Lost One Hundred Years of American Administrative Law* (New Haven, CT: Yale University Press, 2012); Daniel Carpenter, "Completing the Constitution: Progressive-Era Economic Regulation and the Political Perfection of Article I, Section 8," in *The Progressives' Century*, ed. Stephen Skowronek, Stephen Engel, and Bruce Ackerman (New Haven, CT: Yale University Press, 2016), 291–315.

36. Laura Jenson, *Patriots, Settlers, and the Origins of American Social Policy* (New York: Cambridge University Press, 2003); William Novak, *The People's Welfare: Law and Regulation in Nineteenth-Century America* (Chapel Hill: University of North Carolina Press, 1996); Theda Skocpol, *Protecting Soldiers and Mothers: The Political Origins of Social Policy in the United States* (Cambridge, MA: Harvard University Press, 1992).

37. Max Edling, *A Revolution in Favor of Government: Origins of the U.S. Constitution and the Making of the American State* (New York: Oxford University Press, 2003); Paul Frymer, " 'A Rush and a Push and the Land Is Ours': Territorial Expansion, Land Policy and U.S. State Formation," *Perspectives on Politics* 12 (2012): 119–144.

38. Novak draws these connections directly. See also the parallel treatment by Gerald Berk, Daniel Galvan, and Victoria Hattam, eds., *Political Creativity: Rethinking Institutional Order and Change* (Philadelphia: University of Pennsylvania Press, 2013); Morton White, *Social Thought in America: The Revolt against Formalism* (New York: Viking, 1949).

39. James Willard Hurst, *Law and Social Order in the United States* (Ithaca, NY: Cornell University Press, 1977), 25.

40. Novak, "Myth of the Weak American State," 765.

41. Another area already under the authority of the national legislature is the organization and regulation of officeholders. This too had been an ancient hierarchy, with the king at the top. It was ended by Parliament and by the civil war in the seventeenth century. In the United States, this authority was inherited by American legislatures. One of the first laws Congress passed was to adopt practices of English office holding provided at common law into U.S. statutes. We have not listed office holding within the policy space as we discuss it here because its locale is within government itself, but its import will become evident. The subject of nonconstitutional office holding is subject to the same analysis we apply elsewhere. We deal with it briefly in Chapter 3. See Leonard White, *The Federalist: A Study in Administrative History* (Westport, CT: Greenwood Press, 1948), 424–443. For an excellent study of American office-holding policy over time see Nicholas Parillo, *Against the Profit Motive: The Salary Revolution in American Government* (New Haven, CT: Yale University Press, 2013).

2. THE POLICY MOTIVE

1. Karen Orren and Stephen Skowronek, *The Search for American Political Development* (New York: Cambridge University Press, 2004), 22–23.

2. Max Edling, *A Revolution in Favor of Government: Origins of the U.S. Constitution and the Making of the American State* (New York: Oxford University Press, 2003).

3. Philip Hamburger, "The Constitution's Accommodation of Social Change," *Michigan Law Review* 88 (1989): 239; Howard Gillman, "The Collapse of Constitutional Originalism and the Rise of the Notion of the 'Living Constitution' in the Course of American State Building," *Studies in American Political Development* 11 (1997): 191–247.

4. James Kent, *Commentaries on American Law* (New York: O. Halstead, 1827), 2: 201–209.

5. There was the odd exception, for instance, when national government was the employer.

6. Cited in Russell Kirk, *John Randolph of Roanoke: A Study in American Politics*, 4th ed. (Indianapolis, IN: Liberty Fund, 1997), 214.

7. Cited in Russell Kirk, *The Conservative Mind: From Burke to Elliot*, 7th rev. ed. (Washington, D.C.: Regnery, 1985), 159.

8. Ibid., 163. Randolph goes further in this passage to impugn the role of interpretation in settling constitutional meaning: "Shall we get some learned and cunning clerk to say whether the power to do this is to be found in the constitution, and then, if he, from whatever motive, shall maintain the affirmative . . . quietly lie down."

9. Richard E. Ellis, *The Union at Risk: Jacksonian Democracy, States' Rights, and the Nullification Crisis* (New York: Oxford University Press, 1987).

10. John C. Calhoun, "Exposition and Protest" (1828); "The Fort Hill Address: On the Relations of the States and the Federal Government" (1831); "Speech on the Revenue Collection Bill" (1833), collected in John C. Calhoun, *Union and Liberty: The Political Philosophy of John C. Calhoun*, ed. Ross M. Lence (Indianapolis, IN: Liberty Fund, 1992). See also James Read, *Majority Rule versus Consensus: The Political Thought of John C. Calhoun* (Lawrence: University Press of Kansas, 2009).

11. John C. Calhoun, *A Discourse on the Constitution and Government of the United States* and *A Disquisition on Government*, in *John C. Calhoun: Selected Writings and Speeches*, ed. H. Lee Cheek, Jr. (Washington, D.C.: Regnery, 2003).

12. Bertrand de Jouvenel, *On Power: Its Nature and the History of Its Growth* [1945] (Boston: Beacon, 1962), 283–316.

13. Note that concern about the primacy of preferences has not been limited to the political Right. For instance, Max Horkheimer, for many the inspiration for the New Left, covered much the same ground in 1947 in taking issue with the modern equation of ends with desires, interests, and capacity. Targeting American pragmatists in particular, Horkheimer's critique culminates with a typical example of such reasoning drawn from John Dewey: "Faith in the power of intelligence to imagine a future which is the projection of the desirable in the present, and to invent the instrumentalities of its realization, is our salvation"; see Max Horkheimer, *The Eclipse of Reason* [1947] (London: Continuum, 1974), 3–39, esp. 32, 37.

14. Karen Orren, "Officers' Rights: Toward a Unified Field Theory of Constitutional Development," *Law and Society Review* 34 (2001): 873.

15. Jeremy Bentham, *Anarchical Fallacies: Being an Examination of the Declaration of Rights Issued During the French Revolution*, in *The Works of Jeremy Bentham*, 11 vols., ed. John Bowring (Edinburgh: William Tait, 1843), 2: 501.

16. For an inventory of claims based on design and structure, see Richard Pious, *The American Presidency* (New York: Basic, 1979), 42–45.

17. Another Southerner, quick to see this quality of Constitutional structure, spoke of a "machine called inference." "A government, by an unlimited power of construction, may stretch constitutions . . . or interpret them, as synods do scripture, according to the temporal interest of the predominant sect"; see John Taylor, *Construction Construed and Constitutions Vindicated* (Richmond, VA: Sheperd and Pollard, 1820), 23.

18. James Madison, "Federalist #51," in John Jay, Alexander Hamilton, and James Madison, *The Federalist Papers* [1788] (New York: New American Library, 1961), 320–335.

19. Note that translations and transpositions of this sort do not necessarily expand policy's domain. Calhoun used the same reasoning from structural principles to promote the concurrent majority and the plural executive.

20. For a discussion of how much authority shifted with the Civil War amendments, see Orren and Skowronek, *The Search for American Political Development,* 133–143.

21. Mary Dudziak, *Cold War Civil Rights: Race and the Image of American Democracy* (Princeton, NJ: Princeton University Press, 2000); Kim Lane Scheppele, "The New Judicial Deference," *Boston Law Review* 89 (2012): 92.

22. We take the term *parastate* from Eldon Eisenach, *The Lost Promise of Progressivism* (Lawrence: University Press of Kansas, 1994).

3. RIGHTS IN THE POLICY STATE

1. Jonathan A. Bush, " 'You're Gonna Miss Me When I'm Gone': Early Modern Common Law Discourse and the Case of the Jews," *Wisconsin Law Review* (1993): 1225–1285.

2. Charles Howard McIlwain, *The High Court of Parliament and Its Supremacy: An Historical Essay on the Boundaries between Legislation and Adjudication in England* (New Haven, CT: Yale University Press, 1910).

3. N. A. M. Rodger, "Queen Elizabeth and the Myth of Sea Power in English History," *Transactions of the RHS* 14 (2004): 153–174; William Palmer, "High Officeholding, Foreign Policy, and the British Dimension in the Tudor Far North, 1525–1563," *Albion* 29 (1997): 579–595; Felix Gilbert, "The English Background of American Isolationism in the Eighteenth Century," *William and Mary Quarterly* 1 (1944): 138–160; also see G. R. Elton, "Review: 'Before the Armada, the Growth of English Foreign Policy, 1485–1588,' by R. B. Wernham," *English Historical Review* 83 (1968): 122–125.

4. A graph showing the convergence between "fiscal-military" and "civil" spending can be found in Steve Pincus and James Robinson, "Wars and State-Making Reconsidered: The Rise of the Developmental State," translated as an online PDF from publication in French at warsandstatemaking@law.nyu.edu.

5. On common law rules and slavery before the Civil War, see Thomas D. Morris, " 'Villeinage . . . as It Existed in England, Reflects but Little Light on Our Subject': The Problem of the 'Sources' of Southern Slave Law," *American Journal of Legal History* 32 (1988): 95–137; and Bradley J. Nicholson, "Legal Borrowing and the Origins of Slave Law in the British Colonies," *American Journal of Legal History* 38 (1994): 38–54.

6. Inter alia, see Ronald Dworkin, *Taking Rights Seriously* (London: Duckworth, 1977), 6 and passim.

7. For an argument different from our own on this point, see Richard H. Pildes, "Why Rights Are Not Trumps: Social Meaning, Expressive Harms and Constitutionalism," *Journal of Legal Studies* 27 (1998): 725–763.

8. Although our emphasis is different, we are hardly the first to recognize these characteristics. See, for instance, T. Alexander Aleinikoff, "Constitutional Law in the Age of Balancing," *Yale Law Journal* 96 (1987): 943–1005; Kathleen M. Sullivan, "Post-Liberal Judging: The Roles of Categorization and Balancing," *University of Colorado Law Review* 63 (1992): 293–317; Judd Mathews and Alex Stone Sweet, "All Things in Proportion? American Rights Review and the Problem of Balancing," *Emory Law Journal* 60 (2011): 797–875.

9. Our observations have obvious relevance to the better-recognized fact of rights' changing distribution among members of society, against which alterations from trumps to chips have often been a trade-off. If there is disappointment in that reality, some consolation may be found in the fact that the rights-as-trumps of elites—property owners and high officers of the church and the state—were the first to see their "rightness" diminished.

10. Town of Castle Rock v. Gonzales, 545 U.S. 748 (2005).

11. Section 1983 reads, "Every person who, under color of any statute, ordinance, regulation, custom, or usage, of any State or Territory or the District of Columbia, subjects, or causes to be subjected, any citizen of the United States or other person within the jurisdiction thereof to the deprivation of any rights, privileges, or immunities secured by the Constitution and laws, shall be liable to the party injured in an action at law, suit in equity, or other proper proceeding for redress."

12. The statute mandates enforcement of a domestic restraining order upon probable cause of a violation, §18–6–803.5(3), while another part directs that police officers "shall, without undue delay, arrest" a suspect upon "probable cause to believe that a crime or offense of domestic violence has been committed," §18–6–803.6(1).

13. 545 U.S. 748, at 784.

14. See generally W. S. Holdsworth, *A History of English Law* (Boston, MA: Little, Brown, 1923), 3: 278–287.

15. 545 U.S. 748, at 761–762.

16. Ibid., at 768.

17. Ibid., at 749.

18. Ibid., at 760, 765.

19. Ibid., at 768.

20. Roger A. Hanson and Henry W. K. Daley, *Challenging the Conditions of Prisoners and Jails: A Report on Section 1983* (Washington, D.C.: U.S. Department of Justice, Bureau of Justice Statistics, 1995), 2–3.

21. 545 U.S. 748, at 793.

22. Ibid., at 775.

23. Ibid., at 778, n.6.

24. Ibid., at 771.

25. Ibid., at 790 (quoting Board of Regents of State Colleges v. Roth, 408 U.S. 564 [1972], at 577).

26. Ibid., at 772.

27. See Sally F. Goldfarb, "Reconceiving Civil Protection Orders for Domestic Violence: Can Law Help End the Abuse without Ending the Relationship?" *Cardozo Law Review* (2008): 1487–1551, 1495.

28. William Blackstone, *Commentaries on the Laws of England* (Chicago, IL: University of Chicago Press, 1979) 1: 430.

29. For a good overview, see Carl Tobias, "Interspousal Tort Immunity in America," *Georgia Law Review* 23 (1988–1989): 359–478.

30. As passed in 1901, the full statute for D.C. reads: "SEC. 1155. Power of Wife to Trade and Sue and be Sued.—Married women shall have power to engage in any business, and to contract, whether engaged in business or not, and to sue separately upon their contracts, and also to sue separately for the recovery, security, or protection of their property, and for torts committed against them, as fully and freely as if they were unmarried; contracts may also be made with them, and they may also be sued separately upon their contracts, whether made before or during marriage, and for wrongs independent of contract committed by them before or during their marriage, as fully as if they were unmarried, and upon judgments recovered against them execution may be issued as if they were unmarried; nor shall any husband be liable upon any contract made by his wife in her own name and upon her own responsibility, nor for any tort committed separately by her out of his presence without his participation or sanction: Provided, That no married woman shall have power to make any contract as surety or guarantor, or as accommodation drawer, acceptor, maker, or indorser."

31. Thompson v. Thompson, 218 U.S. 611 (1910), at 617, 622.

32. Rollin C. Hurd, *A Treatise on the Right of Personal Liberty and Habeas Corpus* (Albany, NY: W. C. Little, 1858), 34–40.

33. Fouke v. People, 4 Colo. App. 519, at 528 (1894).

34. The phrase is from Blackstone, *Commentaries*, 1: 453.

35. Randy Frances Kandel, "Just Ask the Kid! Toward a Rule of Children's Choice in Custody Determinations," *University of Miami Law Review* 49 (1994): 299–376, 315ff; also see Rena K. Uviller, "Fathers' Rights and Feminism: The Maternal Presumption Revisited," *Harvard Women's Law Journal* 1 (1978): 107–130.

36. Kandel, "Just Ask the Kid!" n.131, provides a "typical" statute: "As between parents adversely claiming the custody, neither parent is entitled to it as of right; but other things being equal, if the child is of tender years, it should be given to the mother; if it is of an age to require education and preparation for labor and business, then to the father." Horsley v. Horsley, 175 P. 2d 580, at 583 (Cal. Ct. App, 1946) quoting Cal. Civ. Code 138 (replaced 1970).

37. Robert H. Mnookin, "Child Custody Adjudication: Judicial Functions in the Face of Indeterminacy," *Law and Contemporary Problems* 39 (1975): 226–293, 227.

38. See J. Herbie DiFonzo, "From the Rule of One to Shared Parenting: Custody Presumptions in Law and Policy," *Family Court Review* 52 (2014): 213–239, 217.

39. The Civil Rights Cases, 109 U.S. 3, 25 (1883).

40. Ibid., at 62.

41. Among a huge literature, a comprehensive study is Thomas Morris, *Southern Slavery and the Law* (Chapel Hill: University of North Carolina Press, 1996).

42. Brown v. Board of Education of Topeka, 347 U.S. 483 (1954).

43. Ibid., at 492–493.

44. Holmes v. City of Atlanta, 350 U.S. 879 (1955) (public golf courses); Muir v. Louisville Park Theatrical Ass'n, 347 U.S. 971 (1954) (municipally owned amphitheater); Dawson v. Mayor of Baltimore, 220 F.2d 386 (4th Cir.) (public beaches); 350 U.S. 877 (1955); Gayle v. Browder, 352 U.S. 903 (1956) (public buses); New Orleans City Park Improvement Association v. Detiege, 358 U.S. 54 (1958) (public park).

45. Bolling v. Sharpe, 347 U.S. 497, 500 (1954); emphasis in original.

46. Brown v. Board, at 493.

47. Bolling, 347 U.S., at 499–500. Some of the difference might be explained by the equal protection clause in the Fourteenth Amendment, applicable to the (then) forty-eight states, as opposed to the more nuanced due process provision of the Fifth Amendment. *Bolling*, however, said that the two clauses were "not mutually exclusive," and that "discrimination may be so unjustifiable as to be violative of due process" (ibid., 499).

48. McLauglin v. Florida, 379 U.S. 184 (1964), at 192. The opinion cites, for "rigid scrutiny," Korematsu v. United States, 323 U.S. 214 (1944), at 216, where it was first used. "It should be noted, to begin with, that all legal restrictions which curtail the civil rights of a single racial group are immediately suspect. That is not to say that all such restrictions are unconstitutional. It is to say that courts must subject them to the most rigid scrutiny. Pressing public necessity may sometimes justify the existence of such restrictions; racial antagonism never can."

49. Perry Educ. Ass'n. v. Perry Local Educators' Ass'n, 460 U.S. 37 (1983); Miller v. Johnson, 515 U.S. 900, at 915 (1995); Fla. Star v. B. J. F., 491 U.S. 524, 538 (1989). On strict scrutiny generally, see Richard H. Fallon, Jr., "Strict Judicial Scrutiny," 54 *UCLA Law Review* (2007). 1267/–1337.

50. Reed v. Reed, 404 U.S. 71 (1971) (rational basis, sex, probate administrators); Craig v. Boren, 429 U.S. 190 (1976), at 197–198 (intermediate, sex, alcohol sales); Cleland v. National College of Business, 435 U.S. 213 (1978) (heightened, veteran benefits, education); Arcara v. Cloud Books, Inc., 478 U.S. 697 (1986), at 706–707. "Heightened scrutiny" first appears as a test (rejected as applied to "the poor" at p. 28) in San Antonio Sch. Dist v. Rodriguez, 411 U.S. 1 (1973).

51. See Joseph O. Oluwole and Preston C. Green III, "Harrowing through Narrow Tailoring: Voluntary Race-Conscious Student Assignment Plans, Parents Involved and Fisher," *Wyoming Law Review* 14 (2014): 705–774.

52. Adarand Constructors v. Pena, 515 U.S. 200 (1995).

53. Grutter v. Bollinger, 539 U.S. 306 (2003); and at 280.

54. Ibid., at 327 (quoting Adarand, 515 U.S. at 228).

55. Korematsu, n.48 above.

56. Regents of University of California v. Bakke, 438 U.S. 265 (1978).

57. Ibid., at 299.

58. Ibid., at 314.

59. See, for example, Cooper v. Aaron, 358 U.S. 1 (1958).

60. For a recent decision, see Texas Department of Housing and Community Affairs v. The Inclusive Communities Project, Inc., 135 S. Ct. 2507 (2015).

61. Civil Rights Act of 1964, Section VI. Pub. L. 88–352. 78 Stat. 241. 2 Jul. 1964.

62. Respondent's brief in Bakke, June 11, 1977, 9.

63. For an example of a case arising from such circumstances, see Wygant v. Jackson Board of Education, 476 U.S. 267 (1986). For a critique, see Kenneth L. Karst, "The Revival of Forward-Looking Affirmative Action," *Columbia Law Review* 104 (2004): 60–74.

64. Bakke, 438 U.S., at 400.

65. Gratz v. Bollinger, 539 U.S. 244 (2003).

66. For further examples of the Court's narrow tailoring analysis, see Adarand, supra note 15. See also Ward v. Rock against Racism, 491 U.S. 781 (1989).

67. Gratz, at 275–276.

68. Grutter, at 321 (quoting Grutter v. Bollinger, 288 F.3d 732 [6th Cir. 2002]).

69. Ibid., at 337.

70. Ibid., at 315.

71. Fisher v. University of Texas, Austin, 758 F.3d 633, 676 (5th Cir. 2014).

72. Fisher v. Univ. of Texas, 136 S. Ct. 2198; and at 2209.

73. Ibid., at 2210.

74. Ibid., at 2208.

75. On this system and its role in the subsequent political development in the United States, see Orren, *Belated Feudalism*, passim.

76. 301 U.S. 1 (1937).

77. James Gray Pope, "The Thirteenth Amendment versus the Commerce Clause: Labor and the Shaping of American Constitutional Law, 1921–1957," *Columbia Law Review* 102 (2002): 1–122.

78. 29 U.S.C §102. Justice Frankfurter defended this policy-based approach, rejecting the notion that declaring "the public policy of the United States" in a statute's text was an affront to states' rights. He wrote, "To ask: May Congress adopt a federal law for industrial litigation? is to pose a misleading issue. A candid regard for fact would ask: May Congress exercise its responsibility for formulating rules and practices for controversies that are now determined by individual conceptions of policy more or less conscious in the minds of judges, and conform such notions to explicit legislative expression of national policy?" Felix Frankfurter and Nathan Greene, "Congressional Power over the Labor Injunction," *Columbia Law Review* 31 (1931): 385–415, 395.

79. Archibald Cox and Marshall J. Seidman, "Federalism and Labor Relations," *Harvard Law Review* 64 (1950): 211–245.

80. Chamber of Commerce of the United States of America v. Brown 554 U.S. 60 (2008).

81. Justice Stevens citing California Assembly Bill (AB) 1889, ibid., at 62.

82. Ibid., at 65. Stevens is quoting from Machinists v. Wisconsin Employment Relations Comm'n, 427 U.S. 132 (1976), at 140. The phrase was originally in Archibald Cox, "Labor Law Preemption Revisited," *Harvard Law Review* 85 (1972): 1337–1377, 1351.

83. The modern preemption doctrine is associated with Pennsylvania v. Nelson, 450 U.S. 497 (1956).

84. 314 U.S. 469 (1941).

85. 323 U.S. 516 (1945), at 531.

86. Republic Aviation Corp. v. NLRB 324 U.S. 793 (1945), at 798.

87. Ibid., at 805.

88. See NLRB v. Babcock & Wilcox Co., 351 U.S. 105 (1956), at 112. The same principle was established in Teamsters Union v. Hanke, 339 U.S. 470 (1950), where the Court affirmed a state court injunction against union picketing in front of a family-owned automobile repair shop which, until purchased by the Hanke family, had been conducted as a union shop; and in Teamsters Union v. Vogt, 354 U.S. 284 (1957), where the Court affirmed a second injunction against labor picketing (this time at a gravel pit in Wisconsin), and further bolstered these pro-employer rulings.

89. See, for example, Cynthia L. Estlund, "Labor, Property, and Sovereignty after Lechmere," *Stanford Law Review* 46 (1994): 305–359.

90. Food Employees v. Logan Valley Plaza, Inc., 391 U.S. 308 (1968), at 337.

91. Hudgens v. NLRB, 424 U.S. 507 (1976), at 521.

92. NLRB v. Retail Store Employees Union, 447 U.S. 607, at 618 (concurring opinion).

93. Lechmere, Inc. v. NLRB, 502 U.S. 527 (1992), at 536. In 2003, an appeals court declined to apply an owning company's ban against the leaflets naming itself or its tenants, on the ground that it was "content based," contrary to protection of speech under the California constitution. Glendale Assocs., Ltd. v. NLRB, 347 F.3d 1145.

94. On the history of the FAA, see Stephen L. Hayford, "The Unification of the Law of Labor Arbitration and Commercial Arbitration: An Idea Whose Time Has Come," *Baylor Law Review* 52 (2000): 781–928. For an overview of arbitration statutes in the federal courts, see James E. Berger and Charlotte Sun, "The Evolution of Judicial Review under the Federal Arbitration Act," *NYU Journal of Law and Business* 5 (2009): 745–792.

95. The cases in the trilogy are United Steelworkers of America v. American Manufacturing Co., 363 U.S. 564 (1960); United Steelworkers of America v. Warrior & Gulf Navigation Co., 363 U.S. 574 (1960); and United Steelworkers of America v. Enterprise Wheel and Car Corp., 363 U.S. 593 (1960). An insightful discussion is Katherine V. W. Stone, "The Steelworkers Trilogy and the Evolution of Labor Arbitration," in *Labor Law Stories*, ed. Laura Cooper and Catherine Fisk (New York: Foundation Press, 2004), 149–190.

96. Alexander v. Gardner-Denver Co., 415 U.S. 36 (1974), at 40–41.

97. 556 U.S. 247 (2009).

98. Ibid., at 277.
99. Ibid., at 274.
100. See, e.g., https://www.congress.gov/bill/111th-congress/senate-bill/560.
101. See Floyd D. Weatherspoon, "Incorporating Mandatory Arbitration Employment Clauses into Collective Bargaining Agreements: Challenges and Benefits to the Employer and the Union," *Delaware Journal of Corporate Law* 38 (2013–2014): 1025–1071.
102. For an interesting discussion, see Clyde W. Summers, "The Privatization of Personal Freedom and Enrichment of Democracy: Some Lessons from Labor Law," *University of Illinois Law Review* (1986): 689–724.
103. But see Mathews v. Denver Newspaper Agency LLP, 2008 U.S. Dist. LEXIS 119417 (2008).
104. See, for instance, Justice Souter's Pyett dissent, 556 U.S. 247, at 279, 281.
105. Pope, "The Thirteenth Amendment versus the Commerce Clause," passim.
106. See on this Act and generally, Claire Priest, "Creating an American Property Law: Alienability and Its Limits in American History," *Harvard Law Review* 189 (2006): 385–459, 389 and passim.
107. Ibid., 387. The comment is from Joseph Story, *Commentaries on the Constitution of the United States* (Boston, MA: Hilliard, Gray, 1833), §182.
108. 545 U.S. 469 (2005).
109. Ibid., at 504. Prior to 1875, state government undertook the condemnation of property for the post offices, forts, and customs houses the federal government required; the same applies to state agencies. "Although the 'use by the public' test continues to be raised occasionally by counsel litigating state takings, its effect is virtually nil"; see "The Public Use Limitation on Eminent Domain: An Advance Requiem," *Yale Law Journal* 58 (1949): 599–614, 608.
110. Dana Berliner, "Looking Back Ten Years after Kelo," *Yale Law Journal Forum* 125 (2015): 82–93, 90.
111. On states in the North, see Richard H. Chused, "Married Women's Property Law: 1800–1850," *Georgetown Law Journal* 71 (1982–1983): 1359–1425, 1398–1399.
112. Peggy A. Rabkin, "The Origins of Law Reform: The Social Significance of the Nineteenth-Century Codification Movement and Its Contribution to the Passage of the Early Married Women's Property Acts," *Buffalo Law Review* 24 (1974–1975): 683–760.
113. Karen Orren, "Doing Time: A Theory of the Constitution," *Studies in American Political Development* 26 (2012): 71–81, 72–73.
114. Buchanan v. Warley, 245 U.S. 60 (1917).
115. Booth v. Illinois, 184 U.S. 425 (1902), at 428; Otis v. Parker, 187 U.S. 606 (1903), at 609.
116. 334 U.S. 1 (1948).
117. Moose Lodge no. 107 v. Irvis, 407 U.S. 163 (1972); Donald M. Cahen, "The Impact of *Shelley v. Kraemer* and the State Action Concept," *California Law Review* 44 (1956): 718–736.

118. See, for example, John A. Huston, "Constitutional Law: State Court Enforcement of Race Restrictive Covenants as State Action within Scope of Fourteenth Amendment," *Michigan Law Review* 45 (1946–1947): 733–748.
119. Vynior's Case, 7 Jac. I, Coke's Repts. Part VIII, 8 (1609).
120. Adair v. United States, 208 U.S. 161 (1908).
121. Ibid., at 174.
122. 303 U.S. 552.
123. Ibid., at 561.
124. Cf. NAACP v. Button, 371 U.S. 415 (1963); NAACP v. Claiborne Hardware Co., 458 U.S. 886 (1982).
125. 301 U.S. 1 (1937), at 48–49.
126. United States v. Carolene Products Co., 304 U.S. 144 (1938), n.4. See Jack M. Balkin, "The Footnote," *Northwestern University Law Review* 83 (1988): 275–320. For a different view, see L. A. Powe, "Does Footnote Four Describe?" *Constitutional Commentary* 11 (1994–1995): 197–214.
127. Kurt T. Lash, "James Madison's Celebrated Report of 1800: The Transformation of the Tenth Amendment," *George Washington Law Review* 74 (2006): 165–200, 180–181.
128. 542 U.S. 507, at 534.
129. Hurtado v. California, 110 U.S. 516 (1884), at 531.
130. Hudson County Water Co. v. McCarter, 209 U.S. 349 (1908), at 355.
131. 424 U.S. 319 (1976).
132. An action providing damage suits against federal officeholders was devised by the Supreme Court in *Bivens v. Six Unknown Agents*, 403 U.S. 388 (1971). For a recent example of the Court's general reticence in bestowing Bivens rights, see Ziglar v. Abbasi, 137 S. Ct. 615 (2017).
133. See Aziz Z. Hug, "Judicial Independence and the Rationing of Constitutional Remedies," *Duke Law Journal* 65 (2015): 1–80, 21; Jennifer E. Laurin, "Trawling for Herring: Lessons in Doctrinal Borrowing and Convergence," *Columbia Law Review* 111 (2011): 670–744, 706. A more deliberate strategy is attributed to the shift in Sheldon Nahmod, "Section 1983 Discourse: The Move from Constitutional to Tort," *Georgetown Law Journal* 74 (1989): 1719–1752.
134. Ann Woolhandler, "The Common Law Origins of Constitutionally Compelled Remedies," *Yale Law Journal* 107 (1997): 77–164, 84.
135. Slaughterhouse Cases, 83 U.S. 36 (1872); United States v. Harris, 106 U.S. 629 (1883); United States v. Cruikshank, 92 U.S. 542 (1875).
136. Wadleigh v. Newhall, 136 F. 941 (1905), at 946.
137. 307 U.S. 496.
138. 310 U.S. 586, at 597, 602–607.
139. 319 U.S. 624, at 639–640.
140. 365 U.S. 167. The doubt—even humility—registered along the way is striking. The beginning of the district court's opinion in *Hague* is worth quoting:

This case seeks the solution of the problem inevitable and inherent in a democratic form of government. Upon its sound solution the preservation of that form of government may well be said to depend. For that reason we repeat the hope, expressed at the trial, that this opinion will prove only an indistinct sign-post on the road to the ultimate wisdom of the highest tribunal. We spoke of seeking a solution advisedly. We are going to assume, or should we say presume, that both parties to the litigation are convinced that their opposing points of view are in the interest of that democracy we are sure both believe in. . . . As in many matters of political science there exists a necessity for balance and a consequent inability to agree as to the proper adjustment of the scales. (Committee for Indus. Org. v. Hague, 25 F. Supp. 127 [1938], at 129)

The experimental ethos reflects the inherent instability of constitutional rights in the policy state. The *Hague* majority itself, as we have seen, rested on a three-way rationale.

141. Above, p. 47, n. 20. For a starting point in a large literature see Ronald A. Cass, "Damage Suits Against Public Officers," *University of Pennsylvania Law Review* 129 (1981): 1110–1188.

142. Pierson v. Ray, 386 U.S. 547 (1967), at 555.

143. The case in view here is *Brown v. Allen*, 344 U.S. 443 (1953). But see Eric M. Freeman, "*Brown v. Allen*: The Habeas Corpus Revolution That Wasn't," *Alabama Law Review* 51 (2000): 1541–1624.

144. Fay v. Noia, 372 U.S. 391 (1963).

145. 424 U.S. 319 (1976); Goldberg v. Kelly, 397 U.S. 254 (1970).

146. Wainwright v. Sykes, 433 U.S. 72 (1977); Harlow v. Fitzgerald, 457 U.S. 800 (1982); Teague v. Lane, 489 U.S. 288 (1989).

147. Osborn v. Bank of the United States, 22 U.S. 738 (1824); Chisholm v. Georgia, 2 U.S. 419 (1793).

148. Kawananakoa v. Polyblank, 205 U.S. 349 (1907), at 353.

149. 28 U.S. Code, Sec. 2674. Liability of the United States.

150. 28 U.S. Code, Sec. 2680. Exceptions.

151. United States v. Varig Airlines, 467 U.S. 797 (1984), at 814.

152. United States v. Gaubert, 499 U.S. 315, 325 (1991).

153. For example, Mark C. Niles, "Nothing but Mischief: The Federal Tort Claims Act and the Scope of Discretionary Immunity," *Administrative Law Review* 54 (2002): 1275–1354.

154. For discussions of *Hague* as a "sword," see Charles F. Abernathy, "Section 1983 and Constitutional Courts," *Georgetown Law Journal* 77 (1989): 1441–1492, at 1446 n26; and Kermit L. Hall, James W. Ely, and Joel B. Grossman, *Oxford Companion to the United States Supreme Court*, 2nd ed. (Oxford: Oxford University Press, 2005), 567.

4. STRUCTURE IN THE POLICY STATE

1. James Madison, "Report on the Alien and Sedition Acts, 1800," in *Madison: Writings*, ed. Jack N. Rakove (New York: Library of America, 1999), 619–620.

2. Adam Sheingate, "The Terrain of the Political Entrepreneur," in *Formative Acts: American Politics in the Making*, ed. Stephen Skowronek and Matthew Glassman (Philadelphia: University of Pennsylvania Press, 2007), 13–31.

3. National Federation of Independent Business v. Sebelius, 132 S. Ct. 2566 (2012), at 2650.

4. Edward L. Rubin and Malcolm Feeley, "Federalism: Some Notes on a National Neurosis," *UCLA Law Review* 41 (1994): 903–952; Erwin Chemerinsky, "The Values of Federalism," *Florida Law Review* 47 (1995): 499–540.

5. For an example of the standard periodization, see David Walker, *The Rebirth of Federalism* (New York: Chatham House, 2000), 65–140.

6. For a similar treatment from the perspective of the rise of "programmatic" rights, see R. Shep Melnick, "Federalism and the New Rights," in Symposium issue: "Constructing a New Federalism," *Yale Law and Policy Review* 14 (1996): 325–354.

7. Daniel Deudney, "The Philadephian System: Sovereignty, Arms Control and the Balance of Power in the American States-Union, circa 1787–1861," *International Organization* 49 (1995): 191–228.

8. The threat of collective action by the states is implicit in the Virginia and Kentucky Resolutions of 1798, in the call to the Hartford Convention in 1814, in South Carolina's nullification ordinance in 1832, and in Wisconsin's nullification of the Fugitive Slave Act in 1852. See Richard Ellis, *The Union at Risk: Jacksonian Democracy, States' Rights and the Nullification Crisis* (New York: Oxford University Press, 1987); Jeffrey Selinger, "Making Sense of Presidential Restraint: Foundational Arrangements and Executive Decision Making before the Civil War," *Presidential Studies Quarterly* 44 (2014): 27–50; Leslie Goldstein, "State Resistance to Authority in Federal Unions: The Early United States and the European Community," *Studies in American Political Development* 11 (1997): 159–166; Robert Baker, *The Rescue of Joshua Glover: A Fugitive Slave, the Constitution, and the Coming of the Civil War* (Athens: Ohio University Press, 2006); Mark Graber, *Dred Scott and the Problem of Constitutional Evil* (New York: Cambridge University Press, 2006).

9. William Nelson, *The Fourteenth Amendment: From Political Principle to Judicial Doctrine* (Cambridge, MA: Harvard University Press, 1988), 27–36. The role of self-maintenance in compact theory, where the states themselves assume the primary authority to determine the federal relationship, resonates with the prominent role of self-help and self-enforcement in traditional rights in personal relations.

10. Justice Nelson in Collector v. Day, 78 U.S. 113 (1870), at 124.

11. Nelson, *The Fourteenth Amendment*, 181–196. On the reach of the Fourteenth Amendment, see Slaughter-House Cases 83 U.S. 36 (1872), at 77–78: "where it is declared that Congress Shall have the power to enforce that article, was it intended to bring within the power of Congress the entire domain of civil rights heretofore belonging to to exclusively to the States? . . . such a construction followed by the reversal of the judgments of the Supreme Court of Louisiana in these cases, would constitute this

court a perpetual censor upon all legislation of the States, on the civil rights of their own citizens, with authority to nullify such as it did not approve as consistent with those rights, as they existed at the time of the adoption of this amendment. . . . When . . . these consequences are so serious, so far-reaching and pervading, so great a departure from the structure and spirit of our institutions; when the effect is to fetter and degrade the State governments by subjecting them to the control of Congress in the exercise of powers heretofore universally conceded to them of the most ordinary and fundamental character; when in fact, it radically changes the whole theory of the relations of the State and Federal governments to each other, the argument has a force that is irresistible in the absence of language which expressed such a purposes too clearly to admit of doubt."

12. Civil Rights Cases, 109 U.S. 3 (1883) striking down the core of the Civil Rights Act of 1875, at 13–14. The full passage reads: "Such legislation cannot properly cover the whole domain of rights appertaining to life, liberty, and property, defining them and providing for their vindication. That would be to establish a code of municipal law regulative of all private rights between man and man in society." [The legislation] "steps into the domain of local jurisprudence, and lays down rules for the conduct of individuals in society towards each other, and imposes sanctions for the enforcement of those rules, without referring in any manner to the supposed action of the State or its authorities. If this legislation is appropriate for enforcing the prohibitions of the amendment, it is difficult to see where it is to stop."

13. Justice Sutherland in Carter v. Carter Coal, 298 U.S. 238 (1936), at 308; United States v. E. C. Knight Co., 156 U.S. 1 (1895); Hammer v. Dagenhart, 247, U.S. 251 (1918). On strains on the common law of labor relations in this period generally, see Karen Orren, *Belated Feudalism: Labor, the Law and Liberal Development in the United States* (New York: Cambridge University Press, 1991). On gender, too, the laws of nature prevailed over state and federal law: Bradwell v. Illinois, 83 U.S. 130 (1873): "The paramount destiny and mission of women are to fulfil the noble and benign offices of wife and mother. This is the law of the Creator. And the rules of civil society must be adapted to the general condition of things, and cannot be based upon exceptional cases."

14. Edward Corwin, "The Passing of Dual Federalism," *Virginia Law Review* 36 (February 1950): 1–36.

15. Frank Strong, "Cooperative Federalism," *Iowa Law Review* 23 (1938): 459–518; Stephen Gardbaum, "New Deal Constitutionalism and the Unshackling of the States," *University of Chicago Law Review* 64 (1997): 483–566.

16. John Kincaid, "From Cooperative to Coercive Federalism," *Annals of the American Academy of Political and Social Science, American Federalism: The Third Century* 509 (1990): 139–152; Martha Derthick, *Keeping the Compound Republic: Essays on American Federalism* (Washington, D.C.: Brookings Institution, 2001), 138–152; James Blumstein, "Federalism and Civil Rights: Complementary and Competing Paradigms," *Vanderbilt Law Review* 47 (1994): 1262–1271; Joseph Zimmerman, *Contemporary American*

Federalism: The Growth of National Power (Albany: SUNY Press, 2008), 55–81.

17. David Walker, *The Rebirth of Federalism* (New York: Chatham House, 2000), 260–269; Deil Wright, "Policy Shifts in the Politics and Administration of Intergovernmental Relations, 1930–1990s," *Annals of the American Academy of Political and Social Science, American Federalism: The Third Century* 509 (May 1990): 60–72.

18. Heather Gerken, "Federalism as the New Nationalism: An Overview," *Yale Law Journal* 123 (April 2014): 1626–1639.

19. Michael McGuire, "Intergovernmental Management: A View from the Bottom," *Public Administration Review* 66 (2006): 677–679.

20. See, for example, Walker, *Rebirth*, 19–35; Deil Wright, *Understanding Intergovernmental Relations* (Pacific Grove, CA: Brooks Cole, 1988); Laurence O'Toole Jr. and Robert Christensen, *American Intergovernmental Relations* (New York: Sage, 2013).

21. James Stever, "The Growth and Decline of Executive Centered Intergovernmental Management," *Publius* 23 (1993): 71–84; Bradley Patterson, *The White House Staff: Inside the West Wing and Beyond* (Washington, D.C.: Brookings Institution, 2000), 193–204.

22. Walker, *Rebirth*, 234–241.

23. Jessica Bulman-Posen, "Executive Federalism Comes to America," *University of Virginia Law Review* 102 (2016): 953–1030, at 982, 988–991.

24. Shanna Rose, *Financing Medicaid: Federalism and the Financing of America's Health Care Safety Net* (Ann Arbor: University of Michigan Press, 2013), 173; Frank Thompson and Courtney Burke, "Federalism by Waiver: Medicaid and the Transformation of Long Term Care," *Publius* 39, no. 1 (2008): 22–46.

25. Motoko Rich, "'No Child' Law Whittled Down by White House," *New York Times*, July 6, 2012; "Obama Administration Approves Three More NCLB Flexibility Requests—37 States and DC Now Have Approval for Waivers," U.S. Department of Education, May 2013.

26. Pietro S. Nivola, Jennifer L. Noyes, and Isabel V. Sawhill, "Wave of the Future? Federalism and the Next Phase of Welfare Reform," *Brookings CFF Briefs* 29 (2004): 1–8; Pietro Nivola, "Rediscovering Federalism," *Issues in Governance Studies* 8 (2007): 1–8; Richard A. Epstein, "Government by Waiver," *National Affairs* 7 (2011): 39–54.

27. Joanne Kenen, "Fifty Ways to Run Your Medicaid Program," *CQ Weekly*, June 27, 2011, 1362–1364; Carolyn Penicie, "House Votes to Block Administration from Issuing State Welfare Waivers," *CQ Weekly*, March 18, 2013, 510; John Gramlich, "Precedence and a President," *CQ Weekly*, November 18, 2013, 1938–1944; Jason Millman, "Number of Health Care Reform Law Waivers Climbs above 1000," *The Hill*, March 6, 2011; Senator John Cornyn, "Obamacare and the Rule of Law," *National Review*, August 16, 2013.

28. Rachana Pradham, "How the GOP Could Use Obamacare to Gut Obamacare," *Politico*, October 22, 2015, http://www.politico.com/story/2015/09/obamacare-republicans-kill-waivers-213902?cmpid=sf.

29. Erwin Chereminsky, *Enhancing Government: Federalism for the 21st Century* (Stanford, CA: Stanford University Press, 2008). Compare Chereminsky's assessment with that of Robert Nagel, *The Implosion of American Federalism* (Oxford: Oxford University Press, 2001). Roderick Hills Jr. anchors the problem in neo-federalist reasoning that largely abstains "from any empirical examination of intergovernmental relations" and relies instead on "abstract notions of dual sovereignty and political accountability"; see his "The Political Economy of Cooperative Federalism: Why State Autonomy Makes Sense and 'Dual Sovereignty' Doesn't," *Michigan Law Review* 96 (1998), 813–944, at 817. Similar critiques can be found in Charlton Copeland, "Beyond Separation in Federalism Enforcement: Medicaid Expansion, Coercion, and the Norm of Engagement," *University of Pennsylvania Journal of Constitutional Law* 15 (2012): 91–182; and Erin Ryan, "Negotiating Federalism," *Boston College Law Review* 52 (2011): 1–136.

30. On the question of capacity, see Gerald Rosenberg, *The Hollow Hope: Can Courts Bring about Social Change?* (Chicago: University of Chicago Press, 1991); Keith Whittington, "Dismantling the Modern State? The Changing Structural Foundations of Federalism," *Hastings Constitutional Law Quarterly* 25 (1998): 483–528; Robert Lipkin, "Federalism as Balance," *Tulane Law Review* 79 (2004): 93–165.

31. Susan Rose-Ackerman, Stefanie Egidy, and James Fowkes, *Due Process of Lawmaking: The United States, South Africa, Germany, and the European Union* (New York: Cambridge University Press, 2015), 59–74.

32. National League of Cities v. Usery, 426 U.S. 833 (1976), at 856, Justice Blackmun concurring.

33. Garcia v. San Antonio Metro. Transit Auth., 469 U.S. 528 (1985), at 528, 539, 546–547, 550–551; Herbert Wechsler, "The Political Safeguards of Federalism: The Role of the States in the Composition of the National Government," *Columbia Law Review* 54 (1954): 543–560.

34. On sovereign immunity, see Seminole Tribe of Florida v. Florida, 517 U.S. 44 (1996); Alden v. Maine, 527 U.S. 706 (1999).

35. On Section 5, City of Boerne v. Flores, 521 U.S. 507 (1997).

36. Congress worked around the restrictions imposed by the Court's decision in City of Boerne v. Flores, reviving the goals of the Religious Freedom Restoration Act through new legislation using conditional spending. See Kimberly Sayes-Fay, "Conditional Federal Spending: A Back Door to Enhanced Free Exercise Protection," *California Law Review* 88 (2000): 1281–1322.

37. Nat'l Fed'n of Indep. Bus. v. Sebelius, 567 U.S. 132 (2012), at 2602, resurrecting the "status of states as independent sovereigns in our federal system." Jonathan Varat, "Supreme Court Foreword, October Term, 2011: Federalism Points and the Sometime Recognition of Essential Federal Power," *Loyola of Los Angeles Law Review* 46 (2013): 411–456.

38. United States v. Lopez, 514 U.S. 549 (1995), at 549.

39. Seth Safra, "The Amended Gun-Free School Zones Act: Doubt as to Its Constitutionality Remains," *Duke Law Journal* 50 (2000): 637–662; Vikram

David Amar, "The New 'New Federalism': The Supreme Court, in *Hibbs* (and *Guillen*)," *Green Bag 2D* 6 (Summer 2003): 349–357.

40. United States v. Morrison, 529 U.S. 598 (2000).
41. Robert Christiansen and Charles Wise, "Dead or Alive? The Federalism Revolution and Its Meaning for Public Administration," *Public Administration* Review 69 (2009): 920–931.
42. Gonzales v. Raich, 545 U.S. 1 (2005).
43. Alison L. La Croix, "The Shadow Powers of Article I," Chicago Public Law and Legal Theory Working Paper No. 457, The Law School, the University of Chicago, January 2014. La Croix discusses the General Welfare Clause and the Necessary and Proper Clause as "doctrinal workarounds" (30–33).
44. Gonzales v. Raich, 545 U.S. 1 (2005), at 46; O'Connor, Rehnquist, Thomas, JJ, dissenting. Ilya Somin, "A False Dawn for Federalism: Clear Statement Rules after Gonzales v. Raich," *Cato Supreme Court Review* (2006): 113–140.
45. Gregory v. Ashcroft, 501 U.S. 452 (1991).
46. New York v. United States, 505 U.S. 144 (1992).
47. Printz v. United States, 521 U.S. 898 (1997).
48. William Eskridge and Philip Frickey call this "stealth constitutionalism" in "Foreword: Law as Equilibrium," *Harvard Law Review* 108 (1994): 26–108, at 85. See also Ernest Young, "The Rehnquist Court's Two Federalisms," *Texas Law Review* 83 (2004): 1–165; William N. Eskridge and Philip P. Frickey, "Quasi-Constitutional Law: Clear Statement Rules as Constitutional Lawmaking," *Vanderbilt Law Review* 45 (1992): 593–646; Ernest Young, "The Story of *Gregory v. Ashcroft*: Clear Statement Rules and the Statutory Constitution of American Federalism," in *Statutory Interpretation Stories*, ed. William N. Eskridge, Philip P. Frickey, and Elizabeth Barrett (New York: Foundation Press, 2011). In a review of the preemption doctrine in the Roberts Court, Ernest Young concludes: "This is not to say that preemption battles can ever fully transcend the statutory terrain on which they are fought; indeed if there is any clear lesson from the last Term's cases, it is that different statutes yield different results"; see Ernest Young, " 'The Ordinary Diet of the Law': The Presumption against Preemption in the Roberts Court," *Supreme Court Review* 60 (2011): 253–344, at 283–284.
49. New York v. United States, 505 U.S. 144 (1992), Justice White in dissent at 208–209. On the greater threat to federalism from preemption, see Neil Siegel, "Commandeering and Its Alternatives: A Federalism Perspective," *Vanderbilt Law Review* 59 (2006): 1627–1692.
50. New York v. United States, Justice O'Connor quoted at 168–169.
51. Reno v. Condon, 528 U.S. 141 (2000).
52. Stephen Hartzell-Jordan, "*Condon v. Reno* and the Driver's Privacy Protection Act: Was *Garcia* a Bump in the Road to States' Rights?" *North Carolina Law Review* 78 (1999): 217–256; Erwin Chermerinsky, "Right Result, Wrong Reasons: Reno v. Condon," *Oklahoma City University Law Review* 25 (2000): 823–841. Erin Ryan, "Federalism and the Tug of War Within: Seeking Checks and Balances in the Interjurisdictional Gray Area," *Maryland Law Review* 63 (2007): 544–549.

53. Shelby County v. Holder, 570 U.S. (2013).
54. Guy-Uriel E. Charles and Luis Fuentes-Rohwer, "Race, Federalism, and Voting Rights," *University of Chicago Legal Forum* (2015): 113–152.
55. On the separation of powers problems posed more generally by this approach to review, see Rose-Ackerman, Edigy, and Fowkes, *Due Process of Lawmaking*, 59–71.
56. Franklin Roosevelt, "Inaugural Address," March 4, 1933, *The American Presidency Project*, http://www.presidency.ucsb.edu/ws/index.php?pid=14473.
57. James Landis, *The Administrative Process* (New Haven, CT: Yale University Press, 1938), 47; Peter Straus, "The Place of Agencies in Government: Separation of Powers and the Fourth Branch," *Columbia Law Review* 84 (1984): 573–699.
58. Roscoe Pound, "Report of the Special Committee on Administrative Law," *American Bar Association Reports* 63 (1938): 411–456. Pound was the outgoing dean of Harvard Law School and a fierce critic of the New Deal's legal realism. His replacement at Harvard was James Landis. On the relationship between Pound's report and the ABA bill, see Daniel Ernst, *Tocqueville's Nightmare: The Administrative State Emerges in America, 1900–1940* (Oxford: Oxford University Press, 2014), 121, 126; Joseph Postell, "The Anti–New Deal Progressive: Roscoe Pound's Alternative Administrative State," *Review of Politics* 74 (2012): 53–85. On the politics of the ABA report, see James Edward Brazier, "Who Controls the Administrative State? Congress and the President Adopt the Administrative Procedures Act of 1946" (diss., Michigan State University, 1993); George Shepherd, "Fierce Compromise: The Administrative Procedure Act Emerges from New Deal Politics," *Northwestern University Law Review* 90 (1996): 1557–1683.
59. President's Committee on Administrative Management, *"The Administrative Reorganization of the Government of the United States,"* Report of the President's Committee (Washington, D.C.: U.S. Government Printing Office, 1937).
60. Reuel Schiller, "The Era of Deference: Courts, Expertise, and the Emergence of New Deal Administrative Law," *Michigan Law Review* 106 (2007): 399–442.
61. On the "hole" in the constitutional structure within which administration would arise, see Jerry Mashaw, *Creating the Administrative Constitution: The Lost 100 Years of American Administrative Law* (New Haven, CT: Yale University Press, 2012). Mashaw documents the spirit of pragmatism that filled that hole with administrative instruments prior to age of industrialism, and he seeks to counter on that ground the notion that the creation of the modern state was a great departure, one negotiated in the Progressive Era and the New Deal. His leading case in point, regulation of steamship boilers by a national commission in antebellum America, prefigures the creation of the Interstate Commerce Commission to regulate the railroads in 1887, and Mashaw draws the implication that this early precedent diminishes the significance of the latter-day departure. We would draw the contrast between the relatively straightforward public safety question of regulating exploding steamboat boilers on interstate waterways and the

continuous forty-year institutional push and pull (1877–1920) over how to regulate the nation's railroads. The difference suggests to us a categorically different kind of problem, one that implicated all the interests that had been made interdependent by a national railroad network: corporations, farmers, creditors, laborers, and states. Indeed, the contentious negotiations over railroad regulation did not subside until labor interests were explicitly incorporated into the administrative calculus in 1920. See Karen Orren, *Belated Feudalism, Labor the Law and Liberal Development in the United States* (New York: Cambridge University Press, 1992), 160–208; Ruth O'Brien, *Workers' Paradox: the Republican Origins of New Deal Labor Policy, 1886–1935* (Chapel Hill: University of North Carolina Press, 1998).

62. See Stephen Skowronek, *Building a New American State: The Expansion of National Administrative Capacities, 1877–1920* (New York: Cambridge University Press, 1982). See also Joanna Grisinger, "The (Long) Administrative Century: Progressive Models of Governance," in *The Progressives' Century*, ed. Stephen Skowronek, Bruce Ackerman, and Stephen Engel (New Haven, CT: Yale University Press, 2016), 360–381.

63. See the graphic representation of expanding points of political intervention in Peter Strauss, "From Expertise to Politics: The Transformation of American Rulemaking," *Wake Forest Law Review* 31 (1996): 745–777, at 768–772.

64. Reorganization Act of 1939, PL 76–19. 53 Stat. 561 (1939); Franklin Roosevelt, "Executive Order 8248 Reorganizing the Executive Office of the President," September 8, 1939, *The American Presidency Project*, http:/www.presidency.ucsb.edu/ws/index.php?pid=15808.

65. Peri Arnold, *Making the Managerial Presidency: Comprehensive Reorganization Planning* (Princeton, NJ: Princeton University Press, 1986), 81–117; Matthew Dickinson, *Bitter Harvest: FDR, Presidential Power and the Growth of the Presidential Branch* (New York: Cambridge University Press, 1997).

66. Administrative Procedure Act of 1946. PL 79–404. 60 Stat. 237 (1946).

67. On the APA as protection for New Deal policy, see Shepherd, "Fierce Compromise," and McNollgast, "The Political Origins of the Administrative Procedure Act," *Journal of Law, Economics, and Organization* 15 (1999): 180–217.

68. Mathew McCubbins, Roger Noll, and Barry Weingast, "Administrative Procedures as Instruments of Political Control," *Journal of Law, Economics, and Organization* 3 (1987): 243–277.

69. Legislative Reorganization Act of 1946. PL 601. 60 Stat. 812 (1946); Roger Davidson, "The Advent of the Modern Congress: The Legislative Reorganization Act of 1946," *Legislative Studies Quarterly* 15 (1990): 357–373; Julian Zelizer, *On Capitol Hill: The Struggle to Reform Congress and Its Consequences, 1948–2000* (Princeton, NJ: Princeton University Press, 2004), 130–131. On the relative weakness of congressional incentives to build institutional capacity and the clustering of those concerns around periods of presidential aggrandizement, see Eric Schickler, *Disjointed Pluralism: Institutional Innovation and the Development of the U.S. Congress* (Princeton, NJ: Princeton University Press, 2001), 140–141, 263–268.

70. Employment Act of 1946. PL 79–304. 50 Stat. 23 (1946); Stephen Bailey, *Congress Makes a Law: The Story behind the Employment Act of 1946* (New York: Columbia, 1950), 1–36; Alan Brinkley, *The End of Reform: New Deal Liberalism in Recession and War* (New York: Knopf, 1996), 227–264.

71. On the particular agencies targeted by conservatives in the struggle over administrative reform—most especially the National Labor Relations Board but also the Securities and Exchange Commission and the Federal Power Commission—see Brazier, "Who Controls the Administrative State," 242; and Shepherd, "The Administrative Procedures Act."

72. Robert Anthony, "Interpretive Rules, Policy Statements, Guidances, Manuals and the Like—Should Federal Agencies Use Them to Bind the Public?" *Duke Law Journal* 41 (June 1992): 1311–1384; Edward Rubin, "It's Time to Make the Administrative Procedure Act Administrative," *Cornell Law Review* 89 (2003): 95–190.

73. William Simon, "The Organizational Premises of Administrative Law," *Law and Contemporary Problems* 78 (2015): 61–100: "Agencies that seek to make themselves accountable through rulemaking face high costs that they could avoid by resort to less transparent forms of administration. And courts are encouraged to focus their accountability-inducing efforts on the agencies that take the most initiative to make themselves accountable" (79). James Hamilton and Christopher Schroeder, "Strategic Regulators and the Choice of Rulemaking Procedures: The Selection of Formal vs Informal Rules in Regulating Hazardous Waste," *Law and Contemporary Problems* 57 (1994): 127, 147; M. Elizabeth Magill, "Agency Choice of Policy Making Form," *University of Chicago Law Review* 71 (2004): 1383–1447; Rubin, "It's Time."

74. On the eclipse of faith in administrators as bearers of the public interest, see Charles Reich, "The Law of the Planned Society," *Yale Law Journal* 75 (1966): 1226–1270.

75. See Richard Stewart, "The Reformation of American Administrative Law," *Harvard Law Review* 88 (1975): 1667–1813; Robert Rabin, "Federal Regulation in Historical Perspective," *Stanford Law Review* 38 (1986): 189–1326, at 1290–1293; Richard Stewart, "The Discontents of Legalism: Interest Group Relations in Administrative Regulation," *Wisconsin Law Review* (1985): 1272–1295; William Simon, "The Organizational Premises of Administrative Law."

76. Karen Hult and Charles Walcott, *Empowering the White House: Governance under Nixon, Ford, and Carter* (Lawrence: University Press of Kansas, 2004).

77. Arnold, *Making the Managerial Presidency*, 282–286; Hugh Heclo, "OMB and Neutral Competence," *Public Interest* 38 (1975), 80–99; Terry Moe, "The Politicized Presidency," in *The New Direction in American Politics*, ed. John Chubb and Paul Peterson (Washington, D.C.: Brookings Institution, 1985), 235–273. Larry Berman, *The Office of Management and Budget and the Presidency, 1921–1979* (Princeton, NJ: Princeton University Press, 1979), 105–130; Richard P. Nathan, *The Administrative Presidency* (New York: Wiley, 1983), 28–57; John Hart, *The Presidential*

Branch: From Washington to Clinton, 2nd ed. (Chatham, NJ: Chatham House), 38–147.

78. Cornelius Kerwin and Scott Furlong, *Rulemaking: How Government Agencies Write Law and Make Policy* (Washington, D.C.: CQ Press, 2011), 123–125; on the shift from neutral competence to political responsiveness in personnel management, see J. Edward Kellough and Sally Coleman Selden, "The Reinvention of Public Personnel Administration," *Public Administration Review* 63 (2003): 171.

79. Ronald Reagan, "Executive Order 12291—Federal Regulation," February 17, 1981, *The American Presidency Project*, http:/www.presdiency.ucsb.edu/ws/index.php?pid=43424.

80. Curtis Copeland, "Federal Rulemaking: The Role of the Office of Information and Regulatory Affairs," *Congressional Research Service*, Report 32397, June 9, 2009; Benjamin Mintz and Nancy Miller, "A Guide to Federal Agency Rulemaking, Administrative Conference of the United States," Office of the Chairman, second ed. 1991; Robert Percival, "Who's in Charge? Does the President Have Directive Authority over Agency Regulatory Decisions?" *Fordham Law Review* 79 (2011): 2487–2540.

81. William Jefferson Clinton, Executive Order 12866: Regulatory Planning and Review, September 30, 1993, *The American Presidency Project*, http://presidency.ucsb.edu/ws/index,php?pid=61560; Steven Croley, "White House Review of Agency Rulemaking: An Empirical Investigation," *University of Chicago Law Review* 70 (2003): 821–886.

82. General Accounting Office, *Rulemaking: OMB's Role in Reviews of Agencies Draft Rules and the Transparency of Those Reviews* (Washington, D.C.: U.S. GAO, 2003). Jennifer Nou, "Agency Self-Insulation under Presidential Review," *Harvard Law Review* 126 (2013): 1756–1837; Liza Shultz Bressman and Michael Vandenbergh, "Inside the Administrative State: A Critical Look at the Practice of Presidential Control," *Michigan Law Review* 105 (2006): 47–99; Joseph Cooper and William West, "Presidential Power and Republican Government: Theory and Practice of OMB Review of Agency Rules," *Journal of Politics* 50 (1988): 864–895.

83. Congressional Budget and Impoundment Control Act of 1974. PL-93-344. 88 Stat. 297 (1974). James Sundquist, *The Decline and Resurgence of Congress* (Washington, D.C.: Brookings Institution, 1981), 201–227.

84. Paul Light, *Monitoring Government: Inspectors General and the Search for Accountability* (Washington, D.C.: Brookings Institution, 1993).

85. Sean Fahrang, *The Litigation State: Public Regulation and Private Lawsuits in the United States* (Princeton, NJ: Princeton University Press, 2010).

86. Andrew Rudalevige, *The New Imperial Presidency, Renewing Presidential Power after Watergate* (Ann Arbor: University of Michigan Press, 2006), 101–138. The quest for "transparency" evident in the "sunshine" laws is taken up in Chapter 5.

87. Experience under the Clean Air Act of 1970s also indicates that frequent amendments to detailed statutes has the countervailing effect of keeping policy in a perpetual state of litigation. On the exceptional character of the

Clean Air Act, see Terry Moe, "The Politics of Bureaucratic Structure," in *Can the Government Govern?* ed. John Chubb and Paul Peterson (Washington, D.C.: Brookings Institution, 1989), esp. 306–320. See also Rabin, "Federal Regulation," 655–686.

88. Mathew McCubbins, Roger Noll, and Barry Weingast, "Structure and Process, Politics and Policy: Administrative Arrangements and the Political Control of Agencies," *Virginia Law Review* 75 (1989): 431–482; Mathew McCubbins and Thomas Schwartz, "Congressional Oversight Overlooked: Police Patrols versus Fire Alarms," *American Journal of Political Science* 28 (1984): 165–179; Kathleen Bawn, "Political Control versus Expertise: Congressional Choices about Administrative Procedures," *American Political Science Review* 89 (1995): 62–73.

89. Legislative Reorganization Act of 1970. PL 91–510. 94 Stat. 1140 (1970).

90. Julian Zelizer, *On Capitol Hill* (New York: Cambridge University Press, 2004), 125–132; Gregory Wawro, *Legislative Entrepreneurship in the U.S. House of Representatives* (Ann Arbor: University of Michigan Press, 2001), esp. 157–158; Schickler, *Disjointed Pluralism*, 194–195.

91. Joel Aberbach, *Keeping a Watchful Eye: The Politics of Congressional Oversight* (Washington, D.C.: Brookings Institution, 1990), esp. 59–72, 90–104, 208–209.

92. In the 1970s and 1980s, the political science literature on Congress was roiled by a related but more specific question: whether and to what extent the committee system undermines the institutional authority of Congress by extending its privileges to preference outliers. Most of this work focused on lawmaking rather than administrative oversight. See Kenneth Shepsle, *The Giant Jigsaw* (Chicago: University of Chicago Press, 1978); and the critical retort by Keith Krehbiel, *Information and Legislative Organization* (Ann Arbor: University of Michigan Press, 1992). Shepsle's brief for the power of committee outliers was echoed in the study of oversight by Barry Weingast and Mark Moran, "The Myth of the Runaway Bureaucracy: The Case of the FTC," *Regulation* (1982): 33–38; and Barry Weingast and Mark Moran, "Bureaucratic Discretion or Congressional Control? Regulatory Policy Making by the Federal Trade Commission," *Journal of Political Economy* 91 (1983): 765–800. This work asserted congressional control over the bureaucracy, albeit control by self-promoting committee members. It drew a stiff refutation from Terry Moe, "An Assessment of the Positive Theory of Congressional Dominance," *Legislative Studies Quarterly* 12 (1987): 475–520. Moe's alternative, more compatible with the view presented here, emphasized multiple overseers carving out options on intervention from different sites, and in the process, undermining the integrity of bureaucratic forms. See Moe, "Politics of Bureaucratic Structure." For a recent study of the redirection of resources through committee intervention, see J. R. De Shazo and Jody Freeman, "The Congressional Competition to Control Delegated Power," *Texas Law Review* 81 (2003): 1443–1519. On "conditional committee capture," see Richard Hall and Bernard Grofman, "The Committee Assignment Process and the Conditional Nature of Committee Bias," *American Political Science Review* 84 (1990): 1149–1166.

93. James Maxeiner, "Symposium Article: The Federal Rules at 75: Dispute Resolution, Private Enforcement or Decisions According to Law," *Georgia State University Law Review* 30 (2014): 983–1026; Martin Redish, "Class Action and the Democratic Difficulty: Rethinking the Intersection of Private Litigation and Public Goals," *University of Chicago Legal Forum* 1 (2003): 71–139; Paul Carrington, "Moths to the Light: The Dubious Attractions of American Law," *University of Kansas Law Review* 46 (1998): 673–686; Paul Carrington, "The American Tradition of Private Law Enforcement," *German Law Journal* 5 (2004): 1413–1429.

94. Goldberg v. Kelly, 397 U.S. 254 (1970); Charles Reich, "The New Property," *Yale Law Journal* 73 (1964): 733–787.

95. Jerry Mashaw, "The Supreme Court's Due Process Calculus for Administrative Adjudication in *Mathews v. Eldridge*: Three Factors in Search of a Theory of Value," *University of Chicago Law Review* 44 (1976): 28–59; Jerry Mashaw, " 'Rights' in the Federal Administrative State," *Yale Law Journal* 92 (1983): 1129–1173; more generally, see Jerry Mashaw, *Due Process in the Administrative State* (New Haven, CT: Yale University Press, 1985); Jonathan Weinberg, "The Right to be Taken Seriously," *University of Miami Law Review* 67 (2002): 149–216.

96. Rabin, "Federal Regulation"; Richard Stewart, "The Reformation of American Administrative Law," *Harvard Law Review* 88 (1985): 1760–1800. A similar pattern may be read through Court responses to the civil rights movement: Office of Communication of the United Church of Christ v. FCC, 359 F. 2d 994 (D.C. Cir. 1966); Office of Communication of the United Church of Christ v. FCC, 425 F.2d 542 (D.C. Cir. 1969). On these and the environmental cases, see Rabin, "Federal Regulation."

97. Scenic Hudson Preservation Conference v. Federal Power Commission, 354 F.2d 608 (2d. Cir. 1965).

98. Citizens to Preserve Overton Park, Inc. v. Volpe, 401 U.S. 402 (1971).

99. Kennecott Copper Corp. v. EPA, 462 F.2d 846 (D.C. Cir. 1972); also National Tire Dealers and Retreaders Association v. Brinegar, 491 2d 31 (D.C. Cir. 1974).

100. Portland Cement Ass'n v. Ruckelshaus, 486 F. 2d 375, 402 (D.C. Cir. 1973), at 402; also U.S. v. Nova Scotia Food Products Corp., 568 F2d 240 (2d Cir. 1977).

101. Rabin, "Federal Regulation," 1307.

102. Vermont Yankee Nuclear Power Corp. v. National Resources Defense Council, Inc., 435 U.S. 519 (1978).

103. Ibid., at 553, 554, 549.

104. Motor Vehicles Manufactures Association v. State Farm, 463 U.S 29 (1983).

105. Ibid., at 57, 42.

106. Ibid., at 59.

107. Chevron U.S.A. v. National Resources Defense Council, Inc., 467 U.S. 837 (1984), at 865–866. Also Anne Joseph O'Connell, "Political Cycles of Rulemaking: An Empirical Portrait of the Modern Administrative State," *Virginia Law Review* 94 (2008): 889–986; Anne Joseph O'Connell, "Agency Rulemaking and Political Transitions," *Northwestern University Law Review* 105 (2011): 471–543; Copeland, "Federal Rulemaking," 13.

108. Kerwin and Furlong, *Rulemaking*, 260.

109. William Eskridge Jr. and Lauren E. Baer, "The Continuum of Deference: Supreme Court Treatment of Agency Statutory Interpretations from *Chevron* to *Hamdan*," *Georgetown Law Journal* 96 (2008): 1157.

110. Massachusetts v. Environmental Protection Agency, 549 U.S. 497 (2007); Jody Freeman and Adrian Vermeule, "*Massachusetts v. EPA*: From Politics to Expertise," *Supreme Court Review* (2007): 51–110.

111. City of Arlington, TX. v. Federal Communications Commission, 569 U.S.___ (2013), at 1877–1886, Roberts, Kennedy, and Alito, JJ dissenting; Samuel Feder, Matthew Price, and Andrew Noll, "*City of Arlington v. FCC*: The Death of *Chevron* Step Zero?" *Federal Communications Law Journal* 66 (2014): 48–70.

112. King v. Burwell, 576 U.S. ___ (2015); Jody Freeman, "The *Chevron* Sidestep: Professor Freeman on *King v. Burwell*," Harvard University Environmental Law Program, Emmett Clinic Policy Initiative, June 25, 2015, http://environment.law.harvard.edu/2015/06/the-chevron-sidestep/; also Michigan v. Environmental Protection Agency, 576 U.S. (2015); Blake Emerson, "Administrative Answers to 'Major Questions': On the Democratic Legitimacy of Agency Statutory Interpretation," *Minnesota Law Review* 102 (2018), forthcoming.

113. Walter Oleszek, *Congressional Procedures and the Policy Process*, 3rd ed. (Washington, D.C.: Congressional Quarterly, 1989): 74–77; Eric Petashnik, "Congress and the Budget since 1974," in *The American Congress, The Building of Democracy*, ed. Julian Zelizer (New York: Houghton Mifflin, 2004), 668–686.

114. Immigration and Naturalization Service v. Chadha, 462 U.S. 919 (1983).

115. John Copelan Nagle, "Corrections Day," *UCLA Law Review* 43 (1996): 1267–1319.

116. Congressional Review Act of 1996. PL 104–121. 110 Stat. 847 (1996).

117. "Brushing Back a Lawless EPA," *Wall Street Journal*, December 22, 2015.

118. Strauss, "From Expertise to Politics," esp. 768–772; Morton Rosenberg, "Congressional Review of Agency Rulemaking: An Update and Assessment of the Congressional Review Act after a Decade," *Congressional Research Service Report*, Report 30116, May 8, 2008; Cornelius Kerwin and Scott Furlong, "The Mysteries of the Congressional Review Act," *Harvard Law Review* 122 (2009): 2162–2183. The transition from the Obama administration to unified Republican control in the Trump administration was accompanied by a burst of activity under the Review Act.

119. Edward Purcell Jr., "The Class Action Fairness Act in Perspective: The Old and the New in Federal Jurisdictional Reform," *University of Pennsylvania Law Review* 156 (2008): 1823–1927.

120. Negotiated Rule Making Act of 1990. PL 101–648. Stat. 4969 (1990).

121. Susan Rose-Ackerman, "Consensus versus Incentives: A Skeptical Look at Regulatory Negotiation," *Duke Law Journal* 43 (1994): 1206–1220.

122. Kerwin and Furlong, "Mysteries of the Congressional Review Act," 205–210; Philip Harter, "Negotiating Regulations: A Cure for Malaise," *Georgetown Law Journal* 71 (1982): 1–118; Gary Coglianese, "Assessing Consensus: The Pressure and Performance of Negotiated Rule Making," *Duke Law Journal* 6 (1997): 1255–1349.

123. "Blood sport" from Thomas McGarity, "Administrative Law as Blood Sport: Policy Erosion in a Highly Partisan Age," *Duke Law Journal* 61 (2012): 1671–1762.

124. For a modern restatement of the idea that there is little to the power of the modern presidency that Congress could not at any time take back, see Charles Black, "The Working Balance of the American Political Departments," *Hastings Constitutional Law Quarterly* 1 (1974): 13–20.

125. Henry Jones Ford, *The Rise and Growth of American Politics: A Sketch of Constitutional Development* (New York: MacMillan, 1898), 56.

126. Ibid., at 357.

127. Ibid., at 279.

128. Ibid., at 292–293.

129. Abraham Lincoln, *Collected Works* (New Brunswick, NJ: Rutgers University Press, 1953), 3: 278.

130. For an assessment of developments in the last decades of the nineteenth century, when Ford was writing about the mobilizing potential of the presidency, see Daniel Klinghard, *The Nationalization of American Political Parties, 1980–1896* (Cambridge: Cambridge University Press, 2010). Still, as late as 1890, the Whig tradition of executive deference to Congress was still a factor in major policy disputes. In that year, Benjamin Harrison, a persistent and avid advocate of the Federal Elections Bill, rejected his advisers urging to weigh in directly on a close Senate contest by engaging the public directly in his cause. Karen Orren, "Benjamin Harrison," in *Reader's Companion to the American Presidency*, ed. Alan Brinkley and Davis Dyer (Boston: Houghton Mifflin, 2000), 269–275.

131. On presidential parties as coalitions of intense "policy demanders," see Marty Cohen, David Karol, Hans Noel, and John Zaller, *The Party Decides: Presidential Nominations before and after Reform* (Chicago: University of Chicago Press, 2008). Also Kathleen Bawn, Martin Cohen, David Karol, Seth Masket, Hans Noel, and John Zaller, "A Theory of Political Parties: Groups, Policy Demands, and Nominations in American Politics," *Perspectives on Politics* 10 (September 2012): 571–597.

132. Sidney Milkis, "Progressivism and the Rise of Executive Centered Partisanship," in *The Progressives' Century: Democratic Reform, Constitutional Government and the Modern American State*, ed. Stephen Skowronek, Bruce Ackerman, and Stephen Engel (New Haven, CT: Yale University Press, 2016). Sidney Milkis and Daniel Tichenor, "Direct Democracy and Social Justice: The Progressive Party Campaign of 1912," *Studies in American Political Development* 8 (1994): 282–239; Sidney Milkis, *Theodore Roosevelt, the Progressive Party and the Transformation of American Democracy* (Lawrence: University Press of Kansas, 2009).

133. Franklin Roosevelt, "Address Accepting the Presidential Nomination at the Democratic National Convention in Chicago," July 2, 1932, *The American Presidency Project*, http://www.presidency.ucsb.edu/ws/index.php?pid =75174.

134. Harold Bass Jr. "Presidential Party Leadership and Party Reform: Franklin Roosevelt and the Abrogation of the Two Thirds Rule," *Presidential Studies*

Quarterly 18 (1988): 303–317; Marc Landy and Sidney Milkis, *Presidential Greatness* (Lawrence: University Press of Kansas, 2000), 169–170.

135. Louis Overacker, "Labor's Political Contributions," *Political Science Quarterly* 54 (1939): 56–68; William Leuchtenburg, *Franklin Roosevelt and the New Deal, 1932–1940* (New York: Harper, 1963), 183–190; David Greenstone, *Labor in American Politics* (New York: Knopf, 1969), 39–52; David Plotke, *Building a Democratic Political Order: Reshaping American Liberalism in the 1930 and 1940s* (New York: Cambridge University Press, 1996), 153–156; Daniel Schlozman, *When Movements Anchor Parties: Electoral Realignments and American History* (Princeton, NJ: Princeton University Press, 2015).

136. Ronald Schurin, "The President as Disciplinarian: Wilson, Roosevelt and Congressional Primaries," *Presidential Studies Quarterly* 28 (1998): 409–421. More generally, see Sidney Milkis, *The President and the Parties: The Transformation of the American Party System since the New Deal* (New York: Oxford University Press, 1993).

137. "We very definitely did not want Nixon to be perceived as the Republican candidate for President, but as Richard Nixon running for reelection"; see Peter Dailey, president, the November Group, 1972 Nixon advertising agency, quoted in Robert Agranoff, "The New Style of Campaigning: The Decline of Party and the Rise of Candidate-Centered Technology," in *The New Style of Election Campaigns*, ed. Robert Agranoff (Boston, MA: Holbrook, 1976), 3.

138. Nelson Polsby, *The Consequences of Party Reform* (New York: Oxford University Press 1983), 64.

139. Cohen et al., *The Party Decides*. These authors argue, too strongly in our view, that the parties remain in charge. Nonetheless, they view the parties as disembodied, free-floating elites linked together through informal communications networks, and the control they describe is less institutional than symbiotic. The conclusion that no one is in charge of these informal relationships would seem to be borne out in the 2016 primary contests.

140. For example, the Bipartisan Campaign Reform Act of 2002 and Citizens United v. Federal Election Commission, 558 U.S. 310 (2010). See Sidney Milkis and John York, "Barack Obama, Organizing for Action, and Executive Centered Partisanship," *Studies in American Political Development* 31 (2017): 1–23.

141. Theodore Roosevelt, *An Autobiography* (New York: Da Capo, 1913), 476–492.

142. Scott James, *Presidents, Parties and the State: A Party System Perspective on Democratic Regulatory Choice, 1884–1936* (New York: Cambridge University Press, 2000), 123–199.

143. Arthur Link, *Woodrow Wilson and the Progressive Era, 1910–1917* (New York: Harper, 1954), 235–240; Elizabeth Sanders, *Roots of Reform: Framers, Workers, and the American State* (Chicago: University of Chicago Press, 1999), 379–380.

144. On FDR and the NRA, see Ellis Hawley, *The New Deal and the Problem of Monopoly* (Princeton, NJ: Princeton University Press, 1966); on LBJ

and the War on Poverty, see John Donovan, *The Politics of Poverty* (New York: Bobbs-Merrill, 1973); David Zarefsky, *Lyndon Johnson's War on Poverty: Rhetoric and History* (Tuscaloosa: University of Alabama Press, 1986).

145. Sidney Milkis, Daniel Tichenor, and Laura Blessing, "'Rallying Force': The Modern Presidency, Social Movements and the Transformation of American Politics," *Presidential Studies Quarterly* 43 (2013): 641–670. Stephen Skowronek, "Twentieth Century Remedies," *Boston University Law Review* 94 (2014): 795–805.

146. Moe, "Politicized Presidency."

147. Bradley Peterson Jr., *The White House Staff: Inside the West Wing and Beyond* (Washington, D.C.: Brookings Institution, 2000), 173–184. Karen Hult and Charles Walcott, *Empowering the White House: Governance under Nixon, Ford and Carter* (Lawrence: University Press of Kansas, 2004), 78–105; Joseph Pika, "The White House Office of Public Liaison," *Presidential Studies Quarterly* 39, (2009): 549–573; Katherine Krimmel, "Special Interest Partisanship: The Transformation of American Political Parties," paper presented at the 2011 Annual Meeting of the American Political Science Association.

148. Milkis and York, "Barack Obama."

149. Maeva Marcus, *Truman and the Steel Seizure Case: The Limits of Presidential Power* (New York: Columbia, 1977).

150. Harry S Truman, "Radio and Television Address to the American People on the Need for Government Operation of the Steel Mills," April 8, 1952, *The American Presidency Project*, http://www. presidency.ucsb.edu/ws/index.php?pid=14454&st=&st1.

151. Youngstown Sheet and Tube v. Sawyer, 343 U.S. 579 (1952).

152. On the ambiguities of the decision, see Patricia L. Bellia, "The Story of the *Steel Seizure* Case," in *Presidential Power Stories*, ed. Christopher Schroeder and Curtis Bradley (New York: Foundation Press, 2009), 233–285; Grant McConnell, *The Steel Seizure of 1952* (Tuscaloosa: University of Alabama Press, 1960).

153. 343 U.S. 579, at 588.

154. Ibid., at 589–615; quoted passages at 589, 602, 611, 613.

155. Ibid., at 634–667. Martin Sheffer, "The Attorney General and Presidential Power: Robert H. Jackson, Franklin Roosevelt and the Prerogative Power," *Presidential Studies Quarterly* 12, no. 1 (Winter 1982): 54–65.

156. Terry Moe and William Howell, "The Presidential Power of Unilateral Action," *Journal of Law, Economics, and Organization*, 15 (1999), 132–177; William Howell, *Power without Persuasion: The Politics of Direct Presidential Action* (Princeton, NJ: Princeton University Press, 2003); William Howell with David Milton Brent, *Thinking about the Presidency: The Primacy of Power* (Princeton, NJ: Princeton University Press, 2013); Eric Posner and Adrian Vermeule, *The Executive Unbound: After the Madisonian Republic* (New York: Oxford University Press, 2011).

157. Bruce Ackerman, *The Decline and Fall of the American Republic* (Cambridge, MA: Harvard University Press, 2010), 88–116.

158. Hamdan v. Rumsfeld, 548 U.S. 557 (2006), Scalia in dissent: http://acslaw
.org/aclsbolg/under-the-radar-does-scalia's-dissent-in-Hamdan-boost-the
-validity-of-presidential-signing-statements?.

159. T. J. Halstead, "Presidential Signing Statements: Constitutional and Insti-
tutional Implications," Congressional Research Service Report 33667, Up-
dated September 2007; Stephen Engel, *American Politicians Confront the
Court: Opposition Politics and Changing Responses to Judicial Power*
(New York: Cambridge University Press, 2011), 348–354; Phillip Cooper,
"George W. Bush, Edgar Allan Poe and the Use and Abuse of Presidential
Signing Statements," *Presidential Studies Quarterly* 35 (2005): 515–532;
James Pfiffner, *Power Play: The Bush Presidency and the Constitution*
(Washington, D.C.: Brookings Institution, 2008), 184–229. In a reassessment
of claims about the significance of signing statements, Ian Ostrander and
Joel Sievert draw a distinction between protecting constitutional pre-
rogatives and making policy: Ian Ostrander and Joel Sievert, "What's So
Sinister about Presidential Signing Statements?" *Presidential Studies
Quarterly* 43 (2013): 58–80.

160. Kenneth Mayer, *With the Stroke of a Pen: Executive Orders and Presidential Power* (Princeton, NJ: Princeton University Press, 2001); Howell, *Power
without Persuasion*; Phillip Cooper, *By Order of the President: The Use and
Abuse of Executive Direct Action* (Lawrence: University Press of Kansas,
2002); Andrew Rudalevige, "The Obama Administrative Presidency:
Finding New Meanings in Old Laws," paper prepared for "L'heritage
Obama," Foundation des Etats Unis/Université de Paris, December 12,
2016.

161. Howell, *Thinking about The Presidency: The Primacy of Power*, 21–30; Rudalevige, *New Imperial Presidency*, 174–175; Michael Glennon, *National
Security and Double Government* (Oxford: Oxford University Press, 2015).

162. Richard Allen, a national security advisor under Reagan, put it this way: "In
the 1980s, national security is in itself an all-encompassing term too often
narrowly construed as having to do only with foreign policy and defense
matters. In reality, it must include virtually every facet of international activity, including (but not limited to) foreign affairs, defense, intelligence,
research and development policy, outer space, international economic and
trade policy, monetary policy and reaching deeply even into the demands of
the Departments of Commerce and Agriculture. In a word, 'national security' must reflect the Presidential perspective, of which diplomacy is but a
single component." See "Foreign Policy and National Security: The White
House Perspective," in *Agenda '83: A Mandate for Leadership*, ed. Richard
Nolwill (Washington, D.C.: Heritage Foundation, 1983), 6.

163. Mitchel Sollenberger and Mark Rozell, *The President's Policy Czars: Un-
dermining Congress and the Constitution* (Lawrence: University Press of
Kansas, 2012), 6–8. Bradley Patterson Jr., *The White House Staff: Inside the
West Wing* (Washington, D.C.: Brookings Institution, 2000), 283–281.

164. Barack Obama, "Statement on Signing the Consolidated Appropriations Act, 2012," December 23, 2011, *The American Presidency Project*,
http://www.presidency,ucsb.edu/ws/index.php?pid=97996; also Barack

Obama, "Statement on Signing the Department of Defense and Full Year Continuing Appropriations Act, 2011," *The American Presidency Project*, http://www.presidency.ucsb.edu/ws/index.php?pid=90269. Mitchel Sollenberger and Mark Rozell, "Prerogative Power and Executive Branch Czars: President Obama's Signing Statement," *Presidential Studies Quarterly* 41 (2011): 819–833.

165. National Labor Relations Board v. Noel Canning, 573 U.S. (2014).

166. See Alex Bolton, "Senate Guts Filibuster Power, *The Hill*, November 21, 2013, http://ithehill.come/homenews/senate/191042-dems-reid-may-go-nuclear-thursday; Walter Oleszek, Mark Oleszek, Elizabeth Rybicki, and Bill Heniff Jr., *Congressional Procedures and the Policy Process*, 10th ed. (Washington, D.C.: CQ Press, 2016), 314–315.

167. Sarah Binder and Steven Smith, *Politics or Principle? Filibustering in the U.S. Senate* (Washington, D.C.: Brookings Institution, 1997).

168. Gregory Wawro and Eric Schickler, *Filibuster: Obstruction and Lawmaking in the U.S. Senate* (Princeton, NJ: Princeton University Press, 2006); Gregory Koger, *Filibustering: A Political History of Obstruction in the House and Senate* (Chicago: University of Chicago Press, 2010), 37–96.

169. Bruce Oppenheimer, "Changing Time Constraints on Congress: Historical Perspectives on the Use of Cloture," in *Congress Reconsidered*, ed. Lawrence Dodd and Bruce Oppenheimer (Washington, D.C.: Congressional Quarterly, 1985), 393–413.

170. Koger, *Filibustering*, 169.

171. Steven Smith, *The Senate Syndrome: The Evolution of Procedural Warfare in the Modern U.S. Senate* (Norman: University of Oklahoma Press, 2014).

172. Koger, *Filibustering*, 172; *Congressional Record*, 91st Congress, 1st sess., January 27, 1969, 1867. Frances Lee, "Senate Deliberation and the Future of Congressional Power," *PS* 43 (2010): 227–229.

173. On judicial empowerment through congressional gridlock, see Richard Hasen, "The End of the Dialogue: Political Polarization, the Supreme Court and Congress," *Southern California Law Review* 86 (2013): 205–262; on executive bypass, see Michael Barber and Nolan McCarty, "Causes and Consequences of Polarization, American Political Science Association," *Task Force on Negotiating Agreement in Politics* (2006): 44–45; Bulman-Posen, "Executive Federalism."

174. Wawro and Schickler, *Filibuster*, 16–17.

175. Frances Lee, "Senate Deliberation and the Future of Congressional Power," 227–229.

176. Barbara Sinclair, *Unorthodox Lawmaking: New Legislative Processes in the U.S. Congress* (Washington, D.C.: CQ Press, 2012), 68–69; Oleszek et al., *Congressional Procedures*, 256–266.

177. Smith, *Senate Syndrome*, 91.

178. Koger, *Filibustering*, 53–55; on the institutionalization of party control in the House as it took hold between the Civil War and the imposition of the Reed Rules in 1890, see Jeffrey Jenkins and Charles Stewart III, *Fighting for the Speakership: The House and the Rise of Party Government* (Princeton, NJ: Princeton University Press, 2013), 240–302.

179. Zelizer, *On Capital Hill*, 31–42. On the Democratic Study Group, see James Sundquist, *Politics and Policy: The Eisenhower, Kennedy and Johnson Years* (Washington, D.C.: Brookings Institution, 1968), 395–405.

180. Sinclair, *Unorthodox Lawmaking*, 148–152; Oleszek et al., *Congressional Procedure*, 168–175.

181. Sinclair, *Unorthodox Lawmaking*, 10–49.

182. Russell Berman, "The Humbling of Paul Ryan," *Atlantic*, May 26, 2016, http://www.theatlantic.com/politics/archive/2016/05/the-humbling-of-paul-ryan/4845291.

183. For a review of the political science literature, see Sarah Binder, "The Dysfunctional Congress," *Annual Review of Political Science* 18 (2015): 85–101. Also see David Mayhew, *Divided We Govern: Party Control, Lawmaking, and Investigations, 1946–1990* (New Haven, CT: Yale University Press, 1991); E. Scott Adler and John Wikerson, *Congress and the Politics of Problem Solving* (New York: Cambridge University Press, 2012); Thomas Mann and Norman Ornstein, *The Broken Branch: How Congress Is Failing America and How to Get It Back on Track* (New York: Oxford University Press, 2006); Thomas Mann and Norman Ornstein, *It's Even Worse Than It Looks: How the American Constitutional System Collided with the New Politics of Extremism* (New York: Basic Books, 2012).

184. Shep Melnick, "The Conventional Misdiagnosis: Why 'Gridlock' Is Not Our Central Problem and Constitutional Revision Is Not the Solution," *Boston University Law Review* 94 (2014): 767–793.

185. William Casto, "The Early Supreme Court Justices' Most Significant Opinion," *Ohio Northern University Law Review* 29 (2002): 173–207. On the origins and historical fraying of the political question doctrine, see Nada Mourtada-Sabbah and Bruce Cain, eds., *The Political Question Doctrine and the Supreme Court of the United States* (Lanham, MD: Lexington, 2007).

186. Marbury v. Madison, 5 U.S. 137 (1803); Stuart v. Laird, 299 U.S. 1803.

187. Theodore Roosevelt, quoted in Stephen Engel, *American Politicians Confront the Court: Opposition Politics and Changing Responses to Judicial Power* (New York: Cambridge University Press, 2011), 244–245.

188. Cooper v. Aaron, 358 U.S. 1 (1958).

189. Charles Geyh, *When Courts and Congress Collide: The Struggle of Control of America's Judicial System* (Ann Arbor: University of Michigan Press, 2006).

190. As noted in Chapter 3, the doctrinal shift is often traced to footnote four of United States v. Carolene Products Co., 304 U.S. 144 (1938), where the Court signals a turn to laws targeted at discrete and insular minorities.

191. Engel, *American Politicians*, 302–371; also Geyh, *When Courts and Congress Collide*.

192. Jeffrey Rosen, interview with Chief Justice John Roberts, "Roberts Rules," *Atlantic*, January–February 2007; Lincoln Caplan, "John Roberts's Court," *New Yorker*, June 29, 2015; Robert Barnes, "The Political Wars Damage Public Perception of the Supreme Court," *Washington Post*, February 4, 2016.

5. POLITICS IN THE POLICY STATE

1. John Dewey, *Liberalism and Social Action* [1935] (New York: Capricorn, 1963), 45–49: "The crisis of liberalism is connected with the failure to develop an adequate conception of intelligence integrated with social movements."

2. Frank Goodnow, *The American Conception of Liberty and Government* (Providence, RI: Standard, 1916), 29.

3. Mary Parker Follett, *The New State: Group Organization and the Solution of Popular Government* (New York: Longmans, 1918), 127–128.

4. Woodrow Wilson, *Congressional Government: A Study in American Politics* [1885] (Gloucester, MA: Peter Smith, 1973), 187.

5. Herbert Croly, *Progressive Democracy* (New York: MacMillan, 1914), 41.

6. M. J. C. Vile, *Constitutionalism and the Separation of Powers* (Indianapolis, IN: Liberty Fund, 1998), 289–323.

7. Ibid., 314.

8. See Michael Lacey and Mary Furner, eds., *The State and Social Investigation in Britain and the United States* (New York: Cambridge University Press, 1993).

9. Walter Lippmann, *Drift and Mastery: An Attempt to Diagnose the Current Unrest* [1914] (Englewood Cliffs, NJ: Prentice Hall, 1961), 150–151. Don Price offers a similar if more sober assessment in *The Scientific Estate* (New York: Oxford University Press, 1965), 274–275: "Science supplies much of the factual knowledge that men must agree on (at least they must agree on most of it) if their arguments about the choices that are open to them are to be conducted on some rational and orderly basis. It sweeps away superstitions that paralyze political responsibility. It opens up new opportunities and new possibilities for cooperation, and thus makes the concept of the public interest more meaningful, though at the same time more complicated and difficult to define."

10. John Dewey, *Democracy and Education* (New York: MacMillan, 1916), 5: "Men live in a community by virtue of the things which they have in common . . . What they must have in common in order to form a community or society are aims, beliefs, aspirations, knowledge—a common understanding—like-mindedness as the sociologists say."

11. Nicole Mellow, "The Democratic 'Fit': Party Reform and the Eugenics Tool," in *The Progressives' Century: Political Reform, Constitutional Government, and the Modern American State*, ed. Stephen Skowronek, Stephen Engel, and Bruce Ackerman (New Haven, CT: Yale University Press, 2016), 197–218.

12. Croly, *Progressive Democracy*, 376–377.

13. See, for example, Price, *Scientific Estate*; Aaron Wildavsky: *Speaking Truth to Power: The Art and Craft of Policy Analysis* (Boston, MA: Little, Brown, 1979); David Dickson, *The New Politics of Science* (Chicago, IL: University of Chicago Press, 1992); Bruce Smith, *The Advisers: Scientists in the Policy Process* (Washington, D.C.: Brookings, 1992); Sheila Jasanoff, *The Fifth Branch: Science Advisers as Policy Makers* (Cambridge, MA: Harvard

University Press, 1990); Thomas Gieryn, *Cultural Boundaries of Science: Credibility on the Line* (Chicago, IL: University of Chicago Press, 1999).

14. Michael Polanyi, "The Republic of Science," *Minerva* 1 (1962): 54–73.

15. Dwight D. Eisenhower, "Farewell Radio and Television Address to the American People," The American Presidency Project, http://www.presidency.ucsb.edu/ws/?pid=12086.

16. The creation of the Office of Information and Regulatory Affairs in the Office of Management and Budget, discussed in Chapter 4, was a potent response to this demand for peer review. OIRA review provided a technocratic check on agency rule making but not a politically independent one.

17. Jasanoff, *Fifth Branch*, esp. 234–237; on "boundary work" as the foundation of science more generally, see Gieryn, *Cultural Boundaries*.

18. Thomas McGarity and Wendy Wagner, *Bending Science: How Special Interests Corrupt Public Health Research* (Cambridge, MA: Harvard University Press, 2008), 150–156.

19. William Aiken, *Technology and the American Dream* (Berkeley: University of California Press, 1977).

20. Franklin D. Roosevelt, "State of the Union Message to Congress," January 11, 1944," The American Presidency Project, www.presidency.ucsb.edu/ws/?pid=16518.

21. Lauchlin Currie, "Lauchlin Currie's Memoirs: The New Deal," *Journal of Economic Studies* 31 (2004): 201–234, esp. 227–229.

22. The turn in priority from fiscal policy to monetary policy during the 1970s, and the accompanying decline in the power of the Council of Economic Advisors, coincided with a transfer of leadership at the Federal Reserve Board to professional economists. The first economist to head the Board was Arthur Burns, appointed by Richard Nixon in 1970. Since then all Fed chiefs but one has been an economist.

23. Claudia Goldin and Lawrence F. Katz, *The Race between Education and Technology* (Cambridge, MA: Harvard University Press, 2008), esp. 324–325.

24. Noah Smith, "Free Trade Is No Longer a No Brainer," *Bloomberg View*, October 7, 2015; Jackie Calmes, "Economists Sharply Split over Trade Deal Effects," *New York Times*, February 1, 2016.

25. Roger Hickey, "Economist Jeffrey Sachs Says NO to TPP and TAFTA Trade Deals," *Huffington Post*, November 15, 2014.

26. David Ricci, *The Transformation of American Politics: The New Washington and the Rise of Think Tanks* (New Haven, CT: Yale University Press, 1993); Andrew Rich, *Think Tanks, Public Policy, and the Politics of Expertise* (New York: Cambridge University Press, 2004).

27. Rich, *Think Tanks, Public Policy, and the Politics of Expertise*, 211.

28. For an illustration of the divide in the area of social policy see Kent Weaver, *Ending Welfare as We Know It* (Washington, D.C.: Brookings Institution, 2000), 364–385.

29. Chairman Glenn Seaborg quoted in Brian Balogh, *Chain Reaction: Expert Debate and Public Participation in American Commercial Nuclear Power, 1945–1975* (New York: Cambridge University Press, 1991), 301.

30. Ibid., 300–301.

31. "Hillary Clinton Acceptance Speech at the Democratic National Convention," July 28, 2016, time.com/3920332/transcript-fu.

32. See, for example, Bruce Cain, *Democracy More or Less: America's Political Reform Quandary* (New York: Cambridge University Press, 2015); Bruce Cain, Russell Dalton, and Susan Scarrow, *Democracy Transformed: Expanding Political Opportunities in Advanced Industrial Democracies* (Oxford: Oxford University Press, 2003); David Magleby, "Let the Voters Decide? An Assessment of the Initiative and Referendum Process," *University of Colorado Law Review* 66 (1995): 13–46; David Broder, *Democracy Derailed: Initiative Campaigns and the Power of Money* (New York: Harcourt, 2000).

33. John Keane, *The Life and Death of Democracy* (New York: Simon and Schuster, 2009); John Keane, "Democracy: The Rule of Nobody," formal lectures delivered at Wissenschaftszentrum Berlin für Sozialforschung, July 14, 2004. In a different vein, see Philip Howard, *Rule by Nobody: Saving America from Dead Laws* (New York: Norton, 2014).

34. Michael Wines, "Push to Alter Constitution, via the States," *New York Times*, August 23, 2016, A1.

35. On TR's proposal, see Sidney Milkis, *Theodore Roosevelt, the Progressive Party, and the Transformation of American Democracy* (Lawrence: University Press of Kansas, 2009), 219; on the Kemp proposal, see Magleby, "Let the Voters Decide," 42.

36. Adam Sheingate, *Building a Business of Politics: The Rise of Political Consulting and the Transformation of American Democracy* (New York: Oxford University Press, 2016), 21–25.

37. Jonathan Kahn, *Budgeting Democracy: State Building and Citizenship in America, 1890–1928* (Ithaca, NY: Cornell University Press, 1997), 93–119.

38. Lotte E. Feinberg, "Mr. Justice Brandeis and the Creation of the Federal Register," *Public Administration Review* 61 (2001): 359–370.

39. Michael Schudson, *The Rise of the Right to Know: Politics and the Culture of Transparency, 1945–1975* (Cambridge, MA: Harvard University Press, 2015).

40. David Truman describes this as "morbific politics" in *The Governmental Process: Public Interests and Public Opinion* (New York: Knopf, 1971), 520–535; Grant McConnell describes public-private relations in *Private Power and American Democracy* (New York: Knopf, 1966).

41. Schudson, *Rise of the Right to Know*, 37–54.

42. Quote in Trip Gabriel, "A Table Full of Trump Voters," *New York Times*, January 13, 2017, 12.

43. This discussion draws on Jason Ross Arnold, *Secrecy in the Sunshine Era: The Promises and Failures of U.S. Open Government Laws* (Lawrence: University Press of Kansas, 2014), 97–133; Mary Graham, *Presidents' Secrets: The Use and Abuse of Hidden Power* (New Haven, CT: Yale University Press, 2017), 161–162. Cheney and Clinton quoted on 106 and 110.

44. Public Citizen v. Department of Justice, 491 U.S. 440 (1989), at 88.

45. Freedom of Information Act, PL 89-487, 80 Stat. 250, 5 U.S.C. 552.

46. For examples, see Arnold, *Secrecy*, 75–76.

47. Critical Infrastructure Information Act of 2002, PL 107-296, 116 Stat. 2135, 6 U.S.C. 106; Graham, *Presidents' Secrets*, 173.

48. Graham, *Presidents' Secrets*, 227–332; McGarity and Wagner, *Bending Science*, 350–356.

49. See Roberta Ann Johnson, *Whistleblowing: When It Works and Why* (Boulder, CO: Reinner, 2003), 6.

50. Ibid.; Sissela Bok, "Whistleblowing and Leaks," in *Transparency and Secrecy*, ed. Suzanne Piotrowski (New York: Rowman and Littlefield, 2010), 134–147; U.S. Merit Systems Protection Board, *Whistleblowing in the Federal Government: A Report to the President and the Congress of the United States* (Washington, D.C.: Government Printing Office, 1993).

51. David Cole, "What Should We Do about Leakers?" in *After Snowden: Privacy Secrecy and Security in the Information Age*, ed. Ronald Goldfarb (New York: St. Martin's, 2015), 126.

52. Graham, *Presidents' Secrets*, 88–94.

53. A good entry point into a vast literature is Nolan McCarty, Keith T. Poole, and Howard Rosenthal, *Polarized America: The Dance of Ideology and Unequal Riches* (Cambridge, MA: MIT Press, 2016). Also Nolan McCarty, "The Policy Effects of Polarization," in *The Transformation of American Politics: Activist Government and the Rise of Conservatism*, ed. Paul Pierson and Theda Skocpol (Princeton, NJ: Princeton University Press, 2007), 223–255.

54. Arthur H. Miller, Warren E. Miller, Alden S. Raine, and Thad A. Brown, "A Majority Party in Disarray: Policy Polarization in the 1972 Election," *American Political Science Review* 70 (1976): 753–778.

55. McCarty et al., *Polarized America*, 26–27.

56. Alexander Hamilton, "Federalist No. 17," in John Jay, Alexander Hamilton, and James Madison, *The Federalist Papers* (New York: Mentor, 1961), 118–121.

57. Marc Stears, *Progressives, Pluralists, and the Problems of the State: Ideologies of Reform in the United States and Britain, 1909–1926* (New York: Oxford University Press, 2002), 127–167.

58. Dewey, *The Public and Its Problems*.

59. See, for example, Craig Fehrman, "All Politics Is National," *538*, November 7, 2016; David Schleicher, "All Politics Is National," *Atlantic*, July 13, 2012; Larry Sabato, "All Politics Is National," *Larry Sabato's Crystal Ball*, Virginia Center for Politics, July 29, 2010.

60. http://usgovernmentspending.com/us-federal-spending.php?chart=FO-total&gove=total.

61. Veronique de Rugy, "President Reagan, Champion Budget Cutter," *American Enterprise Institute*, June 9, 2004. We report the growth in nondefense discretionary spending not because we estimate the impact of defense and mandatory (entitlement) spending on the policy state to be negligible; to the contrary, it is immense. But the cost pressures of entitlements, debt payments, military obligations, and periodic spikes in defense spending may leave the impression that the policy state is now simply servicing its accumulated commitments. The onset of budget wars attests to these fiscal

constraints and the political divisions that they expose. That said, the real absolute growth in nondefense discretionary spending speaks more directly to the costs of establishing and implementing new programs and rules, activities which bear most directly on the policy state changes we have analyzed.

62. Matthew J. Dickinson, "The President and Congress," in *The Presidency and the Political System*, 10th edition, ed. Michael Nelson (Washington, D.C.: CQ Press, 2013), 418–419.

63. See, for instance, Alan Abramowitz and Steven Webster, "All Politics Is National: The Rise of Negative Partisanship and the Nationalization of U.S. House and Senate Elections in the 21st Century," paper for the Annual Meeting of the Midwest Political Science Association, Chicago, April 16–19, 2015.

64. Barbara Sinclair, *Party Wars: Polarization and the Politics of National Policy Making* (Norman: University of Oklahoma Press, 2006), 308.

65. Nelson W. Polsby, "The Institutionalization of the U. S. House of Representatives," *American Political Science Review* 62 (1968): 144–168, esp. 148–149.

66. David P. Thelen, *Robert M. La Follette and the Insurgent Spirit* (Boston, MA: Little, Brown, 1976), 21.

67. Henry Chu, "Beilenson to Retire at End of Term," *Los Angeles Times*, November 2, 1995.

68. Frances E. Lee, "Patronage, Logrolls, and 'Polarization': Congressional Parties of the Gilded Age, 1876–1896," *Studies in American Political Development* 30 (2016): 116–127.

69. On polarization as less ideological than as "improved teamsmanship," see Francis Lee, *Beyond Ideology: Politics Principles and Partisanship in the U.S. Senate* (Chicago: University of Chicago Press, 2009).

70. Kevin R. Kosar, "Why I Quit the Congressional Research Service," *Washington Monthly*, January–February 2015.

71. Jonathan Capehart, "Pelosi Defends Her Infamous Health Care Remark," *Washington Post*, June 20, 2012.

72. "Congressmen Admit to Not Reading the NDAA before Voting for It; 'I Trust the Leadership,'" *RT*, December 5, 2014.

73. James M. Curry, *Legislating in the Dark: Information and Power in the House of Representatives* (Chicago: University of Chicago Press, 2015), chap. 7.

74. Whole Woman's Health v. Hellerstedt, 136 Sup. Ct. 2292 (2016).

75. Ibid., at 2300.

76. Ibid., at 2321.

77. Ibid., at 2330.

78. United States v. Texas, 136 S. Ct. 2271.

79. 86 F. Supp. 3d 591 (2015); 809 F. 3d 134 (2015).

80. The notice and comment provision requires that proposals for new rules be announced in the *Federal Register* and that a given period be allotted, typically sixty days with thirty days for replies, within which time interested members of the public may offer their views.

81. See discussion in Chapter 4, "The Place of Administration," pp. 118–120.

82. Attorney General's Manual on the Administrative Procedure Act, Prepared by the United States Department of Justice, Tom C. Clark, Attorney General, 1947, 26.

83. Respondent's brief, United States v. Texas, Supreme Court, December 29, 2016, at 63.

84. Petitioner's brief, United States v. Texas, Supreme Court, March 1, 2016.

85. Ibid., at 45.

86. Cass R. Sunstein, " 'Practically Binding': General Policy Statements and Notice-and-Comment Rulemaking," http://ssrn.com/abstract=2697804.

87. Vermont Yankee Nuclear Power Corp. v. Natural Resources Defense Council, 435 U.S. 519 (1978).

88. Sunstein, "Practically Binding," 21.

89. Cass R. Sunstein, "The Most Knowledgeable Branch," *University of Pennsylvania Law Review* 164 (2016): 1607–1648, 1614.

90. Jeremy Bentham, *Anarchical Fallacies; Being an Examination of the Declarations of Rights Issued During the French Revolution*, in *Works of Jeremy Bentham*, vol. 2, ed. John Bowring (Edinburgh: William Tait, 1843), 2: 501.

91. Auer v. Robbins 519 U.S. 452 (1997).

92. Sunstein, "The Most Knowledgeable Branch," 1647.

93. Cass R. Sunstein and Adrian Vermeule, "The New Coke: On the Plural Aims of Administrative Law" (2015), 1, http://ssrn.com/abstract=2631873.

94. Philip Hamburger, *Is Administrative Law Unlawful?* (Chicago: University of Chicago Press, 2014).

95. See, for instance, Chris Walker, "Is It Time to Revisit Auer Deference? Some Preliminary Empirical Findings," *Yale Journal on Regulation: Notice & Comment*, December 2, 2014, http://yalejreg.com/nc/is-it-time-to-revisit -auer-deference-some-preliminary-empirical-findings-by-chris-walker/.

96. Jack Goldsmith, *Power and Constraint: The Accountable Presidency after 9/11* (New York: Norton, 2012), 232.

97. Ibid., at 240.

98. Ibid., at 243.

99. Oliver Wendell Holmes, "The Path of the Law," *Harvard Law Review* 10 (1897): 457–478.

100. Richard Posner, "The Academy Is Out of Its Depth," Supreme Court Breakfast Table, *Slate*, June 24, 2016.

101. Jessica Chasmar, "Richard Posner, Federal Judge, Apologizes for 'Careless' Remarks about U.S. Constitution," *Washington Times*, July 6, 2016.

102. Joan McCarter, "Memo to Republicans: Trump Isn't a Policy Guy and GOP Voters Don't Care," *Daily Kos*, June 8, 2016; Michael Grunwald, "Trump's One Unbreakable Policy: Skip the Details," *Politico Magazine*, July 17, 2016.

Acknowledgments

This book is the culmination of a long collaborative reflection on problems of state development in the United States. In previous work, now decades old, one of us wrote about the emergence of an "administrative state" in America, the other, about the emergence of a "fully legislative polity." Since then we have grappled with those formulations in light of ongoing exchanges and mounting political stress. *The Policy State* presents an analysis that is, we believe, adjusted to the contemporary political scene. Although the book draws on our individual research programs, it is very much a synthetic statement.

We are grateful to Michael Aronson of Harvard University Press for encouraging us when we first pitched the idea, to John Kulka for taking up the project after Michael's retirement, and to Ian Malcolm for shepherding the manuscript through to publication. We benefited enormously from the two anonymous reviews of the manuscript.

We have had the good counsel of many others along the away. Gerald Berk, Dennis Galvan, and Victoria Hattam gave us the opportunity to introduce our idea at a conference on political creativity at the University of Oregon. Related papers were presented and discussed at a lecture on new research at Baylor University and at a conference on twentieth-century progressivism jointly sponsored at Yale University by the Institution for Social and Policy Studies (ISPS) and the law school. The editors of *The Oxford Handbook on American Political Development*, Rick Valelly, Suzanne Mettler, and Robert Lieberman provided an outlet for an early version of the argument.

Bruce Miroff, Blake Emerson, and John Compton read and commented on several early draft chapters. Michael Dorf and Joshua Chafetz gave an airing to the opening chapters at the Cornell Law School's Constitutional Law and Theory Colloquium. Participants in the Workshop on American Political Development at Yale's ISPS read and discussed each chapter serially. Susan Rose-Ackerman, Steven Calabresi, and Eileen McDonagh read the final manuscript in its entirety, providing extensive comments both on large issues and important details.

We received reactions to various bits and parts from many others over the years. Bruce Ackerman, Jack Balkin, Richard Bensel, Dan Carpenter, Brian Cook, Sam DeCanio, Lynda Dodd, Eldon Eisenach, Stephen Engel, Dan Galvin, Bryan Garsten, Jacob Hacker, Scott James, David Karol, Andrea

Katz, Frances Lee, David Mayhew, Jim Morone, Patrick O'Brien, Ariel Ron, Noah Rosenblum, Sidney Tarrow, Christopher Walker, and Vesla Weaver all helped out with candid thoughts and good leads. John Dearborn, David Lebow, Cody Trojan, Benjamin Waldman, and Lucy Smoot Williams did that and more, providing expert research assistance. All this guidance and encouragement improved the book in countless ways. Whatever errors and misconceptions remain are our own.

Stephen Werner and Susan Jacobs have been not-so-silent partners in this collaboration. They endured our seemingly interminable, often untimely phone calls and helped us keep our work on this project in perspective. With their support and good humor, we made it through, lifelong friendships intact.

Index